Prai

FAITH IN TH

GW00724525

"Christians must neither ignore the variety of religions around them nor capitulate to the lie that there are many paths to God. McDowell skillfully weaves together the biblical truth of Christ's uniqueness with an informed consideration of our neighbors' belief systems. The result is a great encouragement to evangelism."

—Joel R. Beeke
President, Puritan Reformed Theological Seminary
Grand Rapids, MI

"What Bruce McDowell provides for us in this remarkable book are the many reasons why we may have utter confidence in the traditional biblical stance. Instead of downplaying the difficult teaching on the exclusivity of the gospel, he turns it into one of our greatest strengths. Read it and be heartened."

—William Edgar
Professor of Apologetics
Westminster Theological Seminary
Philadelphia, PA

"Navigating our way as Christians through the raging waters of dogmatic relativism requires clear captains. Bruce McDowell is just such a guide, and I know that you'll find *Faith in the Mosaic* a valuable compass."

—Michael Horton
J. Gresham Machen Professor of Theology
Westminster Seminary California
Author of *Core Christianity*

FAITH

IN THE

MOSAIC

FAITH

IN THE

MOSAIC

BRUCE A. McDOWELL

CLC
PUBLICATIONS
Fort Washington, PA 19034

Faith in the Mosaic
Published by CLC Publications

U.S.A.
P.O. Box 1449, Fort Washington, PA 19034

UNITED KINGDOM
CLC International (UK)
Unit 5, Glendale Avenue, Sandycroft, Flintshire, CH5 2QP

ISBN (paperback): 978-1-61958-247-7
ISBN (e-book): 978-1-61958-248-4

Cover design by Mitch Bolton.

Contents

Preface

For many years, Western society has tended toward the secular. According to Pew Research Center, in 2014, 77 percent of Americans described themselves as "religiously affiliated," down from 83 percent in 2007, while the number who said they were "absolutely certain" God existed fell from 71 percent to 63 percent in the same time period.[1] With the large wave of immigration from the Two-Thirds World to Western societies and the rapid growth of a monistic spiritual worldview, secularization has slowed. The trend has morphed into a predominance of postmodern pluralism or has become, as British American scholar Peter Jones describes it, a "postsecular" era. It is an age of maintaining secular critical thought while having an openness to issues of the spirit. Jones writes, "It signals the end of materialistic secular humanism and a final synthesis of mind and spirit in a cultural affirmation of Oneist [monistic] untruth."[2] Tim Keller, pastor of Redeemer Presbyterian Church in New York City, wrote as follows:

> If you read Eric Kaufmann's *Shall the Religious Inherit the Earth?* (2010) and follow the latest demographic

research, you will know that the world is not inevi-
tably becoming more secular. The percentage of the
world's population that are non-religious, and that
put emphasis on individuals determining their own
moral values, is shrinking. The more conservative religious faiths are growing very fast. No one studying
these trends believes that history is moving in the direction of more secular societies.[3]

Led by the culture makers in positions of influence, the past
trend toward secularism in the West usually meant getting rid
of Christian vestiges displayed in public spaces. Thus crosses,
the Ten Commandments, and Christmas crèches were removed.
With the newer trend toward pluralism, however, Christian,
Jewish, Muslim, Hindu, Buddhist, and First Nations symbols
are displayed, such as those we see on the popular "coexist"
bumper sticker. Now US postages stamps are published honoring Christmas, Hanukkah, Kwanzaa, Eid, and Chinese New
Year. If an area is designated for religious use on public property
or at a school, it is usually meant to be used by those of all faiths.
The way in which secularists deal with religion has moved toward a pluralist's approach. This includes welcoming Muslim,
Wiccan, Universalist, Roman Catholic, and Protestant prison
and military chaplains.

This often introduces new challenges to our pluralistic society,
however. Already, we here in the United States see trends such
as secular university chapels meant for people of all faiths being
taken over by Muslim students, with all trappings of Christianity removed, including the pews. At public forums such as
school graduations, the mention of Jesus in opening prayer is

disallowed. A moment of silence is preferred over a prayer in public venues. Christmas is no longer celebrated as the birth of Christ, simply as a holiday of the season along with Hanukkah, but the mayor of Philadelphia has made the two major Muslim Eid holidays official city holidays. Muslim public school students there are given permission to leave school on Fridays at noon to attend prayer at their local mosques, yet in many schools it is difficult or impossible to form a Christian club or sing Christmas carols with Christ-centered words. On some college campuses, Christian ministries are not permitted or, if they are, they are required to allow nonbelievers to be officers in their leadership.[4] Additionally, these Christian groups are given more restrictive guidelines than other campus clubs, such as those pertaining to advertising and "giving out free materials, such as Christian books."[5] In other words, true pluralism has died.

New expressions of religion are appearing on our landscape. Now numerous neighborhoods in North America and Europe hear the call to prayer before dawn as new mosques are being built with large infusions of Middle Eastern oil money. The student body at a public high school in Upper Darby, a community outside of Philadelphia, comprises immigrants from all over the world, representing at least ninety languages. The same area is home to the largest concentration of Sikhs in the United States. Additionally, Hindu and Buddhist temples and meditation centers are popping up in communities nationwide.

Christians no longer live in isolated clusters in which most people believe as we do. In the previous generation, Christianity was the accepted religion of Western culture. Bible reading and prayer to the Christian God was part of the daily schedule in schools. Now believers in Christ interact with people from many different faith traditions. Most in North America believe it is important to maintain active, healthy relationships with people of other religious faiths. They are predisposed toward not judging those from other faiths as to whether these individuals know God, how spiritual they are, or if their faith leads to salvation. However, this is usually because they are not well-informed on the principles of their own faith or knowledgeable about the other religions, as opposed to being purposely accepting of other faiths.[6] On the other hand, 60 percent of people of non-Christian faith in the United States, most of whom are immigrants and refugees, say that they do not know a Christian. These newcomers are isolated from the Christian community, which has yet to reach out to them; they remain mostly in their own subcultures, as do many Christians.

While secular humanism has pockets of predominance in academia, Hollywood, and some cultural communities, the trend today is the vast majority of people claiming to have spirituality. Thus our society has become one in which "the cultured elites are trying to preside over a people who are very spiritual," leading to continual conflicts.[7] The difference today over a few decades ago is that while in the past spirituality through Christ was very much out of step with the trend toward secularism, now it is seen as one option among many forms of spirituality. The rub, however, comes when Christians proclaim Christ as the exclusive means for redemptive spirituality. Inherent in this pluralism is a rapidly rising new agnosticism that requires conformity from all in society to what has recently become our new civil religion.[8]

This rising spirituality does not mean that there is a corresponding rise in belief in God, since formerly held categories for spirituality no longer hold. Surveys indicate that more people pray than believe in God. Anthony Giddens, professor of sociology at the University of Cambridge, explains.

> First, religion should not be identified with monotheism. . . . Most religions involve several deities. . . . In certain religions there are no gods at all. Second, religion should not be identified with moral prescriptions controlling the behavior of believers. . . . Third, religion is not necessarily concerned with explaining how the world came to be as it is. . . . Fourth, religion cannot be identified with the supernatural, as intrinsically involving belief in a universe "beyond the realm of the senses."[9]

What we now increasingly encounter is people seeking mystical communion with the spirit world, and this does not fit our categories for religion. It includes an amoral value system with selective tolerance for those who do not conform to its sense of destiny.

Academics and policymakers work at eliminating Western civilization from university study curricula and keeping Christian morals from producing value judgments in student and faculty behavior. A current political movement in the United States seeks to eliminate most vestiges of Christianity from Christian colleges, including mandatory chapel attendance and Bible classes, prayer, curriculums based on a Christian worldview, and adherence to a doctrinal statement.[10] Colleges that impose traditional Christian rules of morality and conduct on issues regarding gender identity and sexual orientation could be stripped of public funding[11] and open themselves up to lawsuits.[12] Some are even advocating that Christian colleges be stripped of their accreditation.[13] At the same time, all sorts of ideologies, worldviews, and religions are introduced as truths at "secular" universities and are considered appropriate because they are seen as acceptable pluralism and multiculturalism in our postmodern milieu. Christianity is not considered to be part of that mix. At an Ivy League university, a Christian administrative faculty member was dismissed by the dean of her department for having Christian verses on display in her office and meeting with students for prayer and Bible study. In today's pluralist environment, talking about and expressing one's faith in public is strongly discouraged, as faith is believed to be a private matter.

Peter Jones, Christian apologist and cultural analyst, describes our current climate. "Political correctness denies any distinctions between cultures, religions, and value systems. Thus, politically correct multiculturalism dominates the public square and the university campus and affects domestic and foreign policy."[14] It has become official United States policy to fund lobbyists and train activists to demand gay rights, gay marriage, and abortion rights, and to deny foreign aid to majority countries that refuse to comply with our monistic religious-based cultural imperialism.

Secular university campuses have shifted toward emphasizing pluralism and multiculturalism, and not just at a practical level where all religious views get a voice at the table; rather, welcoming diversity is now an ideology and movement. Two types of pluralism have emerged. The first is a militant form that says one can have a voice at the table only as long as one espouses views that are pluralistic. The second form, which is true pluralism, allows for all with differing religious and philosophical viewpoints to express them, no matter how committed people are to their ideals.[15] Obviously, the first form is more oppressive and restrictive, while the second allows for true diversity and freedom. The challenge is when one group's freedom takes over another group's right to freely exercise or express their faith.

Now even many church-related colleges are teaching religion as if all options are equally valid in our multicultural context.[16] Christianity, for these institutions, is just one option with no eternal truth valid for all. But as Alister McGrath explains, "The whole issue of religious pluralism has been fatally flawed by a mentality that demands that all shall be reduced to the same mold. . . . Dialogue implies respect, but it does not presuppose agreement."[17]

This context of our current daily lives challenges our faith. It has become closer to the pluralistic religious mixture prevalent in the Roman Empire, in which early Christians learned to live out their faith. Consequently, it makes it harder for Christians to remain neutral and passive about our faith in Christ. The former trend toward cultural Christianity has now been replaced with many who claim to be spiritual but do not associate with organized religion or identify themselves as Christian.

As true Christians, how should we think about those who do not subscribe to faith in Christ? How should we perceive their eternal destiny in light of Christianity's definitive belief in the true and only God, biblical authority, and exclusivity to salvation through Christ alone? Are we the only ones who are right? How can we know? In a time when so many are looking for tolerance, freedom, peace, and unity, how should we respond from a Christ-centered perspective? With all the daily bad news in this world, what can we expect from the future? Is there hope?

This book wades through these questions and offers thoughts to help those of us who are believers relate to people who observe other faiths or no apparent faith at all.

I thank the Lord for my wife Anne, for her encouragement and support in writing this book, and for the congregation of Tenth International Fellowship at Tenth Presbyterian Church, where I first presented these themes.

1

Is Seeing God in Nature Sufficient for Salvation?

Romans 1:18–25

What can be known about God is plain to [humanity], because God has shown it to them. For his invisible attributes, namely, his eternal power and divine nature, have been clearly perceived, ever since the creation of the world, in the things that have been made.

Romans 1:19–20

As Western society has rapidly moved toward being post-Christian, many people are looking for spiritual experiences and some type of god to worship. Often they are confused and not sure where to look as they compare various religions and ideologies. Many end up holding to a syncretistic mixture of assorted philosophies and ideas. But to various degrees, their thoughts generally turn away from the Christian view of a distinction between the Creator and His creation to a monistic view of all things being one, as in the Eastern religions.

Consequently, many have turned back to nature as their source. This turn, however, is away from the creator God who has spoken to everyone and toward a mystical god to whom people seek to become united by looking within themselves.

This has been described as turning from a Twoist worldview to a Oneist perspective. Scripture reveals that although everyone should know something about their creator, they "suppress the truth" and have "exchanged the truth about God for a lie" (Rom. 1:18, 25). Because of this "God gave them up to a debased mind" (1:28) and this has resulted in an unrighteous, pagan manner of living. How then can people know that there is a God distinct from them to whom each of us is accountable? Most people enjoy seeing beautiful scenes of nature—Niagara Falls, the Grand Canyon, Yosemite National Park, the Milky Way. These sights can lead one to reflect on where all this marvel came from and how it came to be. But can a person go into the woods, up on a mountain, or to the beach to meditate and thereby come to know God? Can he or she discover a personal relationship with the living God in this way? Is communing with nature sufficient for our salvation?

The Bible, God's special revelation to us, makes it clear in Romans 1:18–20 that God does reveal Himself through His creation. While He does not reveal the message of salvation in creation, He reveals enough about Himself that we should be moved to seek Him and honor Him as the creator of all things.

But why is this even an issue?

Looking back in history we see that man and woman initially did know God intimately. Humanity did not evolve from a beast, progressing from worshiping spirits in rocks, trees, and animals (animism) to various gods with separate functions (polytheism) to one god for a particular nation or tribe (henotheism) to finally one supreme being (monotheism).

Actually, the opposite is the case. Humankind was created by God and originally had a very close relationship with this personal God. Adam and Eve, however, rejected the authority of God over them and wanted to become like God themselves. Consequently, they and their descendants worshiped the creation rather than the creator of all things. Idolatry includes anything we give our ultimate allegiance to (including ourselves and our desires—money, sex, and power) and any false view of the true creator God.

Departure from worship of the one true God into polytheism is thought to have developed particularly after God confused men's languages and dispersed the peoples at the building of the Tower of Babel (see Gen. 11). Each people group acquired its own national god following this event. Having lost the understanding of the unity and absoluteness of one supreme God, people began to venerate other gods. Idolatry, however, begins in the heart, and it has made itself manifest from the Fall, when Adam and Eve wanted to be like God and rejected submission to His lordship (see 3:1–6).

Though we are a marred version of His image, God has continued to make Himself known in a limited sense to people through His creation.

The Revelation of God in Nature

So what do we know about God from creation? First, we know His "invisible attributes, namely, his eternal power and divine nature" (Rom. 1:20). God's creation shows us that in His wisdom, He planned, designed, and had the power to create everything. Scientists with eyes of faith are continually amazed to see in their research how only a Divine Designer could have made possible the intricacies of connection, functionality, and beauty in every aspect of our physical world, from the structure of the atom to the creation of a zygote to the expanse of the galaxies in the universe. The creation also reveals God's eternal nature. This is expressed in the age of the universe and the repeated cycles of the seasons.

Swiss theologian Emil Brunner has said, "The first and most important thing we know about God is that we know nothing about him except what He himself makes known."[1] In Psalm 19, David described God's revelation beautifully in two parts: first, through His speech proclaimed in the glory of the heavens, which we call "general revelation," and second, in the Word of God that enlightens the eyes and renews the mind, known as "special revelation."

Let's look at the general revelation that is seen through nature. King David extols the glory of God's creation.

> The heavens declare the glory of God,
>> and the sky above proclaims his handiwork.
> Day to day pours out speech,
>> and night to night reveals knowledge.
> There is no speech, nor are there words,
>> whose voice is not heard.
> Their voice goes out through all the earth,
>> and their words to the end of the world.
> In them he has set a tent for the sun,
>> which comes out like a bridegroom leaving his chamber,
>> and, like a strong man, runs its course with joy.

Its rising is from the end of the heavens,
  and its circuit to the end of them,
  and there is nothing hidden from its heat.
                                    (Ps. 19:1–6)

David further extols the power, glory, and strength of God as displayed in a storm coming across the Mediterranean Sea to Lebanon to the wilderness of Kadesh. Through this display of power, God speaks.

The voice of the LORD is over the waters;
  the God of glory thunders,
  the LORD, over many waters.
The voice of the LORD is powerful;
  the voice of the LORD is full of majesty.

The voice of the LORD breaks the cedars;
  the LORD breaks the cedars of Lebanon. . . .

The voice of the LORD flashes forth flames of fire.
The voice of the LORD shakes the wilderness;
  the Lord shakes the wilderness of Kadesh.

The voice of the LORD makes the deer give birth
  and strips the forests bare,
  and in his temple all cry, "Glory!"
                                    (29:3–9)

This psalm illustrates how Yahweh ("the LORD") speaks audibly through the thunderbolts and the trembling earth. It is written in protest against worship of the pagan Canaanite storm god, Baal.

Since "the earth is the LORD's, and everything in it, / the world, and all who live in it" (Ps. 24:1, NIV), all His creation is His temple, in which all He has made cries out in worship, "Glory!" The mighty power of God is heard through the voice of the seas pounding their waves and telling us that "the LORD on high is mighty!" (93:4)

Invisible Attributes of God

God does speak to us of His invisible attributes through His creation. The psalmist made this clear: we know of God's glory and handiwork through the cycle of day and night and the radiant heat of the sun.

What can we know of God from observation through creation? First, we can see that God is distinct from His creation. He is its creator and ruler, but He is not part of it. He is architect and designer of all the beauty we behold, and He sustains it all by His power.

We find in Scripture that God is both transcendent and immanent—both above and beyond His creation yet close and personal. Both aspects of God are described by Paul to the Ephesians as "one God and Father of all, who is over all and through all and in all" (Eph. 4:6). His transcendence is seen in the fact that He is over all, sovereignly determining the course of every event, while His immanence is explained in the truth that He is our Father and is in all creation through His Spirit. God has also revealed His goodness and kindness to us in nature, for all He created He declared "good" (see Gen. 1). When Paul was on his first missionary journey in the city of Lystra, God used him to heal a man crippled since birth. The Lycaonians, believing Paul and Barnabas were the gods Hermes and Zeus disguised as humans, wanted to worship them, but Paul protested.

> Men, why are you doing these things? We also are men, of like nature with you, and we bring you good news, that you should turn from these vain things to a living God, who made the heaven and the earth and the sea and all that is in them. In past generations he allowed all the nations to walk in their own ways. Yet he did not leave himself without witness, for he did good by giving you rains from heaven and fruitful seasons, satisfying your hearts with food and gladness. (Acts 14:15–17)

God reveals His goodness and kind provision for our lives in His promise to sustain us daily (see also Ps. 104:14–15, 27–28; 145:15). In some sense all religions recognize this, although they are misdirected as to whom they should give thanks. Most do not recognize the love and grace of a personal God. Rather, they attribute earthly blessings to the gods of nature as part of a Oneist worldview or, in Islam, an unknowable, transcendent god.

In addition, God reveals His righteousness, faithfulness, love, justice, and integrity in a world order that, in both its physical and moral aspects, is part of His one-kingdom rule. The psalmist declares, "The LORD reigns, let the earth rejoice! . . . Clouds and thick darkness are all around him; / righteousness and justice are the foundation of his throne. . . . The heavens proclaim his righteousness, / and all the peoples see his glory" (97:1–6). He tells us that through God's general revelation, all people can see the glorious attributes of God's character, even though its brilliant fullness is veiled in dark clouds. When the psalmist tells us, "You open your hand; / you satisfy the desire of every living thing," we can see for ourselves: "The LORD is righteous in all his ways / and kind in all his works" (Ps. 145:16–17) and "The LORD is good to all, / and his mercy is over all that he has made" (145:9). Again, the psalmist declares as follows:

> Say among the nations, "The LORD reigns!
>   Yes, the world is established; it shall never be moved;
>   he will judge the peoples with equity."
>
> . . . Then shall all the trees of the forest sing for joy
>   before the LORD, for he comes,
>   for he comes to judge the earth.
> He will judge the world in righteousness,
>   and the peoples in his faithfulness.
>
> (Ps. 96:10–13)

Attributes Clearly Perceived

Paul also tells us that God's eternal power is clearly perceived: "What can be known about God is plain to them, because God has shown it to them. For his invisible attributes, namely, his eternal power and divine nature, have been clearly perceived, ever since the creation of the world, in the things that have been made" (Rom. 1:19–20).

God's eternal power and divine nature can be seen in how brief our lives are in the context of the age of the universe, said to be about 13.8 billion years old, or in the distance of the stars from us. The most distant observable galaxy from Earth is believed to have formed more than 13.4 billion years ago, but it is more than 32 billion light years away because of the continuing expansion of the universe! Solomon wrote that God "has put eternity into man's heart, yet so that he cannot find out what God has done from the beginning to the end" (Eccles. 3:11). Because we have such a short lifespan, we cannot see the pattern of events that God has ordered; we simply see that it is long-lasting: "A generation goes, and a generation comes, / but the earth remains forever" (1:4). Yet we can discern that there must be a supreme power overseeing all that occurs to reach its designer's ultimate purpose. The Lord's reign as King has been since before His creation: "The world is established, firm and secure. / Your throne was established long ago; / you are from all eternity" (Ps. 93:1–2, NIV).

Additionally, the unmeasurable expanse of the universe demonstrates the transcendent power of God who created it. The psalmist declares, "[Yahweh] determines the number of the stars; / he gives to all of them their names" (147:4). The mind-boggling vastness of 100 billion stars in the Milky Way Galaxy alone and 170–200 billion galaxies in the observable universe, each star named by God, indicates His abundant power and understanding "beyond measure" (147:5). Even without the aid of the Hubble Space Telescope, everyone can observe the amazing light, energy, design, and creativity of the universe on a clear night. Don Richardson relates the story of Pachacuti, king of the great Inca civilization in Andean South America from 1438 to 1471. Besides building fortresses, cities, temples, and monuments, Pachacuti reached out for and found through observation a God far greater than the popular god of his own culture. He had been devoted to worship of Inti, the sun god, but he came to doubt Inti's credentials when he observed that the sun never did anything original but always followed the same routine (see Eccles. 1:5). Moreover, the solar radiance could be dimmed by any passing cloud. If Inti were truly God, then no mere created thing could dim its light. Pachacuti realized he had been worshiping a mere thing.

This reminds us of Paul's testimony to the people of Lystra: "In past generations he allowed all the nations to walk in their own ways. Yet he did not leave himself without witness" (Acts 14:16–17). Pachacuti took what he observed from nature and combined it with an ancient tradition within his own culture's almost forgotten memory—that of Viracocha, the Lord, the omnipotent creator of all things. Consequently, he called a congress of the priests of the sun and taught them what he had discovered. His teaching is summarized as follows:

> He is ancient, remote, supreme, and uncreated. Nor does he need the gross satisfaction of a consort. He manifests himself as a trinity when he wishes, . . . otherwise only heavenly warriors and archangels surround his loneliness. He created all peoples by his "word," as well as all huacas [spirits]. He is man's Fortunus, ordaining his years and nourishing him. He is indeed the very principle of life, for he warms the folk through his created son, Punchao [the sun disk]. He is a bringer of peace and an orderer. He is in his own being blessed and has pity on men's wretchedness. He alone judges and absolves them and enables them to combat their evil tendencies.[2]

Prayer was then directed by the Incas to Viracocha, the creator God, with deep awe and humility. Unfortunately, this new teaching was only given to the royal and upper-class Incas.

What we see in this example, however, is that many truths of the true God may yet be found through His general revelation. Even some long-forgotten truth about God, passed down from true worshipers, may be revived. It bridges the revelation of God through Christ to make the gospel of grace known. We also see God's design and power when we look at humankind. King David expressed his awe of seeing God's majestic signature stamped on all that He has made.

> When I look at your heavens, the work of your fingers,
>   the moon and the stars, which you have set in place,
> what is man that you are mindful of him,
>   and the son of man that you care for him?
>
> Yet you have made him a little lower than the heavenly beings
>   and crowned him with glory and honor.
> You have given him dominion over the works of your hands;
>   you have put all things under his feet.
>
> (Ps. 8:3–6)

This dominion, given to humankind at creation (see Gen. 1:26), is evident in all that we seek to do—from growing crops and domesticating animals (see Gen. 2:15; 4:2; Ps. 104:14–15) to building cities (see Jer. 29:5) and exploring both space and the human genome. Our existence as creative, conceptional, rational creatures cannot be explained through evolution or a mystical oneness of a universal mind that is not distinct from us. Antony Flew, one of the best-known twentieth-century atheists, became a theist toward the end of his life. This was because "he was unable to account for the mystery of the personal, thinking, planning, self-critical, and self-conscious human being, who cannot be explained purely from physics or chemistry. He stated, 'It is simply inconceivable that any material matrix or field can generate agents who think and act. Matter cannot produce conceptions and perceptions. . . . Such a world . . . has to originate in a living Source, or Mind.'"[3] Thus, we see that God has crowned humankind "with glory and honor" as He exercises dominion, which points us to the existence of the One who made us. The creative hand of God is distinguishable in human consciousness, development of language, appreciation of beauty, capacity for love, and yearning for justice.

Because He gave us consciences, we see the imprint of God in our lives in a way that distinguishes us from the rest of creation. The sense of morality instilled in us is one of the good, common-grace gifts that reflects God's character. Yet this sense can be sharpened with acute sensitivity to what is good, just, loving, and honoring to God to become a "good" or "clear conscience" (Acts 23:1; 24:16; 1 Tim. 1:5, 19; 3:9; 2 Tim. 1:3; Heb. 5:14; 13:18; 1 Pet. 3:16, 21) or it can be dulled so that it becomes almost nonexistent through continual rejection of that which prompts it. It then becomes a "seared" conscience (1 Tim. 4:2) that is "evil" (Heb. 10:22). Depending on the state of one's conscience, even those without the law of God "by nature do what the law requires. . . . They show that the work of the law is written on their hearts, while their conscience also bears witness, and their conflicting thoughts accuse or even excuse them" (Rom. 2:14–15). Paul quotes Psalm 19:4 to prove that God has made His voice heard throughout the world of the Gentiles (non-Jews who did not receive God's Word) as a means for calling people to faith in Him, saying, "I ask, have they not heard? Indeed they have, for 'Their voice [i.e., creation's voice] has gone out to all the earth, / and their words to the ends of the world'" (Rom. 10:18).

French scientist and Christian philosopher Blaise Pascal wrote, "Instead of complaining that God had hidden himself, you will give him thanks for having revealed so much of himself."[4]

We know nothing about God, His plans, or His purposes apart from what He reveals to us. The Lord spoke to Israel through Moses saying, "The secret things belong to the LORD our God, but the things that are revealed belong to us and to our children forever" (Deut. 29:29). The fact that there are secret things of God means that we need to have trust, faith, and obedience in a state of humbleness toward Him, even when we don't understand His ways. What God has revealed in creation, we can treasure as a revelation of His glorious invisible attributes. Through that knowledge, we are accountable to Him and we should seek Him.

Seeking God

Does God hear the prayers of those who truly seek Him? We learn the answer is "yes" from Psalm 14:2: "The LORD looks down from heaven on the children of man, / to see if there are any who understand, / who seek after God." Although He speaks clearly to us through His creation, His Word is special revelation of His great promises. The personal knowledge we need of Him for life and godliness has been determined by God; we receive it through His divine power displayed in Jesus Christ (see 2 Pet. 1:3–4).

We see an example of a man seeking and finding God and then having the gospel explained to him in Acts 10. That man was Cornelius, a Gentile centurion of "the Italian Cohort, a devout man who feared God with all his household, gave alms generously to the people, and prayed continually to God. . . . He saw clearly in a vision an angel of God. . . . [The angel] said to him, 'Your prayers and your alms have ascended as a memorial before God'" (10:1–4). He was a Gentile who may not have had the Old Testament Scriptures or at least was not a Jew with the Jews' benefits of revelation, but he was clearly seeking God with all the light he had received (see Acts 10:34–35). It appears that Cornelius may have been a proselyte without knowledge of Christ. God responded to him with special revelation, and an angel followed by giving Peter a vision and sending him to Cornelius to present the gospel.

When I was in Colombia, I heard the testimony of the witch-doctor head of the Chimila Indian community that was in the Sierra Nevada Mountains near Santa Marta. He'd had a vivid dream the night before Pastor Jaime Leal first came to the community and preached the gospel. In the dream, he heard that a white man was going to come and bring a message from God and the community was to believe this message. He had told his dream to another leading man in the community. Over the next weeks, as the witchdoctor heard the gospel message that Pastor Leal preached, he came to believe along with a number of others in the community, who were then baptized. Previously, there had never been any true believers in Christ in that indigenous community.

Similarly, we find Muslims around the world who have had a dream or vision of Jesus appearing to them. Recently, I heard the testimony of a young refugee woman from an Iranian Muslim family tell of how she started to have regular dreams of Jesus when she was eight years old. When a neighbor heard about those dreams, she gave the girl an old Bible. The girl enjoyed reading the stories. Years later, she met a group of Muslim-background believers with whom she prayed. Upon moving to Turkey to escape harassment and detention from the police in Iran, she was baptized at a local church. This is just one of many examples of those whom God calls to Himself even before they have ever heard the gospel preached. Then God leads them to hear or read the gospel to believe in salvation. In other words, even those who receive dreams and visions from God still need to hear the gospel to activate its written revelation.

What we see consistently throughout both Scripture and experience is that God calls a person to seek Him and that person then responds in faith. Jesus said, "My sheep hear my voice, and I know them, and they follow me" (John 10:27).

Suppressing the Truth

God has plainly made Himself known so that all people might seek Him out. But instead of seeking Him, most people "suppress the truth" (Rom. 1:18) that God has revealed about Himself. They do not allow this truth to work in their lives. They refuse to be accountable to God for how they live their lives; they want to live their own way rather than be convicted by God's truth and repent. As a result, people refuse the truth (see 1:21–22) and turn the truth into a lie (see 1:25).

This devolution leads people to totally abandon the truth so that they end up living like a beast in their thinking and living. We see an example of this suppression of the truth and its subsequent transformation into idolatry when Moses traveled up Mount Sinai to receive the Ten Commandments from God. Upon returning to the people of Israel after forty days, he found

them worshiping a golden calf (see Exod. 32:19–24). This aban-
donment of their allegiance to the God who had delivered them
out of slavery and miraculously led them through the Red Sea
by His Spirit demonstrates the hardness of heart and blindness
these people had to the goodness and power of God.

They returned to the degenerate idolatry of animism and
fetishism, sorcery and magic, revelry and drunkenness and ca-
rousing of the Egyptians. What the Israelites returned to is called
"Oneism" by cultural analyst and New Testament scholar Peter
Jones, a worldview that sees the world as self-creating or perpet-
ually existing, in which "everything is made up of the same stuff,
whether matter, spirit, or a mixture."[5] Such sameness is a worship of nature called "paganism." This worldview rejects "Two-
ism," the only alternative, of a personal transcendent God who
created all things out of nothing and made distinctions within
His creation.

This second worldview, based on otherness, is frequently
called "theism." Both worldviews cannot be true simultaneous-
ly—one is ultimately true and the other false.[6] Paul made it clear
that those who have given up the knowledge of the glory of God
for images of His creation and are thus given up to impurity
have "exchanged the truth about God for a lie and served the
creature rather than the Creator" (Rom. 1:25). Paul then warned
his mentee, Timothy.

> The Spirit expressly says that in later times some
> will depart from the faith by devoting themselves to
> deceitful spirits and teachings of demons, through
> the insincerity of liars whose consciences are seared,
> who forbid marriage and require abstinence from

> foods that God created to be received with thanks-
> giving by those who believe and know the truth.
> (1 Tim. 4:1–3)

This describes our own day of a return to paganism. Pagan gods are idols—gods that do not exist. They are lies and vanity, and their worship is worship of demons (see Deut. 32:17; 1 Cor. 10:20; Rev. 9:20). Those who remain in paganism apart from God's revelation live in darkness, ignorance, vain human wisdom, deception, and unrighteousness (see 1 Cor. 1:19–21; 2:5, 13; 6:9; Eph. 5:6–8). Paganism is a deliberate suppression of the truth to follow "ungodly passions." Those who adhere to paganism rely "on their dreams, defile the flesh," and "reject authority" (Jude 8).

Today we are seeing a revival of paganism in the Western world. Owning images of a Hindu deity, making fruit offerings and burning joss sticks to spirits represented in a Buddha or bodhisattva for protection and good fortune is common not just among immigrants but Western-born people as well. It is now commonplace to hear of Wiccan gatherings, Sophia goddess worship, yoga classes in which the instructor not only teaches the technique of the practice but also the spiritual concepts behind it, demonstrations of traditional animistic rituals, television shows on communicating with the dead, psychics channeling through spirit guides in an altered state of consciousness with the universal mind, horoscope readings, people bowing in prayer five times a day toward a black meteorite in the Kaaba, and a total rejection of traditional Christian moral and sexual values. The sexual identity confusion so prevalent in our society comes from a rejection of God as creator of humanity in His image as male and female and a welcoming of the view that everything in the universe is one.

Such a monistic worldview leads to loss of a clear sexual identity and gender confusion.[7] In seeking a classless egalitarian society, gender distinction is targeted for eradication along with the institution of marriage. What is it that leads people to reject the creator God as revealed through both His creation and Scripture? First, people hate God's sovereignty, His most basic attribute. If God is not sovereign, then He is not God. He hardens the hearts of some—like Sihon, king of Heshbon, and Pharaoh, mentioned nine times in Exodus—and He softens the hearts of others, like the Gentiles at Antioch in Pisidia and Lydia at Philippi (see Exod. 4:21; Deut. 2:30; Lam. 3:65; John 12:40; Acts 13:48; 16:14; Rom. 9:18). He is ruler and head over all, He dispenses wealth and honor, and He gives strength and power. But people rebel against God's authority and rule over them. This was Adam's problem in the garden of Eden, which led to the Fall—separation from a relationship with God. He wanted to be sovereign himself. Humankind is not holy and people don't want their shameful sin exposed. They don't want anyone to know them too deeply, as to what they really think and what they are really like. They are overwhelmed with fear of being undone in the presence of God, who actively punishes rebellion and wickedness and seeks to establish righteousness (see Exod. 15:11; Isa. 6:3; 1 Pet. 1:16; Rev. 4:8). But God knows all about us—our innermost thoughts and motivations—and men and women cannot hide from Him (see Ps. 139:1–6).

Finally, people hate God for His immutability. God does not change (see Mal. 3:6; James 1:17). People think that if God stops being sovereign or holy, or if His memory fails Him, they could continue comfortably in their sin in the afterlife forever, since they are eternal beings. But God will always be sovereign, omniscient, omnipresent, holy, just, and righteous. Seeking to suppress this truth will get people nowhere but condemnation to an eternity of punishment without God. Men and women need a God who remains the same always and knows them thoroughly and yet, through His grace, loves them anyway. Thus, in the verse "Jesus Christ is the same yesterday and today and forever" (Heb. 13:8), people can have great hope and security if they are in right relationship with God.

Wrath of God

We now come to the subject Paul introduced Romans 1 with: the wrath of God. "For the wrath of God is revealed from heaven against all ungodliness and unrighteousness of men, who by their unrighteousness suppress the truth" (1:18). God exercises wrath because He is a righteous and holy God who cannot stand the presence of evil (see Ps. 5:4; Hab. 1:13). He is justly angry, with a personal revulsion for humanity's ungodliness (see Ps. 5:5–6) in which they have not honored the Lord as God or given thanks to Him (see Rom. 1:21). Rather, people wickedly "became fools, and exchanged the glory of the immortal God for images resembling mortal man and birds and animals and creeping things" (1:22–23). What's more, people have indulged "in the lusts of their hearts to impurity, to the dishonoring of their bodies among themselves," and "exchanged the truth about God for a lie and worshiped and served the creature rather than the Creator, who is blessed forever!" (Rom. 1:24–25). The wrath of God was revealed from heaven against the ungodly in the days of Noah, when the flood came and destroyed the earth. God's wrath continues to be seen today in famine, hurricanes, tornados, lightning, volcanoes, and earthquakes. Hurricanes such as Katrina on the Gulf Coast of the United States and Mitch in Central America created unimaginable devastation. In 1998, on the island of Guanaja off the coast of Honduras, Hurricane Mitch blew every leaf of vegetation and nearly every wooden house off the island with two-hundred-mile-an-hour winds that continued for four days. Such events cause people to fear God and realize that they need to be ready to meet their Maker. After the devastation, I was part of a team that both helped rebuild and witnessed to people. Several individuals turned in faith to the Lord.

Then too we see the devastating effects of disease. Take, for instance, the bubonic plague that killed about 35 million people in China followed by almost half the population of Western Europe in the fourteenth century. In 1918–1919, right after World War I, the Spanish flu epidemic spread across the United States and then to other countries, killing more than 25 million people in one year. It likely mutated from a swine virus and became airborne. Where I live, in Philadelphia, 158 out of every one 1,000 people died.

Today we have the scourge of AIDS, which is rapidly spreading around the world. In some southern African countries, around 40 percent of the population is infected with HIV. Now we face the threat of avian flu possibly mutating. In 2014, at the height of the Ebola virus crisis in West Africa, the disease was spreading out of control with an approximately 70 percent death rate. How do we interpret these events? Is God in control? As our sovereign creator who does whatever He pleases (see Ps. 115:3), of course He is. Many causes of death exist; but without a doubt, if the Lord tarries, someday every one of us will die and face the judgment seat of Christ, where our King will separate the sheep from the goats (see Matt. 25:31–46). God can use our experiences with disaster, drought, flood, pain, suffering, and illness as His means of speaking to us to get our attention. Perhaps He is speaking to us to let us know that we are not God and that we are not in control of our destiny. King David cries out for justice, saying, "Arise, O Lord! Let not man prevail; / let the nations be judged before you! / Put them in fear, O Lord! / Let the nations know that they are but men!" (Ps. 9:19–20). The question is: Are we listening?

Without Excuse

Paul brings his thoughts to a climax in this portion of Romans 1 by saying, "So they are without excuse" (1:20). Since God has made Himself plainly known through what people can perceive with their senses in the world around them, men are without excuse for their disobedience to Him. Yet men and women seem to have an infinite capacity for making excuses for their blameworthy behavior: "It wasn't my fault." "Nobody told me." "I had good intentions." "Stop being so critical!"

No, they should have known better. As Proverbs reminds us, "All the ways of a man are pure in his own eyes, / but the Lord weighs the spirit" (16:2; see also 21:2). All nature loudly speaks to people that they are accountable to their creator and must seek Him and find Him. The psalmist David explains, "The Lord has made himself known; he has executed judgment; / the wicked are snared in the work of their own hands" (Ps. 9:16).

Still, even though what is seen in creation gives humanity no excuse to sin, people must hear the word of Christ to be saved. Natural revelation does not deal with our sin, guilt, and shame, nor does it offer people forgiveness and personal love. R.C. Sproul has said, "The world's best geographer cannot show us the way to God, and the world's best psychiatrist cannot give us a final answer to the problem of our guilt. There are matters contained in Holy Writ that 'unveil' for us that which is not exposed to the natural course of human investigation."[8] Nor is human reason or wisdom sufficient to bring us to saving faith, since it has been corrupted and is not able to tell us what is only "spiritually discerned" (1 Cor. 2:14), since "the god of this world has blinded the minds of the unbelievers" (2 Cor. 4:4). Therefore Paul says, "Where is the one who is wise? Where is the scribe? Where is the debater of this age? Has not God made foolish the wisdom of the world? For since, in the wisdom of God, the world did not know God through wisdom, it pleased God through the folly of what we preach to save those who believe" (1 Cor. 1:20–21).

Eighteenth-century deists and rationalists believed in the total sufficiency of general revelation and natural religion guided by reason. But Thomas Aquinas wrote, "Human salvation demands the divine disclosure of truths surpassing reason."[9] Even those truths that are revealed in general revelation to philosophers and scientists take much study and remain incomplete and uncertain to these researchers. Therefore special revelation from God and its authority are needed for all. Although general revelation provides us with knowledge of God's existence and some of His attributes, such as His eternity, power, creativity, goodness, justice, and common grace toward all, it leaves us with no knowledge of Jesus Christ, who came to reveal the Father to us and the way to Him. Therefore general revelation cannot help us as sinners in need of a Savior. It offers nothing of grace for sinners and forgiveness, but rather sometimes reveals God's wrath (see Rom. 1:18). When God first created the world, grace and forgiveness were unnecessary. But for the fallen human race, grace and forgiveness are the essence of our faith and trust in Christ. Although general revelation conveys some truths about God and His creation, it gives us no interpretation of the facts and history, so it changes nothing about our existence. Yes, God has given everyone a conscience so that general revelation somewhat enlightens people's minds and restrains evil, but it has no power to regenerate people's human nature and transform the creation that suffers from frustration and bondage to decay (see 8:20–21). Through what is revealed in nature, fear of God may be instilled, but love and trust are revealed through His Son.

Additionally, natural revelation is insufficient for any people because no group has remained satisfied with natural religion. The religion of the deists, the rational philosophers' moral reason, and the piety and obedience of people apart from some revelation remain abstract. These ideas have never founded any religion or church. Therefore, natural religion has never really existed. "All religions are concrete and rest on revelation."[10]

If general revelation is insufficient, does this mean that the person who has never heard of Christ in some remote part of the world will be condemned to hell? The implication behind this question is that such a person is "innocent," having never had the opportunity to believe in Christ. It implies that God would be unjust to condemn such a person to hell and therefore if He did, He could not be a good God.

It is true that God would be unjust if He condemned some-one for what He had never had the opportunity to do. However, failing to believe in Jesus is not the basis for the "innocent" who has never heard of Jesus being condemned. Rather, as Romans 1 teaches us, condemnation comes when people fail to do what they know they should do: seek out, worship, and thank the God who has revealed Himself in His creation. We all have failed in this obligation. We all have a conscience with the law written on our hearts, even as pagans without God's written revelation do; and since we have failed to live up to the law's standards, we are therefore subject to God judging the secrets of our hearts by Christ Jesus (see Rom. 2:15–16).

But one may object, seeing that many people around the world who do not know Jesus are quite religious and pray to their gods. Humanity the world over is religious. However, this universality of religion actually points to people's godlessness be-cause their efforts actually point to their effort to escape from facing the true God. Humanity's tendency is to invent religion not to seek God, but to run away from Him. People repress the revelation God has given them in nature and instead set up false gods of their own imagination. They do this because they don't like the God to which natural revelation leads them.[11] Those who "forget God" shall go down to hopeless death forever (Ps. 9:17–18).

However, God has given humankind His clear, true revelation in His Word. He gave it by the inspiration of His Spirit through His prophets and apostles. The author of Hebrews wrote, "Long ago, at many times and in many ways, God spoke to our fathers by the prophets, but in these last days he has spoken to us by his Son, whom he appointed the heir of all things, through whom also he created the world" (1:1–2). The Word helps us understand who God is in a much fuller way; we come to know Him personally in a relationship through His Son. As John's Gospel says, "No one has ever seen God; the only God, who is at the Father's side, he has made him known" (1:18). When we know Christ, all things become clearer. With the veil lifted from our eyes, His Word applied to our hearts by the Spirit helps us see and understand His creation as something that is transformed from black and white to full, brilliant color.

> God's revelation in nature may be likened to a concert performed by an orchestra. Some people who come to listen hear only the instruments as they express the melody and harmony of the music. But others who come are familiar with the composer and know the words that go with the music. These hear more than the music.
>
> In much the same way, only those who have a personal relationship with the Creator through Jesus Christ can really see in all of creation the fullness of what God intended to communicate through it.[12]

This fuller special revelation is absolutely necessary for saving faith. This is what Paul argues further on in Romans: "Faith comes from hearing, and hearing through the word of Christ" (10:17). He is saying that preachers have to be sent so that people may hear and believe and be saved (see Rom. 10:14–15). Yet, interestingly, Paul goes on to quote from Psalm 19:4, saying, "But I ask, have they not heard? Indeed they have, for 'Their voice has gone out to all the earth, / and their words to the ends of the world'" (Rom. 10:18). Apparently Paul used this quote to enhance the teaching of the entire psalm—the first half that speaks of creation or general revelation and the second half concerning special revelation, which is the Word of God. Today the Word of God has been preached widely, just as the skies have proclaimed the glory of God; thus we, just like the Jews, are without excuse. Having heard the preaching of Christ as Savior of the world, all men and women are called to repentance and faith in Him.

Discussion Questions

1. What do we know about God from observing His creation?

2. What did you know about God before you ever heard from or read the Bible?

3. Did you seek God before learning about Him or were you trying to avoid Him?

4. Before becoming a Christian (if you are one), what was your concept of God like?

5. Why do people suppress the knowledge of God and how do they do it?

6. Why are all people without excuse for their forgetfulness of God?

7. Why is hearing the proclamation of God's Word and its revelation of Jesus Christ necessary for all people, even those who have never heard of Him?

2

The Authority of the Bible Among Multiple Revelations
2 Timothy 3:14–17

All Scripture is breathed out by God and profitable for teaching, for reproof, for correction, and for training in righteousness.

2 Timothy 3:16

Almost daily, we hear many truth claims. Each one has its own source of authority. Most Americans believe that "truth can be discovered only through logic, human reasoning and personal experience."[1] Additionally, in our postmodern age, we find that many claim that there are multiple truths, even though these truths may contradict one another. These people don't seem bothered by the contradictions, believing subjectively that whatever is true for someone else is fine, even though it may not be true for the next person. From their perspective, there is no such thing as one truth. In a world that is moving beyond postmodernism, many seek spirituality and truth within themselves. As David Wells observes, "Spirituality, in the contemporary sense . . . makes no truth claims and seeks no universal significance. It lives out its life within the confines of private experience. 'Truth' is private, not public; it is for the individual, not for the universe."[2]

The spiritual journey for such persons does not begin from something outside themselves, given by God or from what is authoritative and thus unchangeable. Rather, it begins from themselves and leans on their own authority to decide from where to draw knowledge and inspiration and to determine what is viable to believe. Validation for its value is found in its psychological and therapeutic effects. In such spirituality, there is a continual mixing, matching, and reappropriating of ideas to find out what fits one's quest for something more.[3] Consequently, a 2009 survey revealed that 41 percent of Americans believe that "the Bible, the Koran and the Book of Mormon are different expressions of the same spiritual truths."[4]

Those advocating religious pluralism—who are well-meaning but have a patronizing, defective mind-set—think we are all really saying the same thing. They suppress or evade deep-seated differences between faiths in order to develop a theory that accounts for some commonalities. To do justice to world religions, they need to be seen through the eyes of their adherents rather than through homogenizing tendencies of scholars seeking to develop artificially constructed versions. In other words, these individuals advocate unifying ideals found in various religions that they believe to be important, such as love and peace, but do not necessarily teach major themes of those religions. Their attempt to bring unity introduces distortions to each faith, including a redefinition of God. Such pluralists bring their own particular perspectives that actually mold the absolutist perspective they seek to avoid. Deliberate suppression of differences in order to achieve harmony does not bring true understanding. Certain differing claims in each faith cannot be reconciled. For instance, the New Testament continually portrays Jesus as having died on the cross, while the Qur'an emphatically denies that He did. The Bible emphasizes that after death is the judgment and our eternal destiny, while Hindus insist on there being a transmigration of souls through reincarnation based on people's karma.[5]

How can Christians claim that the Bible is the truth, that it is God's Word? Many in the West today reject submission to any external religious authority such as the Bible. But Jesus prayed to His Father, "Your word is truth" (John 17:17), affirming the eternal Word's authority and validity. If we have faith in Jesus as the Son of God, we also have faith in the truth of His word that affirmed the entire Bible as the very Word of God. But before we expound on what the Bible has to say about itself, let's take a brief comparative look at the "revelations" found in other religions.

Hindu, Buddhist, and Muslim Scriptures

Hindu scriptures were composed from about 1800 BC to 300 BC and consist of hymns and prayers, meticulous instructions for rituals, regulations for life in society, profound philosophical discussions, and many other elements. The most important scriptures are the Vedas, the Upanishads, and the Epics. Included in one of the epics is the Bhagavad Gita or "Song of the Lord," which is the most important and best-loved single document of Hinduism. Another epic is Ramayana. These scriptures are written in Sanskrit.

The Vedas are a collection of hymns that were compiled earlier than 1000 BC but written down about the eighth century BC. They are in honor of the Hindu gods that represent the powers of nature. Hinduism began when, during the fourth century BC, Aryan invaders from Greece under Alexander the Great conquered much of the land that makes up present-day India. They brought with them the pantheon of gods they worshiped and combined them with the meditation techniques of Indian tradition to form what we know today as Hinduism.

A Hindu could deny any distinctive Hindu doctrine, except perhaps karma, and still be a Hindu. Hinduism includes a vast amount of highly differing beliefs and has changed throughout the centuries. Since Hinduism developed over a long period of time through diverse people, it has an unusual variety of religious beliefs and practices as well as vagueness.

> It has no founder and no definite creed, and it recognizes no final or absolute revelation. It absorbs and includes all kinds of religious belief and expression in India—if these will permit it—from the animistic religion of hill tribes and the polytheism of peasants to the lofty monistic philosophy and not uncommon agnosticism of the intellectuals.[6]

With this vagueness defining its beliefs, apart from some core elements, such as the law of karma, Hinduism rejects the exclusiveness of the claims of Christ and the absolute authority of the Christian Scriptures. Hindus would rather incorporate Jesus as just another incarnation of a deity among millions and gladly receive some of His ethical teaching. Gautama Buddha, founder of Buddhism, lived about six centuries before Christ; he was probably born in 563 BC. Gautama's discovery of the Middle Way, or enlightenment, occurred as he sat under what became known as the Bo tree about 528 BC in the Indian state of Bihar.

The enlightenment he discovered was contemporaneous with the Old Testament prophets Zechariah and Haggai. The discovery of Buddha, meaning "enlightened one," at age thirty-five was known as the eightfold path to deliverance from suffering. Gautama traveled around forming monastic communities and preaching his doctrines for forty-five years. He died in Nepal of food poisoning at age eighty, telling his disciples, "Work out your salvation with diligence."

The Buddhist sacred writings are called the Tripitaka or the Pali Canon. It is composed of three parts or "baskets," containing the rules of discipline of the order, the sermons of the Buddha, and philosophical commentaries on the teachings of the Buddha. There are two kinds of Buddhists: Theravada and Mahayana. The Theravada Buddhists are generally atheists in their teaching, but many Mahayana Buddhists have evolved a pantheon of gods (Buddhas and bodhisattvas). "Buddhism rejects the concept of a personal God, and for that matter of any spiritual personality, either human or divine. God, in the Christian sense, is unknown to Buddhists. In place of a personal creator, they uphold karma (cause and effect) as the exclusive principle to explain the universe. What or who initiated karma is undetermined."[7]

"Quite unlike Jesus of the New Testament, Gautama of the Tripitaka (early Buddhist scriptures) did not seem to have clearly claimed that the Saving Truth or the Liberating Path was identical with his own person. He was only the Pathfinder and Truth-discoverer."[8] Jesus, however, claimed to be "the truth" (John 14:6). The gospel of Jesus is characterized by its historicity as opposed to the religion of the Buddhas and bodhisattvas, which is based on mythology.

Muslims claim that Muhammad (AD 570–632) received the Qur'an through the angel Gabriel in a cave on Mount Hira in Arabia. He continued to receive revelations for thirteen years in Mecca and then for ten years in Medina. During Muhammad's lifetime, his revelations were memorized by his companions and later compiled into the written Qur'an. An official version was developed under the third caliph, Uthman, and all other versions and copies were burned.

The Qur'an is believed to be an eternal book sent down to Muhammad by Allah that supersedes all previous revelations. The Qur'an is understood, however, to affirm the truthfulness of the books sent down to the Jews (the Torah and the Psalms) and to the Christians (the Injil, or the gospel book given to Jesus). Additionally, prior to Muhammad, 124,000 prophets are believed to have been sent to all peoples with the message of Islam. Only twenty-five of these are named in the Qur'an, and most of them we find in the Bible as well. While many stories from the Bible may be found in the Qur'an, in the Muslim holy book they are incomplete, distorted, out of any historical context, and without salvific significance. There is confusion between Miriam, the sister of Moses, and Mary, the mother of Jesus, and also regarding which of his two sons Abraham was about to offer as a sacrifice. Muslims claim that the Christian Scriptures affirm the teaching of Islam and predict the coming of Muhammad;

but in many critically important points, the differences between the teachings in these two sources are incompatible.

A few of these differences concern the nature, immanence, and character of the triune God. The Qur'an also denies the divinity of Christ and His death and resurrection for humanity's atonement and justification from sins, and it lacks understanding of the sinful nature of humanity from the Fall. Muslims attempt to explain the differences between the teaching of the Qur'an and the Bible by saying that the Scriptures of the "people of the Book," or the Christians, have been corrupted. That is not stated in the Qur'an nor is there any historical evidence for it. The doctrine developed in Islam's early history as Muslims encountered Christians in debate; it was Islam's explanation for the differences between the two faiths.

Someone may ask, "What about revelations received in other religions? Couldn't Buddha or Muhammad have experienced an encounter with God? Aren't their revelations just as real and true as that of the Bible?" Some in this postmodern age respond to this by saying that one's experience should be the test of truth. But should the visions and experiences of Joan of Arc, Joseph Smith, Muhammad, and Gautama Buddha be put on a different level from that of other ordinary people? If so, by what criteria? Subjective experience does not give us much to go on. For Christians, however, it is only because of the uniqueness of Christ found in Scripture that we do not accept all "revelations" as pretty much on the same level as the Bible. There is nothing in the Bible that tells us what could be determined as revelation outside the Word of God. Jesus and the apostles continually appealed to the Scriptures to establish Christian doctrine by some revelation among the nations outside Israel.

Let us look at why Christians see the Bible alone as the Word of God. We believe the Bible, as pastor Voddie Baucham Jr. explains, "because it's a reliable collection of historical documents written down by eyewitnesses during the lifetime of other eyewitnesses. They report supernatural events that took place and fulfilled the specific prophecies, and they claim that their writings are divine rather than human in origin" (see 2 Pet. 1:16–21).[9]

The Inspiration of the Bible

Evangelical Christians recognize the Bible to be the very Word of God. As such, they understand it to be inerrant. This means that the Bible is completely true and has divine authority; it is without error in all that it teaches and all that it affirms from the original autographs; it has plenary inspiration, meaning that the words that the writers of the Bible wrote were inspired by the Holy Spirit. This is all affirmed in many passages of Scripture. One of the important ones—and the one we will examine in this chapter—is when Paul wrote to his spiritual son, Timothy, saying, "All Scripture is breathed out by God" (2 Tim. 3:16), indicating that since God is a God of truth and faithfulness, all He inspired must also be infallible and authoritative.

When Paul said "all Scripture," he was referring to all of the Old Testament, which was already accepted as Scripture by the Jews. But he referred to at least some of the New Testament, which had been written by then, as Scripture. For example, Paul quotes directly from the Gospel of Luke in First Timothy 5:18, calling it Scripture, and Peter refers to a collection of Paul's letters as Scripture in Second Peter 3:16. So Paul's letters and those of other apostles that had been written or authorized by Christ's apostles were already, at a very early date, considered authoritative as Scripture.[10]

Paul's statement that "all Scripture is breathed out by God" is the first occurrence of this word for "breathed out" in any Greek literature, suggesting that Paul may have coined the term. It puts emphasis on the divine origin and consequently the authority of Scripture. Paul was not saying that the writers were inspired men, but that the words written were spoken by God. Paul also emphasized that all Scripture is authoritative and important, while his and Timothy's opponents emphasized only certain portions, such as genealogies and laws (see 1 Tim. 1:4; Titus 3:9). This is generally the approach taken by cults and other religions whose adherents claim to believe in the Bible but deliberately take certain verses out of context to affirm their false doctrine. The apostle Peter further explained this understanding of God-inspired Scripture, responding to questions about the authority and origin of his and other writings. He testified, "We did not follow cleverly devised myths when we made known to you the power and coming of our Lord Jesus Christ, but we were eyewitnesses of his majesty" (2 Pet. 1:16). Peter had seen Jesus glorified on the Mount of Transfiguration, alongside the prophets Moses and Elijah, and personally heard the voice from heaven by which God said, "'This is my beloved Son, with whom I am well pleased; listen to him.' When the disciples heard this, they fell on their faces and were terrified" (Matt. 17:5–6). Now Peter was saying that there was something even more sure than his eyewitness testimony: the written Scriptures from God. He wrote, "We have the prophetic word more fully confirmed, to which you will do well to pay attention as to a lamp shining in a dark place."

Peter went on to explain why Scripture is so trustworthy: "No prophecy of Scripture comes from someone's own interpretation. For no prophecy was ever produced by the will of man, but men spoke from God as they were carried along by the Holy Spirit" (2 Pet. 1:20–21). We see here that both God and people were active participants in the writing of Scripture. Although God the Holy Spirit was the source of Scripture—and whatever Scripture says, God says—the human writer also spoke out of his particular historical-cultural context, addressing issues pertinent to his immediate audience but moved by the Spirit as to what to write.

Since all Scripture is breathed out by God and authoritative, these sacred writings "are able to make [us] wise for salvation" and are "profitable for teaching, for reproof, for correction, and for training in righteousness" (2 Tim. 3:15–16). The divine origin of Scripture, which is then applied to the reader or hearer by the Holy Spirit, has the power to convert a dead heart of stone to a living heart of flesh. Scripture is then applicable for training in righteousness and godliness—that is, for teaching us to live as followers of Christ. Righteousness is living in conformity to the will of God, which means being daily trained in the Word empowers us to do so more closely as we grow in faith by knowing the Word.

Paul wrote to the Romans a great truth about what Scripture means for our instruction and sure hope: "Everything that was written in the past was written to teach us, so that through the endurance taught in the Scriptures and the encouragement they provide we might have hope" (Rom. 15:4, NIV). Having such endurance and encouragement of the Scriptures that leads to hope is possible only if we believe the Scriptures to be a word from God that is totally true. Otherwise, how can we know what to believe and what not to believe? If we do not receive the Scriptures as fully true, there is no basis for our good hope.

The Authority of the Bible

Although the Bible authenticates itself as authoritative for its moral teaching, its amazing literature, the unity of its message from Genesis to Revelation, and the power of its influence to change lives throughout the world, the main reason we believe it to be inspired and authoritative is out of our loyalty to Jesus. Since we believe that He came from God and spoke from God, His endorsement of the Scriptures must be from God, as well.

Jesus said, "My teaching is not mine, but his who sent me. If anyone's will is to do God's will, he will know whether the teaching is from God or whether I am speaking on my own authority" (John 7:16–17). To do God's will is to have faith, which is rewarded by the ability to understand Scripture, which points to Jesus as the Son of God and Savior of humanity.

When the resurrected Christ appeared to two of His followers on the road to Emmaus, "beginning with Moses and all the Prophets, [Jesus] interpreted to them in all the Scriptures the things concerning himself" (Luke 24:27). Shortly afterward, He appeared to His disciples and said, "Everything written about me in the Law of Moses and the Prophets and the Psalms must be fulfilled" (24:44).

Jesus affirmed as Scripture from God all that we know to be the sixty-six books of the Bible—thirty-nine in the Old Testament and twenty-seven in the New Testament. The way in which He did this was different for the two Testaments, because, obviously, the New Testament had not yet been written. Concerning the Old Testament Jesus made direct statements about its origin and permanent validity. He said, "Do not think that I have come to abolish the Law or the Prophets; I have not come to abolish them but to fulfill them. For truly, I say to you, until heaven and earth pass away, not an iota, not a dot, will pass from the Law until all is accomplished" (Matt. 5:17–18; see also Luke 16:17). He also affirmed, "Scripture cannot be broken" (John 10:35).

Jesus quoted or made reference to many of the Old Testament books, often as they testified to Himself or the Spirit, as authoritatively from God. For example, He said that the Holy Spirit spoke through David when He quoted Psalm 110 (see Mark 12:36). He endorsed Moses as the author of the Torah (see John 7:19, 23)—the first five books of the Bible—and a spokesperson for God. When responding to the Pharisees, Jesus referred to God the creator when reflecting on what Moses wrote concerning marriage (see Matt. 19:4–5).

Jesus affirmed the authority of Scripture not only through what He said about it but also by how He used it. It had a supremely high place in His own life and ministry, and He believed and acted on it. John Stott gives examples of this[11] in how Jesus responded to an uncertainty, question, or problem by His response in the areas of personal duty, official ministry, and public controversy. For example, when tempted in the wilderness by Satan, Jesus responded by quoting Scripture, prefacing each of the three temptations with the words "It is written" (see Luke 4:1–13). For Jesus to obey His Father, He knew He must submit to what stood written in Scripture. There was no room for negotiation. Concerning Jesus' official ministry role, He understood who He was as the Son of God, the anointed King, the suffering Servant, and the glorious Son of Man likely by meditating carefully on the Old Testament prophets and psalms. He came to understand that in order to fulfill Scripture, He would have to suffer, die, and rise again. When Satan expressed doubt as to His identity and Peter questioned Jesus' need to suffer and die, the Lord repeatedly referred to Scripture that needed fulfillment (see, for example, Matt. 26:52–54). In Scripture, Jesus found His messianic role and believed that it must be carried out as written because God had decreed it.

As to how Jesus responded to public controversy, again, He continually referred to Scripture. When asked, "Teacher, what shall I do to inherit eternal life?" Jesus responded with the questions, "What is written in the Law? How do you read it?" (Luke 10:25–26). Jesus rebuked both parties of Jewish religious leaders for their cavalier approach to Scripture. The Pharisees added their traditions to Scripture, which led them not to fulfill the teaching of the Scriptures, thus making them void. The Sadducees subtracted from Scripture by denying the supernatural, showing their ignorance of the power of God. So we conclude that in Jesus' perception and use of Scripture, He was completely submissive to the Word as being of God. Since Jesus had such a view and practice, how can we as His followers do any less?[12]

Jesus named His disciples "apostles" (6:13), which means "sent ones," and said they would go on a teaching and preaching mission, affirming the New Testament writing by passing on His words to the world. Like the Old Testament prophets, they were to speak in Jesus' name. Both the prophets and apostles were equal organs of divine revelation. John Stott provides us with three ways in which the apostles were uniquely equipped for their task, making them an irreplaceable group: "their personal commission, their historical experience and their special inspiration."[13]

Jesus personally chose, commissioned, and authorized His twelve disciples to be apostles for the church (see Luke 6:13). They were not self-appointed, as many religious and cult leaders tend to be. Even Paul was made an apostle, or sent out, by Christ, as Paul describes in his conversion experience (see Acts 26:17; Gal. 1:1).

All the apostles also had historical experience of being with Jesus, most of them from the time of His baptism. Each had been witness to Jesus' resurrection, even Paul (see 1 Cor. 9:1; 15:8–9) and James, Jesus' half brother (see 15:7). Mark writes that Jesus "appointed twelve (whom he also named apostles) so that they might be with him and he might send them out to preach" (Mark 3:14). The disciples' preaching had to come out of their experience of being a witness. Jesus spoke to them saying, "You also will bear witness, because you have been with me from the beginning" (John 15:27). Peter's requirement for the replacement of Judas was that it be someone who had been with Jesus from the time of His baptism until He was taken up in the ascension (see Acts 1:21–22).

Not only did the apostles have a personal commission and a historical experience with Jesus, but they were given a special inspiration by the Holy Spirit. This experience was different from that which every true Christian has. It related to the apostles' teaching ministry that had authority from God. Jesus said, "The Helper, the Holy Spirit, whom the Father will send in my name, he will teach you all things and bring to your remembrance all that I have said to you" (John 14:26). Although the disciples could not bear Jesus' teaching at that time, Jesus told them that when the Spirit of truth came, He would guide them "into all the truth" (John 16:13). These promises foretold the writing of the Gospels, in which Jesus' teaching was remembered, and of the Epistles, in which His teaching was supplemented.

Jesus purposely gave those unique gifts for the writing of the New Testament and the apostles understood their distinctive role in that capacity. They exercised power and expected the churches to submit to their apostolic authority, ordering their epistles to be read in services along with the Old Testament Scriptures (see Col. 4:16; 1 Thess. 5:27; Rev. 1:3). Because the Thessalonians received the word of God from him, Paul was thankful (1 Thess. 2:13). He taught that his writing was not only divine revelation but verbally inspired, saying, "We impart this in words not taught by human wisdom but taught by the Spirit" (1 Cor. 2:13). Additionally, Paul demanded obedience, writing that they "should acknowledge that the things [he was] writing to [them were] a command of the Lord" (14:37). The Galatian believers received Paul "as an angel of God, as Christ Jesus" (Gal. 4:14)—in other words, as God's messenger.

Peter wrote that the brothers had been born again "through the living and abiding word of God" that he had delivered (1 Pet. 1:23). He went on to quote Isaiah, saying, "The word of the Lord remains forever," and concluded, "This word is the good news that was preached to you" (1:25). John wrote in his epistles that not only did he testify to and proclaim what he had seen, touched, and heard of Jesus, but that believing this message was required in order for a person to have fellowship "with the Father and with his Son Jesus Christ" (1 John 1:3).

John called his readers back to what had been proclaimed at the beginning (see 1 John 2:7, 24). In fact, a major test of religious teachers' own knowledge of God was if their lessons conformed to those of the apostles.

John wrote, "We are from God. Whoever knows God listens to us; whoever is not from God does not listen to us. By this we know the Spirit of truth and the spirit of error" (4:6; see also 2 John 9–10; 3 John 9–10).

The early church too recognized the authority of the apostles. The new believers, having just received the Holy Spirit on the day of Pentecost, "devoted themselves to the apostles' teaching" (Acts 2:42). Likewise, if we expect to be Spirit filled, we must do as the early believers did. The apostles taught what had been passed on to them by Christ and recognized that only the apostles had authority to issue commandments. No one was to have any teaching on his own authority (see 2 Pet. 1:20–21).

As the early church decided which books were to be included or excluded in the New Testament canon, the test for including a book was whether it had been written by an apostle or had the imprimatur of the apostles as coming from their circle and teaching.

Each book had to have apostolicity.[14] The apostle Paul said that the church was "built on the foundation of the apostles and prophets, Christ Jesus himself being the cornerstone" (Eph. 2:20). He continued, saying that the mystery of Christ "was not made known to the sons of men in other generations as it has now been revealed to his holy apostles and prophets by the Spirit" (3:5; see also 1 Pet. 1:10–12). Thus the Bible, as revealed to Old Testament prophets and New Testament apostles, is recognized as the only Word of God.

The Sufficiency of Scripture

Although many claim to believe in the inspiration and authority of the Bible, many of these people also deny that it is sufficient. Even some claiming to be evangelicals dabble in dreams, visions, prophecies, esoteric experiences, and the teaching of leaders claiming to have the voice of God—even when that teaching has not been tested by Scripture (see 1 Thess. 5:20–21; 1 John 4:1–6).

A variety of cults have arisen that claim to use the Bible and accept its authority. In reality, however, they ignore the clear teaching of the Bible and add to it writings that they also call Scriptures or claim to be as authoritative as Scripture. Among such groups are the Mormons (the Book of Mormon); the Unification Church, also known as the Moonies (Divine Principle); the Christian Science practitioners (Science and Health with Key to the Scriptures); some Seventh Day Adventists groups (the writings of Ellen G. White); and even the Roman Catholics (the Apocrypha and canon law).

Muslims too affirm the Scriptures of the Jews and Christians yet say that the Scriptures have been corrupted. They insist that the Qur'an is the final revelation through the seal of the prophet Muhammad and the only authoritative revelation today. Many Christians have called Islam a heresy of Christianity because of the many parallels yet significant differences between the two religions.

Baha'u'llah, principle founder of Baha'ism, wrote the Book of Certitude, which proposes the central Baha'i idea of "progressive revelation," the theory that prophets arise and reveal teachings according to the needs and possibilities of the times.[15] Baha'i adherents teach that "all the Prophets of God utter the same speech and produce the same Faith," but "they differ . . . in the intensity of their revelation."[16]

But the Word of God that we know as the Christian Bible is all-sufficient for life and salvation. As Jesus rebuked the Jewish religious leaders for their hardness of heart and lack of belief in Him, He said, "You search the Scriptures because you think that in them you have eternal life; and it is they that bear witness about me, yet you refuse to come to me that you may have life" (John 5:39–40).

And who do the Scriptures testify Jesus is? John states, "He was even calling God his own Father, making himself equal with God" (5:18). Jesus taught the following concerning Himself.

> As the Father raises the dead and gives them life, so also the Son gives life to whom he will. For the Father judges no one, but has given all judgment to the Son, that all may honor the Son, just as they honor the Father. Whoever does not honor the Son does not honor the Father who sent him. Truly, truly, I say to you, whoever hears my word and believes him who sent me has eternal life. He does not come into judgment, but has passed from death to life. (5:21–24)

Jesus claimed deity as the one who gives life, receives honor as God, and judges the world. It is necessary to enter into eternal life by hearing and believing the word of Christ, which essentially is the entire Bible and points to Christ and His work, summarized in the gospel. The Word of God and the truth of God's Word are all combined in the person of Jesus.

If the Word of God is inerrant, reliable, authoritative, and eternal, then why would any further revelation be necessary to confirm the previous revelations, as is claimed by the Qur'an? Why would a new revelation be needed based on a book about Jesus coming to the Native American that included extensive quotes from the King James Bible and had ostensibly appeared on golden tablets given by the angel Moroni to Joseph Smith in Palmyra, New York, as we find in the Book of Mormon? All we need for knowledge of God and a relationship with Him, all we need for life, godliness, guidance, social reformation, hope, and salvation has already been given to us in the Bible. In fact, the Bible warns us against adding to or subtracting from God's revelation. God spoke to the Israelites through the prophet Moses saying, "Do not add to what I command you and do not subtract from it, but keep the commands of the LORD your God that I give you" (Deut. 4:2, NIV; see also 12:32).

These commands are sufficient to confirm that all His Word must be obeyed. Anything that changes it or contradicts it cannot be tolerated. As wise Agur said of God's Word, "Do not add to his words, / or he will rebuke you and prove you a liar" (Prov. 30:6, NIV). In the last revelation given from God through the apostle John, we are given stern warnings.

> I warn everyone who hears the words of the prophecy of this book: if anyone adds to them, God will add to him the plagues described in this book, and if anyone takes away from the words of the book of this prophecy, God will take away his share in the tree of life and in the holy city, which are described in this book. (Rev. 22:18–19)

The Word of God is sufficient because in it is encapsulated "the faith that was once for all delivered to the saints" (Jude 3). Jude admonishes us to "contend for the faith," or oppose false teaching concerning the gospel, and live it out faithfully. This "faith" is the same as that taught by the apostles and held in common by all Christians as a body of belief given by God (see Gal. 1:23; 1 Tim. 3:9). "Anyone who runs ahead and does not continue in the teaching of Christ does not have God; whoever continues in the teaching has both the Father and the Son" (2 John 1:9, NIV).

May we, like Jesus, take the inspiration, authority, and sufficiency of the Bible seriously as the very Word of God. Thomas á Kempis (ca. 1380–1471) wrote, "He who hears the Word of God is freed from a multitude of opinions." By reading and studying the Word, we will come to know our Lord and learn to live in a way that pleases and glorifies Him. It is for that purpose we have been created (see Isa. 43:7).

Discussion Questions

1. What is meant by the inspiration of the Scriptures?

2. How does our view of the uniqueness of Christ relate to our understanding of the authority of Scripture?

3. What are some ways in which Jesus used Scripture to demonstrate its authority?

4. How were the apostles uniquely equipped to give us the New Testament Scriptures?

5. How should we beware of adding to "the faith that was once for all delivered to the saints" (Jude 3)?

6. How should we respect, believe, and live by the Bible alone as the Word of God?

3

The Lord—He Is God!

1 Kings 18:15–46

The fire of the LORD fell and consumed the burnt offering and the wood and the stones and the dust, and licked up the water that was in the trench. And when all the people saw it, they fell on their faces and said, "The LORD, he is God; the LORD, he is God."

1 Kings 18:38–39

We hear today of many gods and many ways to God, and we hear that each religion has truth. How can we sort this out? Is each religion's god the same, just called by a different name?

Some would like us to think so. In the days of Elijah the prophet, the people of Israel became apostate by worshiping the gods of the Canaanite people rather than remaining faithful to the God of Israel who had mightily delivered their forefathers out of slavery in Egypt. During that journey, God made a mockery of the gods of Egypt by demonstrating His power over them in each of the ten plagues. Generations later, the kings of Israel led the people into worshiping the false gods of Baal and Asherah, a carved wooden image and a goddess of the Canaanites.

Elijah challenged the prophets of Baal to a contest to prove which of them worshiped the true and living God. He was an instrument in the protracted war God was waging against the worship of Baal so that "all Israel" would know who was Lord. As we see here in First Kings 18:15–46, much of Scripture is a historical narrative through which God makes Himself known in mighty deeds. Again and again, He shows us that He is the only true God.

Apostasy in Israel

Ahab became king of Israel and ruled for twenty-two years. He worshiped idols as his father, Omri, had done, which led the people of Israel to do so as well. This "aroused the anger of the LORD, the God of Israel, by their worthless idols" (16:26, NIV). Ahab's idolatry provoked the Lord to anger.

> And as if it had been a light thing for him to walk in the sins of Jeroboam the son of Nebat, he took for his wife Jezebel the daughter of Ethbaal king of the Sidonians, and went and served Baal and worshiped him. He erected an altar for Baal in the house of Baal, which he built in Samaria. And Ahab made an Asherah. Ahab did more to provoke the LORD, the God of Israel, to anger than all the kings of Israel who were before him." (16:31–33)

Ahab's wife, Jezebel, had been killing off the prophets of God and amassed 450 prophets of Baal and 400 prophets of Asherah who were supported by the state (see 1 Kings 18:19).

Even today in India, for example, one frequently sees images that people worship. Mohandas Gandhi said, as any Hindu would, "There are innumerable definitions of God because his manifestations are innumerable. They overwhelm me . . . stun me."[1] The difficulty with this view is that those innumerable manifestations are really just the wide variety seen in God's creation. They are separate from God, not part of Him. Similarly, when worshipers honored Baal as the storm god, they were worshiping something completely under the control of the creator of the heavens and the earth. In reality, Baal was nothing. He simply became the focus of demon worship, and the people who considered him a god were afraid not to appease him. They felt subject to his whims.

But what makes us think idol worship is demon worship? God commanded the Israelites to sacrifice their animals at the entrance to the Tent of Meeting as a peace offering to the Lord. This was a means of countering "their sacrifices to goat demons, after whom they whore[d]" (Lev. 17:7). We find in Moses' song to Israel, "They sacrificed to demons that were no gods, / to gods they had never known, / to new gods that had come recently, / whom your fathers had never dreaded" (Deut. 32:17). Paul, warning us against participation in idolatry, says, "What pagans sacrifice they offer to demons and not to God. I do not want you to be participants with demons" (1 Cor. 10:20). So even today, offerings of rice, fruit, and incense before idols and altars in homes and stores are actually presented to demonic spirits. The Lord God is a jealous God (see Exod. 34:14) and He cannot allow any shared allegiances to other gods. In judgment, God brought drought and famine on the land of Israel for three and a half years. It was a demonstration that Baal, the storm god, was not able to control the weather as God could.

Water became scarce and the famine severe (see 1 Kings 18:2). Baal was the principle god in the Canaanite nature religion. Ritual prostitution was used as a means of sympathetic magic by which it was believed the ground would become fertile. Baal was the god who was believed to both own and fertilize the land. Yet the Lord God made it clear that Baal had no power over the production of crops, the bringing of rain, or the land itself.

> I know that the LORD is great,
>   and that our LORD is above all gods.
> Whatever the LORD pleases, he does,
>   in heaven and on earth,
>   in the seas and all deeps.
> He it is who makes the clouds rise at the end of the earth,
>   who makes lightnings for the rain
>   and brings forth the wind from his storehouses.
>
> (Ps. 135:5–7)

Ahab looked for Elijah, putting the blame on him for the disastrous drought that had come over the land of Israel. When Elijah finally showed himself, Ahab said to him, "Is [that] you, you troubler of Israel?" (1 Kings 18:17).

Now, "troubler of Israel" refers back to the time of Joshua when Achan took some of the silver and gold from Jericho that had been devoted to the Lord and hid it in his tent. This brought the anger of the Lord upon Israel and they lost in battle against the city of Ai. Thus Achan was asked, "Why have you brought this trouble on us? The LORD will bring trouble on you today" (Josh. 7:25, NIV). By finding and stoning the troubler of Israel, the nation was released from God's curse. Likewise, Ahab assumed that by killing Elijah, the disaster upon Israel would be released. He held Elijah responsible for a crime against the state worthy of death.

Ahab, however, had a basic misunderstanding about who the real troubler of Israel was. "'I have not made trouble for Israel,' Elijah replied. 'But you and your father's family have. You have abandoned the LORD's commands and have followed the Baals'" (1 Kings 18:18, NIV). Ahab and his family had broken their covenantal loyalty to the Lord.

That is the position we are all in when we sin against the Lord and bow to the idols of our hearts that lead us astray. These idols include whatever we are devoted to as first in our lives besides the Lord: money, career, sports, food, sexual gratification, or other indulgences.

Contest of the Gods

Now Elijah asked Ahab to call all the people of Israel to Mount Carmel for a challenge. Used as a place of worship to the gods, Mount Carmel was a high point on the Mediterranean Sea coast, parallel to the Sea of Galilee. Just as the issue of Achan had been settled before all Israel, so now the real troubler of Israel would be revealed by ordeal.

Elijah asked Ahab to invite the 450 prophets of Baal and the 400 prophets of Asherah to a contest. So Ahab sent out word to all of Israel to appear at Mount Carmel. The people assembled on the appointed day, along with the prophets of Baal. The four hundred prophets of Asherah did not appear, nor did Ahab's wife, Jezebel. Apparently these prophets were under Jezebel's control and were supported by her. She refused to have anything to do with Elijah.

Who were these pagan prophets? Today we would call such prophets shamans, witch doctors, spiritual gurus, or mediums. These prophets obtained their spiritual power through communion with the spirit world. As such, they were able to communicate with departed spirits and animal spirits; see into the past and make predictions regarding the future; and diagnose, cure, or cause suffering. They claimed to be intermediaries between the natural and spiritual worlds by travel through the upper and lower worlds.[2] Because they displayed such power, it is understandable why many in Israel were tempted to follow their leadership. The same sort of false prophets are becoming popular in the West today.

The question as to who was the real troubler of Israel was bound up in the question of who was the true God. So Elijah went before the people on Mount Carmel and challenged them to make a decision: "How long will you waver between two opinions?" (1 Kings 18:21, NIV). The Israelites thought that they could worship both the Lord and Baal and, in doing so, cover all their spiritual bases. Today this kind of thinking is considered to be broad-minded; but to be fully committed to only one God, the triune heavenly Father, Jesus Christ, and Holy Spirit, is thought to be narrow-minded religious extremism. For that reason, a relative of mine and his wife had four weddings to cover all their bases: a civil ceremony, a Roman Catholic church wedding, a Sufi Muslim ceremony, and finally a Hindu yoga blessing from their guru. Elijah, however, challenged this apostate idea:

"If the LORD is God, follow him; but if Baal is God, follow him" (1 Kings 18:21, NIV). To include any other deity in our worship is to deny the supremacy and sovereignty of the only true God. The Lord will not bless any mixture of allegiances. And so my relative's marriage also did not last.

Today too we see this mixture of allegiances to both the Lord and other gods. In Latin America, it is common to see Christo-paganism in which the patron saint of the village or town is worshiped. In these festivals most get drunk, sacrifices of a chicken or some animal are made to the local deities, the image of Mary is paraded through the streets, and citizens pray to an image of a bloody, dead Christ in a glass coffin. In North America, someone may say he believes in God and may attend church on special occasions, but he actually believes that all religions are essentially the same. He thinks they all lead to the same goal. Such a person may also get involved in qigong, Eastern meditation, reading his horoscope, or devoting his life to the acquisition of money as his god. Even some mainline church leaders are leading their flocks in such practices as Islamic prayers,[3] Hindu yoga-altered consciousness to unite the soul with a spirit force, Buddhist mindfulness meditation, or spiritual communion between churches and non-Christian religions celebrating what some call the interspiritual age.[4] We cannot waver, however, between various allegiances and think that God is pleased with us.

Before Elijah went on to prove who was the true God, he drew a contrast in the contest. It was just him—the only one of the Lord's prophets left—against the king and 450 prophets of Baal. Surely in the eyes of the people, the number of prophets would increase the likelihood that Baal would answer their prayers. Both Elijah and the prophets of Baal prepared a bull to be offered on an altar to their respective deity. The prophets of Baal had first choice of the bull for their sacrifice and were given first chance to call upon their god. However, in this ordeal, neither party was to light a fire to the wood under their sacrifice. Rather, the god who answered their prayers by fire would be shown to be the true God. This specific request engaged the faith of Baal's worshipers, who believed their god to control thunder, lightning, fire, and storms.

The prophets of Baal prepared the bull, laid it on the altar, and called upon their god. From morning until noon, they called upon Baal to light the altar by fire. "O Baal, answer us!" they shouted. But there was no response; no one answered. They did an ecstatic ritual dance, limping around the altar to arouse their god. Similar ritual dances are still common among Native American Indian tribes, various African tribes, and other pagan groups who seek a response from their gods.

"At noon Elijah began to taunt them. 'Shout louder!' he said. 'Surely he is a god! Perhaps he is deep in thought, or busy, or traveling. Maybe he is sleeping and must be awakened'" (1 Kings 18:27, NIV). Elijah's taunt shows evidence that he was familiar with their myths about Baal that portrayed him as traveling, fighting at war, visiting the underworld, and even dying and coming back to life. Suggesting that he may be "busy" was a euphemism for Baal taking care of his bodily functions in the privy. His "traveling" appears to be a joke about a god being here and there but not everywhere. The lack of response reminds us of the prophecy of Isaiah in which he describes a man who cuts a tree and uses some of the wood for fire to bake bread and warm himself. With another part of the wood, he fashions a god and worships it.

He prays to it and says, "Deliver me, for you are my god!" They know not, nor do they discern, for he has shut their eyes, so that they cannot see, and their hearts, so that they cannot understand. No one considers, nor is there knowledge or discernment to say, "Half of it I burned in the fire; I also baked bread on its coals; I roasted meat and have eaten. And shall I make the rest of it an abomination? Shall I fall down before a block of wood?" He feeds on ashes; a deluded heart has led him astray, and he cannot deliver himself or say, "Is there not a lie in my right hand?" (Isa. 44:17–20)

After hearing the taunts of Elijah, the prophets of Baal became more agitated. "They cried aloud and cut themselves after their custom with swords and lances, until the blood gushed out upon them" (1 Kings 18:28). Such self-mutilation is seen annually among the Shiite Muslim men as they cut themselves with swords and flagellate themselves with chains until their backs are bloody. It is an effort to receive merit from Allah as they identify themselves with the martyrdom of Hassan and Hussein. Among Filipino Roman Catholics, people have themselves crucified during Holy Week as penance to gain merit with God. But all such efforts are useless. Our God has already provided for atonement for our sin by the crucifixion of Christ. He hears and answers our prayers because of the merit of Jesus, who is alive and ever intercedes for us before the Father. Satan, however, is a deceiver who leads people to self-destruction and death.

We see ancient pagan practices promoted today as the new synthesis of old scientific methodology, with Eastern mysticism and deep spirituality leading toward a cosmology of pantheistic Oneism. Peter Jones explains the teaching of transpersonal psychologist Stanislav Grof, a promoter of the psychology of Carl Jung, as saying, "The basic human problems of aggression and greed can be solved only by becoming a shaman, a human being in direct touch with pagan deities."[5] In other words, Grof says, we need to be in touch with our higher shamanistic self through radical inner transformation to a higher level of consciousness as our only hope for the future.

Grof proposes reaching an altered state of consciousness through "technologies of the sacred," which include trance dancing; sound technologies of drumming, rattling, gongs, and chanting; controlled breathing; meditation and prayer; sensory overload, including extreme pain; psychedelic stimulation (use of drugs); and physiological methods of sleep or food deprivation and bloodletting. These ancient pagan techniques are essential to shamanism.[6] Our world today is not really advancing in the spiritual realm but is instead returning to ancient pagan rites of the occult.

Such spiritual technologies were futile for the shamans of Baal: "As midday passed, they raved on until the time of the offering of the oblation [about three in the afternoon], but there was no voice. No one answered; no one paid attention" (1 Kings 18:29). The ritual prophesying reached a crescendo of uncontrolled, ecstatic raving. The response was as the psalmist describes the gods of the nations.

> Their idols are silver and gold,
>   the work of human hands.
> They have mouths, but do not speak;
>   eyes, but do not see.

They have ears, but do not hear;
  noses, but do not smell.
They have hands, but do not feel;
  feet, but do not walk;
  and they do not make a sound in their throat.
Those who make them become like them;
  so do all who trust in them.

(Ps. 115:4–8)

Whatever power people think their gods have is simply a worthless figment of human imagination. Rather, any power people experience is simply the limited powers of the demonic forces they worship that deceive, debilitate, and destroy, producing fear in the worshiper.

Now that Baal worship proved worthless, Elijah called the people: "'Come near to me.' And all the people came near to him. And he repaired the altar of the LORD that had been thrown down" (1 Kings 18:30). The altar was one of the high places built for worship after the kingdom of Israel was divided between Israel and Judah. Such worship in places not designated by the Lord was forbidden, but using the altars to honor the true God was much better than worshiping the Baals and Asherahs. Elijah rebuilt the altar with twelve stones, representing the twelve tribes of Israel, not just the ten tribes of the northern kingdom or the two tribes of the southern kingdom. God had not rejected His covenant with part of His people. He was calling them all back to the true faith with what was about to happen.

Elijah built an altar in the name of the Lord and dug a trench around it that held about thirteen quarts (fifteen liters). He laid the wood, placed the cut-up bull on it, and asked for four large jars of water to be poured over the altar. The pouring of water over the altar assured the people that Elijah was not doing any tricks, nor could spontaneous combustion light the fire. Three times Elijah ordered the altar to be drenched with water. Thus, twelve large jars of water, representing again the twelve tribes, were used to flood the altar and fill the trench.

At the time of sacrifice, Elijah stepped forward and prayed aloud a simple prayer for all to hear. This prayer to the living Lord of their patriarchs—Abraham, Isaac, and Israel—was in stark contrast to the frenetic shouting, dancing, and self-mutilation the prophets of Baal did to gain the attention of a god who could not hear. Elijah prayed that the people would recognize that the Lord was "God in Israel," recalling to them the covenant with their forefathers, and that he was acting upon the Lord's command. He continued, "Answer me, O Lord, answer me, that this people may know that you, O Lord, are God, and that you have turned their hearts back" (1 Kings 18:37). It is the Lord who saves (see Jonah 2:9), draws people to him (see John 6:44), and enables them to believe (see 6:65).

The Lord—He Is God!

"Then the fire of the Lord fell and consumed the burnt offering and the wood and the stones and the dust, and licked up the water that was in the trench" (1 Kings 18:38). Was this a lightning bolt? Perhaps. But no storm clouds were present. The sky was clear. What a dramatic impact this must have had on the people. Everything was burned up, even the stones, dust, and water! Having served its purpose, the altar was removed by the Lord. We also see a similar burst of fire from the Lord at the Tent of Meeting when Moses and Aaron blessed the people after the sacrifice: "Fire came out from before the LORD and consumed the burnt offering and the pieces of fat on the altar, and when all the people saw it, they shouted and fell on their faces" (Lev. 9:24). On Mount Carmel, revival broke out among the people because the demonstration of the Lord's power and presence made His reality undeniable. It was not a demonstration of which god was greater but of who was the true God—and of the fact that Baal was no god at all. Through this dramatic victory, the knowledge of the Lord was preserved in both Israel and Judah from being wiped out by the forces of Satan and his agent Jezebel.

"Elijah said to them, 'Seize the prophets of Baal; let not one of them escape.' And they seized them. And Elijah brought them down to the brook Kishon and slaughtered them there" (1 Kings 18:40). That seems awfully harsh, one might think today. But remember, they lived in a different age under a theocracy, a society constituted under God. The Lord's command was, "Whoever sacrifices to any god, other than the LORD alone, shall be devoted to destruction" (Exod. 22:20). That is, idolaters were earmarked as offerings to the Lord. Any prophet, family member, or close friend who enticed an Israelite to worship other gods was to be put to death and shown no pity (see Deut. 13:1–11; 17:2–7; 18:20). This warning was to make anyone afraid to do such an evil thing and to eliminate the evildoers as well as the evil itself. Fortunately, we now live in an age of grace in which God's mercy is offered to the weak and Jesus seeks the lost to bring them into a relationship with Him despite their rebellion and idolatry. However, the destruction of those who worship foreign gods is a type of the ultimate destruction all will suffer who refuse to repent and believe in the Lord God, who is our creator and redeemer. In John's vision in Revelation, we are told that "the faithless, . . . the sexually immoral, sorcerers, idolaters, and all liars, their portion will be in the lake that burns with fire and sulfur, which is the second death" (Rev. 21:8). As Christians, we remain in a spiritual battle while we are in this present world. As Paul explains, we need to take our stand against the devil's schemes, "for we do not wrestle against flesh and blood, but against the rulers, against the authorities, against the cosmic powers over this present darkness, against the spiritual forces of evil in the heavenly places" (Eph. 6:12). The weapons we use are the Word of God and prayer. "For though we walk in the flesh, we are not waging war according to the flesh. For the weapons of our warfare are not of the flesh but have divine power to destroy strongholds. We destroy arguments and every lofty opinion raised against the knowledge of God, and take every thought captive to obey Christ" (2 Cor. 10:3–5).

This means that the whole person must be influenced by obedience to Christ. Therefore every idea, motive, desire, and decision has to be subjected to His lordship. Only then do we truly acknowledge Him as our Lord and God. Only in that way do we demonstrate that we really love Him. As we subject ourselves to the Word of God and proclaim this Word to the unbelieving world, we will see victory in our ongoing spiritual battle. But this all must be undergirded by prayer.

Answered Prayer

Elijah believed in prayer. He prayed for the Lord to bring down fire upon the altar and the Lord answered decisively. He then prayed for rain and waited with anticipation for that answer from the Lord. When Baal was clearly proven not to be a god, it was also completely ruled out that the coming rain was from Baal. Only the Lord controls the rain.

"Elijah said to Ahab, 'Go up, eat and drink, for there is a sound of the rushing of rain'" (1 Kings 18:41). He was inviting Ahab to hurry up and participate in the sacrificial meal because rain was coming. "So Ahab went up to eat and to drink. And Elijah went up to the top of Mount Carmel. And he bowed himself down on the earth and put his face between his knees" (18:42). The significance of this position for Elijah is uncertain, but he must have been in prayer for the lifting of the covenant curse over Israel. More than three years before, the Lord sent Elijah to Ahab to say that over the next few years there would be neither dew nor rain, except at his word (see 17:1). Now Elijah prayed for rain.

The true God is a God who answers prayer. Elijah sent his servant seven times to check the horizon over the Mediterranean Sea to see if he saw any clouds coming.

> At the seventh time he said, "Behold, a little cloud like a man's hand is rising from the sea." And he said, "Go up, say to Ahab, 'Prepare your chariot and go down, lest the rain stop you.'" And in a little while the heavens grew black with clouds and wind, and there was a great rain. And Ahab rode and went to Jezreel. And the hand of the Lord was on Elijah, and he gathered up his garment and ran before Ahab to the entrance of Jezreel. (18:44–46)

Elijah's run before King Ahab may have been an indication of his loyalty to the king—as a true servant taking on the role

of an outrunner and as a means of winning him over to worship
Yahweh. Figuratively, the Lord was running behind Ahab in His
thundercloud chariot. As we see in the Psalms, "He makes the
clouds his chariot; / he rides on the wings of the wind" (Ps.
104:3). Elijah was given special strength and stamina by God's
Spirit to run ahead of the king's chariot for about seventeen
miles to his summer palace in Jezreel.

James' comments on this event are an encouragement for us
to pray in faith: "The prayer of a righteous person has great power as it is working. Elijah was a man with a nature like ours, and
he prayed fervently that it might not rain, and for three years
and six months it did not rain on the earth. Then he prayed
again, and heaven gave rain, and the earth bore its fruit" (James
5:16–18). Prayer in faith is evidence of our belief in the true
God who made heaven and earth. He has power over all things.
As worship of the true God was restored in Israel through bold
faith and prayer in Elijah's day, so too will we see the strongholds
of Satan destroyed around the world through our prayers. God
wants us to bring all our concerns to Him in prayer.

Our prayers should begin with acknowledgement of what
distinguishes God from the gods of the ungodly. For example,
"Our Father in heaven, / hallowed be your name" (Matt. 6:9).
Allah, the god of Islam, cannot be called upon as "Father," nor
is he knowable. He does not respond to prayer because he offers neither relationship nor love. But the God of the Bible "is
love" (1 John 4:8), which is only possible because there is love
between the three persons of the one God since eternity past.
Therefore Muslim friends are happy to have Christians pray for
their needs because they have no real expectation of answered
prayer from Allah. A Muslim doctoral student from Sudan who

was studying in the United States went to London to be with his father, the leader of a large Sufi following in several countries, who was ill. He called his Christian friend in Philadelphia from his father's hospital bedside to have him pray for his father's healing because he believed there was power in the prayers of a Christian. A Christian partner in Malaysia told of how, "one village imam flung his Quran onto the floor, crying, 'For twelve years I've prayed to Allah, and nothing, nothing! But Jesus! He sent you guys all the way over here to share the good news? We want your Bible.'"[7]

We all struggle to various degrees with idols in our lives. Will you forsake any syncretistic mixture of allegiance you have both to the true God and to false gods that are worthless, and believe instead in the Lord alone? God the Father gave Jesus, His Son, authority over all people that he might give eternal life to all those the Father had given Him. Jesus prayed to His Father, "This is eternal life, that they know you, the only true God, and Jesus Christ whom you have sent" (John 17:3). The Israelites in Elijah's day came to this same faith. They renewed their covenant with God through Elijah's sacrifice on the altar. That sacrifice anticipated the propitiatory sacrifice of Jesus for our sins. Their sin of idolatry was forgiven and they were brought into a relationship with God by faith. Our sins may be forgiven in that same way. We can be brought into an eternal relationship with the true and living God, who calls us to turn to Him.

> There is no other god besides me,
>   a righteous God and a Savior;
>   there is none besides me.

> Turn to me and be saved,
>> all the ends of the earth!
>> For I am God, and there is no other.
> By myself I have sworn;
>> from my mouth has gone out in righteousness
>> a word that shall not return:
> "To me every knee shall bow,
>> every tongue shall swear allegiance."
>
> (Isa. 45:21–23)

Perhaps you have believed yourself to be a Christian, yet you now realize that you have made something other than the Lord your true focus of worship. Has your work, pursuit of recognition, pride, addiction to pornography, or greed become your true passion and thus become the controlling force in your life? Has it become a false idol for which you need to repent? Come now by faith to be made right with God and walk as His true child. Now is the time to bow the knee and swear allegiance only to the Lord, who is the true God.

This same Lord is the one who has come to us as the Lord Jesus Christ, who has all authority over heaven and earth (see Matt. 28:18). "At the name of Jesus every knee should bow, in heaven and on earth and under the earth, and every tongue confess that Jesus Christ is Lord, to the glory of God the Father" (Phil. 2:10–11). Let us follow the apostle John's concluding admonition: "We know that the Son of God has come and has given us understanding, so that we may know him who is true; and we are in him who is true, in his Son Jesus Christ. He is the true God and eternal life. Little children, keep yourselves from idols" (1 John 5:20–21).

Discussion Questions

1. Is it possible to worship the God of the Bible as a Christian and yet maintain the rituals of worship to another deity?

2. How could you be tempted to compromise worship of the one true God?

3. What should we do with pagan attachments we may have in our home, office, or yard (for example, pictures of Krishna, images of Buddha, a prayer carpet with the Kaaba, ritual masks, fetishes, charms, crystals for healing and prosperity, or Halloween decorations)?

4. How can we demonstrate today that the God proclaimed from Scripture is the one true God? What one historical event proves this beyond doubt?

5. What does our prayer life demonstrate about our faith in God?

4

The Unique Christ in a Pluralistic Age

John 1:14–18

The Word became flesh and made his dwelling among us. We have seen his glory, the glory of the one and only Son, who came from the Father, full of grace and truth.

John 1:14, NIV

We live in an age of many challenges to the Christian faith. It is an age of pluralism in which most every viewpoint is considered valid except the Christian viewpoint. One of the reasons the Christian faith is not accepted along with most other worldviews is because it is exclusive in its claims to truth, particularly as it is found in Jesus Christ. This is because Jesus is unique and He demands His followers' undivided loyalty.

Many people hate this and see Christians as close-minded and narrow. But you cannot be a true believer in Jesus as Lord and Savior and still follow other gods or other ways to God. When you understand the uniqueness of Jesus, you come to see that He answers all our doubts and questions and brings us into an intimate relationship with the living God. Many unique things may be said about Jesus, but we will focus on just a few of them, particularly as they are found in John 1:14–18.

The Eternal Word Became Flesh

The incarnation of Jesus as the eternally begotten Son of God sets the Christian faith apart from all others. Pluralists, who seek to destroy the distinctiveness of Christianity, drive a wedge between the historical person of Jesus and the principles that they allege He represents. The "Christ principle" is said by them to be accessible to those from all religions and is expressed in various but equally valid ways. Advocates of the pluralist agenda, however, demand that we adopt heretical views of Jesus that were considered false by the early church councils in order to fit their mold of "the great religious teachers of humanity."[1] Let us look at what Scripture actually says concerning the identity of Jesus.

Jesus was unique because, as the eternal Word of God, He "became flesh and made his dwelling among us" (1:14, NIV). The fact that the Word became flesh indicates that the Word existed before Jesus became a man. This confirms what John stated at the beginning of his prologue: "In the beginning was the Word, and the Word was with God, and the Word was God" (1:1). We see here that the Word was distinct from God, yet He was God. The Word was already there before the beginning of time and creation (see Gen. 1:1). So we are introduced to two distinct persons of God: the Father and the Word. Yet this God, the Word, became flesh. He became incarnated into the body of a human being, born as a baby by means of a miraculous virgin birth (see Matt. 1:18, 23, 25; Luke 1:34). This conception was made possible by the Holy Spirit (see Matt. 1:18, 20; Luke 1:35), the third person of God, thus showing us the unity and diversity in His three parts. Jesus spoke of this unity between Himself and His heavenly Father: "Anyone who has seen me has seen the Father. How can you say, 'Show us the Father'? Don't you believe that I am in the Father, and that the Father is in me?" (John 14:9–10, NIV).

The virgin birth of Jesus is acknowledged by Muslims. Yet they deny the incarnation of God in human form. They simply say that Jesus was virgin born in the same way they believe Allah created Adam without a human father. The New Testament does compare Adam and Christ but only in the sense that they were both federal heads of their race: Adam of the human race, which led to death for all because we sinned in him; and Christ as head of the church, the elect people of God, through whom we have eternal life since he is the "firstborn from the dead" (Col. 1:18). But being virgin-born, Jesus did not inherit the sinful nature brought upon the entire human race descended from Adam. He remained sinless and holy, as Muslims also acknowledge.

Hare Krishna Hindus may also acknowledge the incarnation of Jesus but will say that He is simply another incarnation of Lord Krishna. Mythical Krishna and the historical Jesus Christ, however, have nothing in common. Jesus was born and lived on earth in real history that can be quite adequately dated in relation to secular historical events. The character of Jesus, "full of grace and truth" (John 1:14), was as perfect as that of God the Father: holy, loving, just, joyful, peaceful, compassionate and kind. The playboy character of Krishna, who pursued goat-herding women called *gopis* and led men into war, is no comparison to Jesus. Moreover, Hinduism is not interested in history but turns toward contemplation and speculative thought. "Traditionally the Hindu does not attach great importance to the events that occur in the three-dimensional world of space and time, or to the human beings that take part in them. . . . Thus the Hindu has in the past been inclined to take pride in the fact that Hinduism is a religion of pure ideas, and in this respect to contrast Christianity unfavourably with it as a religion that is dependent on history."[2] Buddhism has a similar view of history because its ideas are reflections of one's own desires, devoid of objective reality. So, for example, the Amida Buddha (the principle Buddha of Pure Land Buddhism) does not actually exist but is a figment of the imagination, the object of religious art and "human figures made to dance in the background of the emotions."[3]

Yet Jesus came into historical time and space to dwell among us and identify with us as a man so that He could bring us salvation. It was not enough simply to postulate the nature and character of God, but it was primarily through what Jesus was and did that God's nature and character were revealed. Jesus' atoning death and resurrection would be meaningless if they did not actually happen historically and if their significance (as given to them by the apostles who were sent by Jesus with the message of the gospel) is not understood.

Greater Than the Prophets

Jesus was unique in that not only was He a prophet, but He was greater than all the prophets. No religious teacher, prophet, or apostle has been able to affirm what Jesus affirmed concerning Himself. We see first what John the Baptist said about Jesus: "This was he of whom I said, 'He who comes after me ranks before me, because he was before me'" (John 1:15). Normally, at that time, the older person was given greater honor than the younger. John was six months older than Jesus. John's ministry began before that of Jesus, with a great following. But John was not concerned about either of these points. John, rather, saw that Jesus was eternally before him. He saw the uniqueness of Jesus as being without historical origins.

Jesus directly claimed this Himself when He said to the Jews, "'Your father Abraham rejoiced that he would see my day. He saw it and was glad.' So the Jews said to him, 'You are not yet fifty years old, and have you seen Abraham?' Jesus said to them, 'Truly, truly, I say to you, before Abraham was, I am!'" (8:56–58). Abraham lived about two thousand years before Jesus' incarnation. So this claim from both John the Baptist and Jesus points to no other conclusion than that of Jesus' divinity.

Additionally, in claiming to be "I am," Jesus was using the divine name revealed to Moses at the burning bush (see Exod. 3:14), emphatically identifying Himself as God. This name expresses His eternity and oneness with God the Father. "I AM" is the name of God that reveals His character as the dependable and faithful God whom we are to trust. It expresses the nature and character of the God who promises, "I will be with you." Having a name by which He is to be known is an indication that God is a personal God rather than an impersonal, unknowable force.[4]

Another affirmation concerning Jesus comes from the apostle John: "The law was given through Moses; grace and truth came through Jesus Christ" (John 1:17). Although it was good, the law had no power to save. It shows us our sin and need for God's mercy and grace. That grace came through the ministry of Jesus. Moses was a faithful servant in God's house, and he testified to what would come in the future, namely Jesus Christ (see Deut. 18:15, 18–19). Jesus, however, was a son in God's house. He was not just a part of the household, as Moses was, but He was over God's house that is made up of the people of God (see Heb. 3:5–6).

The purity of Jesus' person distinguished Him from all other prophets. He was holy, without sin in thought, word, and deed. This was essential for His role as Savior in being the spotless Lamb of God, a perfect substitutionary sacrifice for our sin. Jesus was sinless despite the fact that He was tempted just like we are (see 4:15). He resisted all temptation and overcame it by the Word of God, as we see when Satan tempted Him in the wilderness after His baptism (see Luke 4:1–13). At Jesus' trial Pilate was able to say, "I find no basis for a charge against this man" (23:4, NIV; see also John 18:38). Even the Qur'an acknowledges that Jesus was sinless, without any fault, and went about doing good through miracles. (Interestingly, the Qur'an speaks of Muhammad needing forgiveness, yet Muslims still venerate him as the seal of the prophets and say that all the prophets were sinless. Likewise, adherents of Baha'i recognize Bahá'u'lláh as divine; yet he assassinated his opponents, and his teaching largely ignores the issues of sin and evil.)

The most significant difference marking the greatness of Jesus over all other prophets and religious leaders was His resurrection from the dead. Muhammad's grave and remains are in Medina and his sword, bow, brass footprint, and a hair from his beard are venerated in the Topkapi Palace in Istanbul. Gautama Buddha is still dead in his grave. Joseph Smith, the founder of Mormonism who claimed to have been given golden plates containing a new revelation by the angel Moroni, is still in his grave in Illinois. Mao Tse-Tung, whom the Chinese worshiped as the Great Helmsman, is entombed in a large mausoleum in Tiananmen Square in Beijing. Bahá'u'lláh is still buried in Akka, Israel.

Yet no one has ever found the body or bones of Jesus. He was witnessed alive by His disciples, the numerous women who followed Him, His half-brother James, Paul, and (on one occasion) by more than five hundred disciples at one time (see 1 Cor. 15:5–8). If Jesus did not rise from the dead, then our faith is futile, we are still in our sins, those who died with faith in Christ are lost, and we have no hope (see 15:17–19).

Grace and Truth Through Jesus Christ

The apostle John testifies concerning the grace and truth that came through Jesus.

> We have seen his glory, the glory of the one and only Son, who came from the Father, full of grace and truth. . . . Out of his fullness we have all received grace in place of grace already given. For the law was given through Moses; grace and truth came through Jesus Christ. (John 1:14, 16–17, NIV)

There are two senses in which grace is used here in this passage. First is "common grace," which is the goodness of God that comes to all people in the form of health, prosperity, knowledge, friendships, good times, and everything else that is of blessing. In this sense, rain comes upon the just and the unjust equally (see Matt. 5:45). Most do not acknowledge, however, that it is from the fullness of Jesus' grace that we have received one blessing after another. He is our creator and the creator of everything in the world.

Second, "special grace" or "redeeming grace" is that which is given only to the elect. God's saving grace revealed through Jesus is the unmerited favor of God toward undeserving humanity. It is God's love and kindness shown to people who actually deserve the very opposite. This is expressed by Paul when he says, "God demonstrates his own love for us in this: While we were still sinners, Christ died for us" (Rom. 5:8, NIV). God is gracious toward us not because of anything we have done but solely because His character is to be gracious. This grace is extended to us through Jesus Christ. John contrasts the grace revealed through Christ to the law revealed through Moses. Although there was grace and truth in Moses' day, it was not fully revealed as it has been in Christ. James Boice explains.

> The contrast is between the law with all its regulations and the new era of salvation by grace through faith apart from the works of the law that has come with Jesus Christ. It is a great contrast. Under the law, God demands righteousness from men; under grace, God gives righteousness to men. Under law, righteousness is based upon Moses and good works; under grace, righteousness is based upon Christ and Christ's character. Under law, blessings accompany

obedience; under grace, God bestows His blessings as a free gift. The law is powerless to secure righteousness and life for a sinful race. Grace came in its fullness with Christ's death and resurrection to make sinful men righteous before God.[5]

This grace is unique to Christ among all the religions of the world. In every religion other than Christianity, one must do something to earn God's favor. Sure, there are some similar aspects of grace in other religions. In Mahayana Buddhism, mythical bodhisattvas are lesser gods that did not enter nirvana so that they could return to help others escape the endless cycles of reincarnation. But their aid is still dependent upon the efforts of their devotees. In Islam, one tries to keep the five pillars of the faith and do what is halal or "permitted," and avoids doing what is haram, or "unlawful" or "forbidden." Additionally, various "good works" of reciting the Qur'an, fasting, making a pilgrimage to a holy site, or giving water to a thirsty animal cleanses one from sin and gives one merit before Allah. It is hoped that at the judgment, one's good works will outweigh one's bad deeds on the scales of justice. Because Allah is believed to be merciful and compassionate, one hopes to enter paradise, yet no one has any assurance of that. It is dependent on the capricious decision of Allah. Hindusim shows an element of grace in its bhakti marga tradition with its distinction between "monkey salvation" and "kitten salvation," seen in the fact that baby monkeys have to cling to their mothers, while the tigress carries her kittens in her mouth. This concept of a more grace-conscious "kitten salvation" did not emerge in Hinduism until a late period, particularly with the writings of Sri Ramanuja (1050–1137), when Syrian

Christianity became well established in southern India. Evangelical theologian Alister McGrath asks, "So, does 'kitten salvation' represent an inherent similarity between Hinduism and Christianity, or does it represent the tendency of some Hindu writers to 'borrow' ideas from Christianity?"[6] Hinduism has strong syncretistic tendencies, so similarity may reflect borrowing rather than convergence of the faiths. Thus there is no comforting grace in the various world religions that assures one of eternal life as we find in Jesus Christ, though we are totally undeserving.

Truth is a great theme in John's writing—he mentions it twenty-five times. In this first instance, as in most of them, he relates it to the character of God. At Jesus' trial he responded to Pilate, saying, "'You say that I am a king. In fact, the reason I was born and came into the world is to testify to the truth. Everyone on the side of truth listens to me.' 'What is truth?' retorted Pilate" (John 18:37–38, NIV). However, Pilate did not wait to hear Jesus say what He had said earlier to His disciples—that He is the truth. Jesus pointed to what was heavenly and eternal rather than to what was merely temporal and earthly. His teaching was not just the opinions of people but truth. Every person's eternal destiny is dependent on this truth found in Christ.

In our world today, we often hear the idea that all religions are equally true. Some see each religion as different spokes on a wheel, all leading to the same goal at the center. However, they overlook the fact that each religion has different truth claims. Although there may be some things in common from one religion to another, especially on moral principles, each religion has mutually exclusive claims. They don't even have the same goal at the center.

What do you do when you have conflicting truth claims? Two contradictory statements cannot both be truth. Logically, if someone claims that the dead are raised to life and others claim that they are not, both claims cannot be true. Only one of them can be true, unless the laws of logic do not apply to reality. However, this is the approach many take today. They say that what is true for you may not be true for me.* They claim that there is no universal truth.

This idea developed out of the philosophy of Georg Wilhelm Friedrich Hegel (1770–1831). It then was applied to theological interpretation by F.C. Baur, David Strauss, and Sören Kierkegaard.* From there, people no longer believed that what was true or false at one time was the same forever. They now believed "what is true for me today may not be true for me tomorrow."*Everything was relative. There was no absolute truth. So a common response to our faith in Christ is, "That's fine for you to believe in Jesus if it helps you. But don't bother me with it. I've found something else that helps me. Both of them are equally good. To each his own." This relative view of truth is something we must take a stand against. True truth is universally true for all people at all times. Otherwise how can it really be true at all? Without truth we have nothing upon which to stake our lives, nor can we have any hope.

When Jesus made the claim, "I am the way and the truth and the life," He was making a most reasonable statement based on the reality of who He was. Is His claim true? He could not make this claim and remain simply a way, a truth, or a life. Truth, by definition, is exclusive. The law of noncontradiction means that both Jesus' exclusive claims and other claims to the true way to God cannot both be true. As Ravi Zacharias says, "It is possible to say all the religions of the world are wrong, but it is not logically sensible to say all the religions are right."[7]

When we are confronted with the claims of Jesus Christ, we must make a clear decision about their validity. As Jesus prepared for His coming death, resurrection, and ascension, He discussed it with His disciples.

"You know the way to the place where I am going."

Thomas said to him, "Lord, we don't know where you are going, so how can we know the way?"

Jesus answered, "I am the way and the truth and the life. No one comes to the Father except through me. If you really know me, you will know my Father as well. From now on, you do know him and have seen him."

Philip said, "Lord, show us the Father and that will be enough for us."

Jesus answered: "Don't you know me, Philip, even after I have been among you such a long time? Anyone who has seen me has seen the Father. How can you say, 'Show us the Father'? Don't you believe that I am in the Father, and that the Father is in me? The words I say to you I do not speak on my own authority. Rather, it is the Father, living in me, who is doing his work. Believe me when I say that I am in the Father and the Father is in me; or at least believe on the evidence of the works themselves." (John 14:4–11, NIV)

How do you respond to Jesus' astonishing claims? Is He the truth He claimed to be, and is that truth universal for all? As C.S. Lewis stated it, either He was a liar, a lunatic, or the Son of God. The evidence is overwhelming that He was the unique, eternal Son of God who has revealed the Father to us. If we believe this to be true, we cannot remain neutral, because Jesus' claim has radical implications for how we are to live our lives by faith.

The Unique One

Jesus was unique in that it is only through Him that we may see God. In the concluding section of our text in John 1, the apostle says, "We have seen his glory, the glory of the one and only Son, who came from the Father. . . . No one has ever seen God, but the one and only Son, who is himself God and is in closest relationship with the Father, has made him known" (1:14, 18, NIV). Some translations say "the only begotten of the Father" and "the only begotten Son" instead of "the one and only Son." Only that which is begotten is identical to the begetter. Jesus is eternally begotten of the Father. He said, "I and the Father are one" (10:30).

In various places in Scripture, we are told that no one has seen God. The Lord said to Moses, "You cannot see my face, for no one may see me and live" (Exod. 33:20, NIV). The Lord caused all His goodness to pass in front of Moses and proclaimed His name, "the LORD," in his presence, but He did not fully reveal Himself. God lives in "unapproachable light, whom no one has ever seen or can see" (1 Tim. 6:16). However, in Christ the unique one, we have "the image of the invisible God" (Col. 1:15). As the eternal Son of God, He became the God-man who reflects and reveals God the Father.

Hebrews describes the Son as "the radiance of God's glory and the exact representation of his being" (Heb. 1:3, NIV). As the radiant brightness of the sun is inseparable from the sun itself, so the radiance of Jesus is inseparable from His deity because He comes from the Father. As the exact representation of God, Jesus is not simply a reflection of God. He is God Himself, "the absolutely authentic representation of God's being."[8] Jesus taught concerning Himself, "No one has seen the Father except the one who is from God; only he has seen the Father" (John 6:46, NIV). This is a clear declaration of Christ's deity. Although no one has seen God, the unique Son of God has made Him known. We find some consequential implications from this revelation of God in Christ. All this has significance for how and where we worship God. Jesus spoke about this to the Samaritan woman at the well who was concerned about the correct place to worship God.

> "Woman," Jesus replied, "believe me, a time is coming when you will worship the Father neither on this mountain nor in Jerusalem. . . . A time is coming and has now come when the true worshipers will worship the Father in the Spirit and in truth, for they are the kind of worshipers the Father seeks. God is spirit, and his worshipers must worship in the Spirit and in truth." (4:21–24, NIV)

Jesus delivered us from the tyranny of location and buildings for our worship. This is in clear contrast to other religions. Rather than having to climb a remote mountain to a Buddhist temple, we can pray to God in our apartment, our office, or on the subway. We have no need to make a pilgrimage to Mecca or bow in prayer toward the Kaaba which is located there five times a day. Muslims and Hindus in India have fought and lost many lives over an ancient Hindu temple at Ayodhya that the Muslims destroyed hundreds of years ago before building a mosque on its site. In 1991, the Hindus destroyed the mosque in an effort to rebuild the Hindu temple. This site is considered extremely holy in Hinduism as the birthplace of the god Ram.

As Christians we have no need to bathe in the polluted Ganges River to have our sins washed away. Our sins have been washed away by the once-for-all-time sacrifice of Christ on the cross, which we look to in faith. As true Christians, we have no holy sites for our worship. We have no need to go to the temple in Jerusalem because the temple of God is within us. Jesus now lives within us by His Spirit and, as believers gather together, we are the cumulative body of Christ. We become the church, each person a living stone in the building. As a corporate body, we worship God as His people united as one. Now we worship in spirit and in truth because we are not focused on what is temporary but on what is spiritual and eternal with the aid of the Spirit of Jesus indwelling us.

A unique quality of Jesus is how He was able to create unity from life's diversity. Many philosophers since ancient Greek times have sought to do that. Ancient philosophy believed that there were four essences to life: air, fire, water, and earth. Quintessence, or the fifth essence, of which the heavenly bodies were believed to be composed, seeks unity out of that diversity. It is the most perfect manifestation of anything. From that, the word "university" refers to people seeking unity in a diversity of academic study. The motto on the US quarter and dollar bill, alongside the American eagle, is e pluribus unum, which means "out of the many one." Our country has sought to have unity despite its diversity of peoples. Some have sought unity in the idea of a one-world government or a United Nations.

But what we find in Scripture is that true unity in diversity is found only in the doctrine of the Trinity. The community of the Godhead—Father, Son, and Holy Spirit—illustrates that the three are one in essence but diverse in function. This mystery was revealed in a totally new way by the incarnation of Jesus Christ followed by His and the Father's sending of the Holy Spirit, also called the Spirit of Jesus (see Acts 16:7; Phil. 1:19). Because we continue to live in Christ by the Spirit sent by Him, we have the continuity of His presence with us to take us to our eternal home. And through the revelation of God the Father through Jesus the Son, who is now present in the believer through the Spirit, we as God's people are made one body. We are now called "a chosen people, a royal priesthood, a holy nation, God's special possession" (1 Pet. 2:9, NIV).

Since we have come to know God through His revelation of Himself in Jesus Christ, we must proclaim Him to the world yet in darkness. As Paul writes, "God, who said, 'Let light shine out of darkness,' made his light shine in our hearts to give us the light of the knowledge of God's glory displayed in the face of Christ" (2 Cor. 4:6, NIV). "Light, knowledge and glory converge in the person of Jesus."[9] By knowing Christ, we come to know God. By knowing God, we come to have eternal life.

Discussion Questions

1. What are two senses in which God's grace is given to us?
   ✷ Describe your own experience with God's redeeming grace.

2. What is the relationship between knowing Jesus and knowing God?

3. What are some unique aspects of Jesus mentioned here in the Gospel of John? Can you think of others that are not mentioned in this passage?

4. What distinguishes Jesus from other founders of religious faiths?

5. How do you understand truth? Do you believe it is possible to hold two contradictory truths at the same time? How does Jesus' claim to be truth enter into your understanding of the truth?

5

No Other Name

Acts 3:1–4:22

*Salvation is found in no one else, for there is no other name under
heaven given to mankind by which we must be saved.*

Acts 4:12, NIV

In an age of empirical pluralism, or the diverse society in
which we live today, it is common to meet or work with people from a wide variety of religions. In America, Christianity
is no longer the dominant perspective in many communities.
Philosophical pluralism, in which all religions and worldviews
are seen as equally valid, is pushed upon us from many sides in
light of the multiple perspectives on ultimate reality and ways to
God that we encounter almost daily. In 2009, a survey indicated
that 59 percent of Americans felt that "all religions are valid."[1]
One's worldview is seen to be simply one's opinion but not absolute truth. Many today assert that it does not really matter what
a person believes, as long as he is sincere. All the sincerity in the

sincerely wrong

world, however, will not lead a person to heaven if he is sincerely wrong—if he is on the wrong path to the knowledge of God and eternal life. The Jewish religious leaders at the time of the apostles were sincere but clearly had a wrong understanding of who Jesus was and His unique role in people's salvation, as seen in the story of a healed beggar in Acts 3 and 4. The ISIS radical Muslims are similarly quite sincere in their beliefs although radically wrong.

Salvation in No One Else

Peter and John went up to the Temple at the time of prayer and met a beggar at the temple gate called Beautiful. This beggar, who was over forty years old, had been crippled from birth. When he begged from Peter and John, Peter asked for his attention and said to him, "Silver or gold I do not have, but what I do have I give you. In the name of Jesus Christ of Nazareth, walk" (Acts 3:6, NIV). The man was miraculously healed. He immediately got up and began walking, leaping, and praising God. As a crowd rushed together to see what happened, Peter and John explained the gospel to them.

> You disowned the Holy and Righteous One and asked that a murderer be released to you. You killed the author of life, but God raised him from the dead. We are witnesses of this. By faith in the name of Jesus, this man whom you see and know was made strong. It is Jesus' name and the faith that comes through him that has completely healed him, as you can all see. (3:14–16, NIV)

This preaching of Jesus and His resurrection aroused the anger of the Jewish priests, temple guard, and Sadducees, so they arrested Peter and John. About five thousand men, however, believed in Jesus.

It was the Sadducees who held the high-priestly office. These men collaborated with the Roman rulers, were upset by anything that disturbed their comfortable status, didn't believe in a personal messiah, and denied the doctrine of the resurrection. They were the rationalists of their day. In a way, one could compare them to many of the leaders of the liberal mainline denominations today who, although in positions of power, deny the miraculous, such as the virgin birth and physical resurrection of Christ, and argue that eventually every "good" person will get to heaven. They deny the necessity of a personal relationship with Christ. For them, missions and evangelism are no longer necessary. They dismiss any committed Christian who disagrees with their position as an uneducated, narrow-minded, radical fundamentalist.

The morning after the miracle, Peter and John appeared before the rulers, elders, and teachers of the law—the three groups that made up the Sanhedrin, Israel's supreme court. The prosecutor asked them, "By what power or what name did you do this?" (Acts 4:7, NIV). They apparently thought that Peter and John had acted through the use of illegal incantation and magic. Peter gave a speech in his and John's defense for having shown kindness to a cripple and gave an account for how he was healed. It was a courageous and aggressive defense of the power of Jesus, who had been rejected and crucified by the religious leaders but raised from the dead by God. The power to heal the cripple was evidence that Jesus was actually alive. True

Peter then made his most clear statement on the unique gift that comes only from Jesus: "Salvation is found in no one else, for there is no other name under heaven given to mankind by which we must be saved" (Acts 4:12, NIV). Note that Peter was filled with the Holy Spirit when he made this statement. His declaration was not an unfounded boast.

As early twentieth-century Princeton theology professor Charles Erdman notes, "His words are at once a rebuke, a challenge, and an invitation."[2] The rebuke was in the leaders' failure to believe in Jesus despite the clear evidence from the teachings of the prophets, the witnesses who had seen the risen Christ, and the miraculous power of Jesus' name to heal. Peter quoted Psalm 118:22: "Jesus is 'the stone you builders rejected, / which has become the cornerstone'" (Acts 4:11, NIV).

Could they refute the evidence of the power of Jesus' name to save, seeing how the crippled man had been made whole in the name of Jesus? The man was now standing with them (see 4:14). Could they refute the clear prophecies of the Scriptures concerning the Messiah, which had been fulfilled in Jesus? These pointed to Jesus being the Savior of the world as the firstborn from the dead. The religious leaders of Israel were also invited to put their trust in Jesus as their Savior, for there was no other way to eternal life. Peter appealed to them to cease their rejection of Jesus. Although He was "the stone that the builders rejected" (1 Pet. 2:7), Jesus had now become the capstone or "cornerstone" of the building of God's temple through which all the "living stones" are drawn together as one edifice (see 2:5–6). In Him, all the nations became one. As Paul writes, "No one can lay any foundation other than the one already laid, which is Jesus Christ" (1 Cor. 3:11, NIV). Although Jesus had been rejected, God exalted

His Son to sit at His right hand, the highest place of honor. He declared Jesus to be Savior and Lord and made clear that nobody else could sit alongside Him in His position of glory, power, and authority. This invitation to put faith in Jesus demonstrated that becoming a Christian was not joining an elitist club. Faith in Christ was for both common fishermen and well-placed people from prominent families in positions of authority. Salvation was a free gift offered to everyone because Christianity itself was both inclusive and exclusive. Philip Ryken, president of Wheaton College, explains it.

> The particularity of Christ should not hide his universality. Although he is the only way to God, he offers the Gospel to everyone. "There is one God and one mediator between God and men, the man Christ Jesus, who gave himself as a ransom for all men" (1 Tim. 2:5–6). Whoever you are, you may and you must come close to God through Jesus Christ.

> To use an analogy, Jesus is like God's telephone number. The God of the universe can only be contacted through Jesus Christ. Philosophical pluralists insist on getting through to God no matter what number they dial. But that is not how the telephone system operates, and it is not how God operates either. Jesus is the only direct line to God.[3]

The religious leaders were astonished at the courage of Peter and John, who were unschooled in seminary, and they noted that they were ordinary men. But it was very evident that the two disciples had been with Jesus. The Lord had instructed them well over a three-year period and they were now filled with the Holy Spirit. Only those who are saved are given the gift of the Spirit to have faith to believe in Christ, repent of their sins, and have power to witness for Him both in word and deed. All these elements are missing from those who do not know the gospel of Christ.

Moreover, if there were a way to salvation apart from Christ, why did Peter make such a bold statement that contradicted the teaching of the Jewish leadership? Why did he risk prison and punishment for his belief if it was not a matter of life and death for all? Certainly everyone's eternal destiny is at stake concerning how we respond to Christ and His gospel. That is something worth going to prison or death for. Therefore, Peter and John replied to the Sanhedrin, which had "commanded them not to speak or teach at all in the name of Jesus," saying, "Which is right in God's eyes: to listen to you, or to him? You be the judges! As for us, we cannot help speaking about what we have seen and heard" (Acts 4:18–20, NIV).

Coming Judgment

The reason that Jesus is the only way to God is that everyone has one main problem: We are all separated from God by our sin. We live in rebellion against God and His law, wanting to rule ourselves rather than submitting to God's rule over us. We are all under condemnation apart from the righteousness revealed by faith in Jesus Christ (see Rom. 3:10–26). The fact that a coming judgment is described numerous times from Genesis to Revelation, in almost every book of the Bible, shows us that everyone is accountable to God for his life and faith or lack thereof.

As Peter preached in the Temple upon healing the crippled man, he reminded his audience of what Moses had said of the Messiah: "The Lord your God will raise up for you a prophet like me from among your own people; you must listen to everything he tells you. Anyone who does not listen to him will be completely cut off from their people" (Acts 3:22–23, NIV). To be cut off meant having no hope of sharing in the eternal blessings offered by God to His people. In the next scene, as Peter and John continue giving a defense before the Sanhedrin for preaching and healing in Jesus' name, Peter said, "There is salvation in no one else, for there is no other name under heaven given among men by which we must be saved" (4:12). Inclusivist[4] theologian Clark Pinnock tries to argue that this verse says nothing about the ultimate fate of the heathen. By saying that it does, we are reading our own ideas into it, he avers.

> Peter is magnifying the name of Jesus and the messianic salvation he has brought. A new era has opened up, the last days have begun. Thus we should not see him as denying that there have been and are lesser instances of saving power at work in the world where Jesus' name is unknown. Peter is magnifying a mighty act of God bringing in the kingdom, not discussing comparative religions.[5]

Pinnock claims Peter's statement does not question the eternal fate of the unevangelized and the role of other religions in God's plan of redemption. However, as I have just demonstrated above, Peter is referring to judgment on those who refuse to listen to the gospel according to the prophecy of Moses and those who remain in Judaism by refusing to acknowledge Jesus as their Messiah. As we look at the context of the whole book of Acts, we see that Jesus wanted His apostles and every believer to go to the ends of the earth to bring the good news of salvation. Not only did Jesus explicitly command that (see Acts 1:8), but we see it in numerous examples: in the preaching in various tongues on the day of Pentecost to those from many countries; in the gospel going from Jerusalem to Judea and Samaria due to persecution; in the Ethiopian eunuch bringing the gospel to his own land; and in the gospel spreading to Damascus, Antioch, Cyprus, Iconium, Lystra, Athens, Corinth, Ephesus, Macedonia, Galatia, Illyricum, Rome, and Spain. The gospel confronted the religions of each of these peoples. Each group of people was urged to repent of their sin and believe in Christ alone.

Pinnock admits that he finds it totally repugnant that most people who have ever lived are outside of salvation at the end of their time, and that this view affects his interpretation of our text. Because he thinks our text is silent on the issue, he says we must take a lenient stance on the fate of the heathen. He says that God is not limited to saving people through human preachers.[6]

But if this is so, why preach at all? Paul asks, "How can they believe in the one of whom they have not heard? And how can they hear without someone preaching to them? And how can anyone preach unless they are sent? . . . Consequently, faith comes from hearing the message, and the message is heard through the word about Christ" (Rom. 10:14–17, NIV). To deny that people need to hear the gospel message in order to be saved is to deny the radical depravity of humankind requiring God's judgment and the need for its solution, found only in the substitutionary atonement of Christ on the cross to cleanse us from all our sin. Pinnock sees God's justice as showing mercy toward sinners who have not been absolved by faith. Rather, the opposite is the case. God's justice requires judgment on sinners. But God's mercy and love bring the elect to salvation exclusively through their faith in Christ, who has borne God's judgment for us on the cross.

When the apostle Peter went to the home of the Gentile Cornelius and preached the gospel to his household members, relatives, and close friends, Peter said of Jesus, "He commanded us to preach to the people and to testify that he is the one whom God appointed as judge of the living and the dead. All the prophets testify about him that everyone who believes in him receives forgiveness of sins through his name" (Acts 10:42–43, NIV). If Jesus is the judge of everyone who has ever lived, then everyone is accountable to Him. His judgment of us will be based on our faith in Him. If "everyone who believes in him receives forgiveness of sins through his name," then Jesus must be the only way to salvation. We have no other means of forgiveness of our sins. We cannot enter the presence of our holy God in a state of sin. Therefore, we must heed what the Spirit says through John: "Whoever believes in the Son has eternal life, but whoever rejects the Son will not see life, for God's wrath remains on him" (John 3:36, NIV).

But is God unjust in condemning some to eternal punishment while electing others to be eternally blessed? Part of the answer is found in Paul's letter to the Romans.

What then shall we say? Is God unjust? Not at all!
For he says to Moses, "I will have mercy on whom I
have mercy, / and I will have compassion on whom I
have compassion." It does not, therefore, depend on
human desire or effort, but on God's mercy. (Rom.
9:14–16, NIV)

Paul continues on to explain that God uses the destruction of
the wicked to display His power, show His wrath, proclaim His
name, and make the riches of His glory known to the objects of
His mercy (see 9:17, 22–23).

All love demonstrates a preference for one over another, as we
see in God's love for His elect. As the good shepherd, Jesus "lays
down his life for the sheep" (John 10:11; see also 10:15), but
Jesus told the unbelieving Jews, "You do not believe because you
are not my sheep. My sheep listen to my voice; I know them,
and they follow me. I give them eternal life" (10:26–28, NIV).
Those who do not believe are condemned, because they reject
the revelation that has already been given to them (see 10:25;
Rom. 1:18–23).

Carl Henry, first editor in chief of *Christianity Today*, further
explains the justice of God.

The modern misjudgment of God flows easily from
contemporary theology's preoccupation with love as
the core of God's being, while righteousness is sub-
ordinated and denied equal ultimacy with love in the
nature of deity.[7]

In other words, those who object to eternal judgment misconceive the nature of God. Those who hold this view deny the primary character of God's holiness and righteousness along with His love. God's justice is based on His own nature, which is intrinsically just. The psalmist says, "Righteousness looks down from heaven" (Ps. 85:11, NIV), and, "Righteousness goes before him" (85:13, NIV). God's righteousness and justice are the norm for every human authority. As Bildad rhetorically asked Job, "Does God pervert justice? / Does the Almighty pervert what is right?" (Job 8:3, NIV). Zephaniah the prophet writes, "The LORD . . . is righteous; / he does no wrong. / Morning by morning he dispenses his justice" (Zeph. 3:5, NIV).

Even at an early stage of God's revelation, Abraham asked the Lord as He was about to destroy Sodom and Gomorrah, "Far be it from you to do such a thing—to kill the righteous with the wicked, treating the righteous and the wicked alike. Far be it from you! Will not the Judge of all the earth do right?" (Gen. 18:25, NIV). Of course God would do right. That is why He preserved Lot and his family rather than destroy them with the cities. But the judgment of Sodom and Gomorrah remains an example to us, as Jesus taught us, of the destruction that God will bring upon those who reject His righteousness, which has been revealed through Himself in the gospel (see Matt. 10:15; 11:23–24).

The Church

Throughout church history, from the time of the earliest Greek fathers (that is, Cyprian of Carthage), the church has held to the maxim "Outside the church, no salvation." This is because the church has been entrusted with the gospel, and it is through the gospel that a person can be saved. The signs and symbols of our salvation and subsequent incorporation into the church are administered through the church in the sacraments of baptism and the Lord's Supper. This does not mean that being incorporated into the institutional church is essential for salvation, but anyone who has accepted Christ in the biblical sense of repentance and faith is a member of the invisible Christian church in which there is a union with the worldwide body.

As we read the book of Acts, we see that the whole thrust of the book is to explain how the gospel spread from Jerusalem to Judea and Samaria and to the ends of the earth. In each aspect of the proclamation of the gospel, we find a clear division between those who had come to know God through Christ and those who were lost, hopeless, condemned for their sins, praying to unknown gods, and separated from God. Those who believed and received the gospel by faith were incorporated into the church. So when Peter said, "There is no other name under heaven given to men by which we must be saved," he was speaking of Jesus as the rejected stone that had become the capstone, like the one on the summit of the Jerusalem temple. Jesus completed the edifice. He became the head of the church, having died for His people that they might be adopted as sons of God. Each believer now became a living stone being built into the spiritual house of God's church (see 1 Pet. 2:5).

The church has been God's plan for the nations since the foundation of the world. That church began with all the people of faith down through the ages, from Adam to Abel to Noah to Abraham, Isaac, and Jacob to Moses to David to the apostles and, finally, to us. The advantage that the people of God had over the Gentiles was that "the Jews were entrusted with the oracles of God" (Rom. 3:2). As God said through Moses, "What great nation is there that has a god so near to it as the LORD our God is to us, whenever we call upon him?" (Deut. 4:7). Israel was the only nation that had God's words and rules (see Ps. 147:19–20). For this reason Jesus responded to the woman at the well, "You worship what you do not know; we worship what we know, for salvation is from the Jews" (John 4:22).

The great mystery revealed in the gospel was that the Jews, who had been God's chosen people, were now to be made one people with the Gentiles through a common faith in Jesus Christ. God's "intent was that now, through the church, the manifold wisdom of God should be made known to the rulers and authorities in the heavenly realms, according to his eternal purpose that he accomplished in Christ Jesus our Lord. In him and through faith in him we may approach God with freedom and confidence" (Eph. 3:10–12, NIV). Obviously those who don't have this faith may not approach God. The condition of those Gentiles who were without the gospel is described earlier in Paul's letter to the Ephesians.

> At that time you were separate from Christ, excluded from citizenship in Israel and foreigners to the covenants of the promise, without hope and without God in the world. But now in Christ Jesus you who once were far away have been brought near by the blood of Christ. (2:12–13, NIV)

What a contrast between the hopelessness of those without Christ and the joy of those who have been brought close to God through their faith. "Consequently," Paul continues, "you are no longer foreigners and strangers, but <u>fellow citizens with God's people</u> and also members of his household, built on the foundation of the apostles and prophets, with Christ Jesus himself as the chief cornerstone" (Eph. 2:19–20, NIV). Here we see that incorporation into the church is based on the special revelation of God found in the Scriptures, given to us by the apostles and prophets based on the incarnation and ministry of Christ. Apart from receiving this gospel, people remain foreigners and aliens to the household of God. They have no hope.

The universal invisible church indicates the boundary between the people of God who will be saved and those who are lost, condemned, and without hope. Every group has to have boundaries to distinguish itself from those outside the group. For the church, the boundary is formed by those who have a knowledge and heartfelt acceptance of the truth found in Jesus. They have trusted in Jesus, who claimed, "I am the way, and the truth, and the life. No one comes to the Father except through me" (John 14:6). This boundary makes it impossible that Jesus, Peter, or Paul could have been universalists or even inclusivists. Those outside this boundary do not have the knowledge of God. For those who are perishing, "the message of the cross is foolishness, . . . but to us who are being saved it is the power of God" (1 Cor. 1:18, NIV).

Paul continually made a sharp distinction between those *inside* and those *outside* the church by the language he used to describe them. Those inside were "saints," "loved by God," "known," "brothers," "children of light," and "believers." Those outside were called "outsiders," "unrighteous," those who "did not know God," the "world," "children of darkness," "unbelievers," "enemies," and "idol worshipers." Those who came to faith were adopted into the family of God and made a break with their natural families and former relationships to become part of a new family that was "in Christ." Participation in the sacraments helped to establish these boundaries and promoted solidarity within the church. All this language of boundaries and separation hardly leads readers of the New Testament to believe that, in the end, there will be a final gathering of everyone into one body. The language throughout the New Testament is of a permanent separation of insiders from outsiders, of the sons of God from the sons of Satan. Judgment on the wicked is not to reform or correct them so that they might do good. The fate of those still in their sins of final, utter hopelessness is beyond the grave.[8]

There is still hope for those who are outsiders to become insiders. As Peter preached to the crowd at the Temple, he said: "Repent, then, and turn to God, so that your sins may be wiped out, that times of refreshing may come from the Lord, and that he may send the Messiah, who has been appointed for you— even Jesus" (Acts 3:19–20, NIV). It is in this message that hope of eternal life is found.

Discussion Questions

1. Why was Peter willing to risk imprisonment and punishment by challenging the Jewish religious leaders?

2. How do preconceived ideas about God affect how we interpret Scripture concerning the fate of those who do not know Christ?

3. How does the doctrine of God's judgment affect the fate of both those who have not heard the gospel and those who have heard it but refuse to receive it?

4. Why is there no salvation outside the church?

5. How does the Bible describe the condition and fate of those outside the church?

6

Enter Through the Narrow Door
Luke 13:22–30

Someone said to him, "Lord, will those who are saved be few?" And
he said to them, "Strive to enter through the narrow door. For many, I
tell you, will seek to enter and will not be able."

Luke 13:23–24

People unfamiliar with the Christian faith aren't asking whether or not they are saved. In the gospel, we have a salvific message. Through the knowledge of our self-revealed God, we become aware of our sin and its ensuing condemnation from which we need to be delivered. Hindus seek to escape the cycle of karma leading to repeated incarnations. Buddhists seek nonexistence to escape suffering. Muslims seek to attain a paradise of pleasure through their own efforts and the capricious will of Allah. Mystical Sufi Muslims seek to attain self-union in order to attain unity with Allah. When Sufi master Abu Yazid al-Bastami (AD 804–874) was asked, "What is the way to God?" he answered, "Leave the way and you have arrived at God." He also said, "I sloughed off my self as a snake sloughs off its skin. Then I looked into myself and saw that I am He."[1] It is evident that today we need to understand our audience when considering the question of salvation. It is a most important question to which we need to direct people so that it becomes an ultimate concern to them.

Do you have any doubts as to whether you will be included among those who will be saved? Will the Lord gladly welcome you into His eternal kingdom? As I have gotten to know students from around the world as well as Americans who have gotten involved in cults, the New Age movement, and liberal theology, I have found that people have a wide variety of views regarding our eternal destiny and how we get there. How should we respond to Jesus saying, "Strive to enter through the narrow door. For many, I tell you, will seek to enter and will not be able" (Luke 13:24), and His telling those left outside, "Depart from me, all you workers of evil!" (13:27)?

Will Only a Few Be Saved?

Imagine being with Jesus as He gradually made His way to Jerusalem over a period of perhaps some weeks, teaching in many towns and villages on His way. Sometime during this period, a Jew from the crowd asked Jesus, "Lord, are only a few people going to be saved?" (13:23, NIV).

This was as relevant a question in Jesus' day as it is today. It was discussed by the rabbis during Jesus' earthly ministry with widely differing conclusions. It was firmly held, however, that all Israel would be saved except for those blatant sinners who excluded themselves. Yet you may have wondered, as those who observed Jesus' ministry must have, how it was that the one who claimed to be the author of life had such a small group of disciples. Was Jesus saying that only this small group of people were to be saved, while Israel as a whole would be lost if they rejected Jesus as the Messiah (see Matt. 8:12)?

Another doubt may have come to mind for Jesus' followers as they looked at the condition of the world at that time, which was much as it is today. The great majority of people pursue a lifestyle totally different from that which Christ has called us to. What does this mean? Does it mean that only a few people will be saved? In the Sermon on the Mount, Jesus answered these questions when he said, "The gate is narrow and the way is hard that leads to life, and those who find it are few" (7:14).

By taking a historical survey of the growth of Christianity since the time of Jesus, we can see that many more people are being saved now than in the early days of the faith. According to statistics from mission historian Ralph Winter, in AD 100 there were three hundred sixty non-Christians for every committed Christian. In AD 1000, the ratio was two hundred twenty to one. In AD 1500, the ratio was down to sixty-nine to one. In 1900, the ratio was twenty-seven to one. In 1950, the ratio was twenty-one to one. In 1980, the ratio was eleven to one. And in 1990, the ratio was seven non-Christians for every one committed Christian in the world. This shows the spectacular growth of the church, which has been greater than the population explosion.[2]

Only God knows, however, how many of those who call themselves Christians are really striving to enter the narrow door. In addition, even with the tremendous growth of the church, out of the over 7 billion people in the world, about 2.3 billion have no gospel witness or almost none within their own people group.

In Luke 13, Jesus does not directly answer the speculative question concerning how many will be saved. Rather, he tells us to be concerned with whether or not we are striving to enter the Kingdom ourselves. Are we in the number, however large or small it is? It is a foolish curiosity to be concerned about whether we are going to heaven with a great crowd or a small group. This question makes it seem as if some do not want to be saved unless a crowd is going with them. They would rather be partying in hell with their friends.

Make Every Effort to Enter

Jesus replied to the crowd listening to Him, "Make every effort to enter through the narrow door" (13:24, NIV). The Greek word for "make every effort" or "strive" means "to take wholehearted action." It refers to the "exerting of concentrated strength."[3] It is used as a technical term for competing in the games. Our word "agonize" comes from it. This word, expressed in the New International Version as "every effort," is "expressive of the difficulty of being saved, as if one would have to force his way in."[4] So no halfhearted effort is enough for what God requires from us. We cannot claim to have Christ as our Savior and then not live for Him as our Lord.

We should note that there is a significant difference between striving and seeking. One could compare it to wishing and willing. One can seek something without real earnestness—a quality needed to really find what one is looking for. Many people would like good things in this life but are not willing to work and sacrifice to have those good things. In the same way, many people would like to go to heaven but are not willing to make the sacrifice of self and the world to obtain it. Halfhearted seeking will not get a person anything in this world or in the next.[5]

This does not mean that human achievement will gain us entrance into God's kingdom. It is true that we are saved only by the grace of God, which is received as a gift. But this does not relieve us from the responsibility of making every effort to enter the Kingdom with all the might and main we have. Our attitude should lead us to total dedication to Christ. We will not enter God's rest if we begin in the Spirit and end up quitting along the way in the flesh. As the Scripture says, "the one who endures to the end will be saved" (Matt. 10:22; 24:13; Mark 13:13). It is not enough to intellectually assent to believing in Jesus, but we must make Him Lord of our life by striving to enter His kingdom. Of course, the Holy Spirit enables us to remain faithful to the end as we strive toward that goal (see Phil. 1:6; 1 Thess. 5:23–24).

Living the Christian life is difficult. Everything in our old self-confident, self-centered nature reacts against the conditions for entrance through the narrow door. "The remainder of our old nature will much weaken and interrupt" our desire to make the Lord first in our life, even though it will never overcome it.[6] We must make every effort—or strive—to enter eternal life into heaven. It cannot be done on any easier terms. The Christian must exercise discipline, obedience, and love throughout life. This has been called by pastor-theologian Liam Goligher "a long obedience in the right direction." Seventeenth-century English pastor Richard Baxter put it as follows:

> The sovereign wisdom of God has made striving necessary to salvation. Who knows the way to heaven better than the God of heaven? When men tell us we are too strict, whom do they accuse, God or us? If it were a fault, it would lie in him that commands, and not in us who obey. These are the men that ask us, whether we are wiser than all the world beside; and yet they will pretend to be wiser than God.[7]

Various passages in Scripture point out this need for us to make every effort to assure our entrance to heaven. Philippians 2:12 says, "Continue to work out your salvation with fear and trembling" (NIV). First Peter 4:18 asks us, "If it is hard for the righteous to be saved, / what will become of the ungodly and the sinner?" (NIV). In Second Peter 1:10, we are admonished to "make every effort to confirm [our] calling and election" (NIV). How do we do this? The apostle Peter tells us how: We are to make every effort to add to our faith goodness, knowledge, self-control, perseverance, godliness, brotherly kindness, and love (see 1:5–7). The author of Hebrews further admonishes us.

> Lay aside every weight, and sin which clings so closely, and let us run with endurance the race that is set before us, looking to Jesus, the founder and perfecter of our faith. . . . Lift your drooping hands and strengthen your weak knees, and make straight paths for your feet, so that what is lame may not be put out of joint but rather be healed. . . . See to it that no one fails to obtain the grace of God. (Heb. 12:1–15)

The Christian is beset by doubts, fears, attacks, and temptations, but it is a life we must strive for. British minister Alexander MacLaren says, "The main struggle of our whole lives should be to cultivate self-humbling trust in Jesus Christ, and to 'fight the good fight of faith.'"[8]

"Away from Me, All You Evildoers"

Jesus tells us that many "will seek to enter and will not be able" (Luke 13:24). We are warned here that having many companions in our present life will be no comfort once the time given to us to come to Christ has passed.

People like to flatter themselves by thinking that they are all right with God, that they have nothing to worry about. They may say, "I'm not as bad a person as he is. I'm a good citizen, I help my neighbors, I attend church, and I give to charity." No outward connection with Christ, partaking of the sacraments, being a faithful church member, sitting under Christian teaching all one's life, or having a vague wish to be saved will assure anyone of entrance through the narrow door to salvation. People who outwardly practice these things think they have an easy entrance into heaven because they know God to be a loving and merciful God and because at some time they may have made some kind of profession of believing in Jesus. But those who live their lives in indifference to the commands and ways of God, those who think they are assured easy entrance to heaven, have been warned that they will be shut out of heaven.

While the door is still open, Jesus invites people to enter His kingdom. But the time will come when He will get up to shut the door. We must take advantage of the opportunity to access the Kingdom while we have opportunity. Note that Jesus says to those who are pleading to be let into heaven, "I tell you, I do not know where you come from. Depart from me, all you workers of evil!" (Luke 13:27). First, notice that the master does not know these people. When one is not known by the Lord, it is equivalent to being shut out of heaven. Mutual knowledge, such as that experienced by the Good Shepherd and His sheep who know His voice, is essential for righteousness, the requirement for entrance to heaven.

Second, it seems a bit shocking that Jesus calls them "workers of evil." He mentions no specific evil deeds, but He is speaking of their moral character. Their moral nature has not been changed, even though they are seeking entrance at the door. They still love evil.

We see a similar response in Jesus' teaching found in Matthew 7:21–23. Jesus had just said that we will recognize false prophets by the fruit of their lives; then He continues.

> Not everyone who says to me, "Lord, Lord," will enter the kingdom of heaven, but the one who does the will of my Father who is in heaven. On that day many will say to me, "Lord, Lord, did we not prophesy in your name, and cast out demons in your name, and do many mighty works in your name?" And then will I declare to them, "I never knew you; depart from me, you workers of lawlessness."

It appears that Jesus is calling those who are deceivers, false teachers, false prophets, and pretenders "workers of lawlessness" or "workers of evil." Isn't it amazing that even those who cast out demons and perform miracles in Jesus' name are called "workers of evil"? Why? Because they never really knew Jesus and have led others away from following Him. But aside from these more specific sins, the Bible teaches us that everyone is a sinner—an evildoer. In the end, there will be only two classes of people: those inside and those outside. It is only those who have put their complete faith and trust in Jesus as their Savior who are truly washed clean of their sins. These are those who have made every effort to enter through the narrow door.

Those to whom the Lord says, "Depart from me, all you workers of evil!" are those who are destined for destruction. This means "exclusion from the joys and pleasures of the presence of God in his Kingdom."[9] The many who will try to enter through the narrow door at that point will find that it is too late. "Jesus does not say that there are many who strive in vain to enter, but that there will be many who will seek in vain to enter, after the time of salvation is past. Those who continue to strive now, succeed."[10]

We must make every effort to enter through the narrow door because the time is short. There is a limit as to when we can enter. Jesus, the owner of the house, will one day get up and close the door. Once it has been closed, the opportunity will have been lost. Despite people's pleading and crying, the Lord will not give them a second chance. The day of salvation is now (see 2 Cor. 6:2).

The Narrow Door

The narrow door is not explained, but it is clear that it means the door to salvation through repentance and faith in Christ.

How can we understand what is meant by the narrow door? It is narrow by the fact that it is restrictive. Only a minority enter through it.

In Jesus' Sermon on the Mount, He teaches almost the same thing when He says, "Enter by the narrow gate. For the gate is wide and the way is easy that leads to destruction, and those who enter by it are many" (Matt. 7:13).

Jesus is telling us that if we neglect to enter through the narrow gate because we are kept back by the multitudes going astray from the Lord, then we must understand that we will be separated from the believers. The world may dazzle some by its appeal to prosperity, passion, power, privilege, prestige, and pride, but the last day will cure them of this. Then it will be too late for people to repent of their ways.

The narrow door also speaks to us of the humility we must have to enter God's kingdom. Rather than the Jewish fleshly idea of entering God's kingdom through some great royal entrance worthy of a palace, Jesus refers to a small entrance through which one would have to bend over and squeeze through.

The humility we must have to enter the Kingdom is spoken of by Jesus as that of a little child (see Mark 10:15; Luke 18:17). In the parable of the Pharisee and the tax collector who both went up to the Temple to pray (see 18:9–14), we see that it was humility and acknowledgement of sin before God that made the tax collector rather than the religious Pharisee justified before God.

The door of faith is narrow because it allows no worldly, self-righteousness glories in. From emperor or president to beggar on the corner, we all must enter the Kingdom stripped of everything. We take in no crowns, titles, diplomas, achievements, or property. The entrance is so low and narrow that we must creep on our knees and leave everything outside. Just as when we enter a place of entertainment or a subway entrance, we must pass through a turnstile that allows only one person at a time. Then this narrow door opens into a palace that Jesus has prepared for us.[11]

In addition, the door is narrow in that it is only through Jesus that one can enter the kingdom of God. In John 10:9, Jesus says, "I am the gate; whoever enters through me will be saved" (NIV). This sure sounds like an exclusive statement about salvation being only through Jesus. Numerous other exclusive passages may also be found in the Scriptures, including John 3:16–18.

> For God so loved the world, that he gave his only Son, that whoever believes in him should not perish but have eternal life. For God did not send his Son into the world to condemn the world, but in order that the world might be saved through him. Whoever believes in him is not condemned, but whoever does not believe is condemned already, because he has not believed in the name of the only Son of God.

In John 14:5–6, the following is evidence. "Thomas said to him, 'Lord, we do not know where you are going. How can we know the way?' Jesus said to him, 'I am the way, and the truth, and the life. No one comes to the Father except through me.'" Peter spoke in his defense before the Sanhedrin. "There is salvation in no one else, for there is no other name under heaven given among men by which we must be saved" (Acts 4:12).

And Paul wrote to Timothy. "There is one God, and there is one mediator between God and men, the man Christ Jesus, who gave himself as a ransom for all" (1 Tim. 2:5–6).

Although liberal theologians will acknowledge that the Scriptures contain these exclusive statements about salvation being only through Jesus, they choose to basically ignore them. For example, Wesley Ariarajah, a Methodist minister from Sri Lanka, published *The Bible and People of Other Faiths*. In it, he tries to point out what Jesus said and did in the Synoptic Gospels—Matthew, Mark, and Luke—to show a different perspective between the apostles and members of the early church who changed their understanding of Jesus from that which Jesus had held Himself. Reverend Ariarajah says that this witness of Jesus is in contradiction to the witness found in these exclusive sayings concerning Jesus. He makes numerous other points, like the one below, that relativize the Bible and our faith.

> Truth in the absolute sense is beyond anyone's grasp, and we should not say that the Christian claims about Jesus are absolute because St John, St Paul and the scriptures make them. There will be others who make similar claims based on authorities they set for themselves. Such claims to absolute truth lead only to intolerance and arrogance and to unwarranted condemnation of each other's faith-perspectives.[12]

Later he says that we should not try to convert anyone. Of course, we understand that we cannot convert anyone since God does the converting of people's hearts as they hear the Word proclaimed.

Reverend Ariarajah also admits that he uses a selective approach to the Bible, justifying it by saying that any perspective on the Bible uses a selective approach to defend its position. He fails to understand the principle that any text must be interpreted in light of the Bible as a whole as well as in the context of the chapter or book the text is in.

What this comes down to is whether we can believe in the authority of the Bible. Is it the Word of God, or does it only possibly contain a word from God as it may speak to one's situation? Reverend Ariarajah does not see the Bible as having unity, absolute truth, or authority beyond a faith commitment that one may or may not make. For him, faith "is based not on certain knowledge but on the certainty of faith itself."[13] But we can have a sure faith because we know it to be founded on truth and history, not an empty hope devoid of content. Faith is a gift from God that is based on the facts of God's acts in history for our salvation. Reverend Ariarajah also speaks of a similar theme found in the writings of John Hick, saying that our faith should be God-centered, rather than Christ-centered, or Christ and the church-centered. John Hick, the well-known liberal theologian on ecumenism, suggests that a reorientation to theocentric thinking will "facilitate a new understanding of religions whereby claims to superiority and exclusivity would dissolve, as would mission. A new era of interreligious ecumenism would dawn."[14]

Hick's concept of God, however, becomes free-floating, as he denies that God can be tied to His self-revelation or that a salvific event can be tied to any particular group. He also denies that Jesus can be seen as God incarnate but rather should be seen mythologically. Hick leaves unresolved whose God or whose understanding of God should be at the center of salvation. In his more recent writings, he has argued "that all religions are salvific paths to the one Divine Real, none being better or worse and none having a privileged or exclusive revelation—despite what their adherents may claim." In Hick's view "the Divine cannot be ultimately regarded as personal or impersonal." Also, "each religion has the presence of the divine in more or less equal measure."[15]

As professor of Catholic Theology Gavin D'Costa writes, "Ironically, in [Hick's] attempt to accommodate the world religions on an equal status, he ends up accommodating none of them, since he can only accept them within his system on his, rather than on their own, terms."[16]

Our claim to absolute truth as Christians does not lead us to intolerance and unwarranted condemnation of other faith perspectives but to a love for our neighbor and a hope that others might know and experience God's liberating power from sin. What we have to share is good news! In speaking to people from other faiths, we should listen and learn and agree with them on what we share in common. But we cannot compromise on the truth claims that the gospel makes on all of us. God is the God of the entire universe, the Creator of all people, and He has revealed Himself to us through Jesus Christ and His Holy Scriptures. He provided for the salvation of all people who He calls from sin through Jesus Christ. As Paul says to the Romans, "Is God the God of Jews only? Is he not the God of Gentiles also? Yes, of Gentiles also, since God is one—who will justify the circumcised by faith and the uncircumcised through faith" (Rom. 3:29–30). A little earlier in Romans 3, in verse 22, Paul writes, "This righteousness is given through faith in Jesus Christ to all who believe" (NIV).

Many Will Not Enter

The image portrayed in our text here in Luke 13 is that of a homeowner locking his front door for the night when some of his servants have not yet returned. This tells us that by a decisive act of Christ in the future, the time for entering through the narrow door to the Kingdom will end.

It is the same as when various stages in our life pass. When one has gone, we cannot go back to it again. We cannot return to our childhood once we have become an adult. We cannot undo a crime once it has been committed. So if we do not enter the narrow door while we have opportunity, we will never have another chance once Jesus closes it. The parable of the rich man and Lazarus confirms this when Abraham in heaven answers the rich man in hell, "Between us and you a great chasm has been fixed, in order that those who would pass from here to you may not be able, and none may cross from there to us" (16:26). ✱

Our text says, "Many, I tell you, will seek to enter and will not be able" (13:24). The person asking whether many people will be saved will be no better off if he is given a direct answer. But what Jesus' questioner does need to know that has eternal significance is that even if many will be saved, what is that to him if he is not among them?

What should this mean for us?

First, we must be sure we are among the number who will be saved. One way in which we might examine ourselves is to ask the following questions: Have we trusted in the Lord's precious promises to us in the Scriptures? Do we seek the Lord first in all areas of our lives? Do we have a desire for a close relationship with the Lord? Do we have a love for our brothers and sisters in the Lord and desire to have fellowship with them? Do we examine our own lives to see if there are areas where we need to repent and change to be more Christlike? Is the fruit of the Spirit—love, joy, peace, patience, kindness, goodness, faithfulness, gentleness, and self-control—becoming more evident in our lives?

Second, we should develop a burden and love for the lost, that they might know the way of salvation through our witness. The witness of every Christian is the way God has chosen to bring the salvation message to the world (see Matt. 28:19–20; Acts 1:8; 2 Cor. 5:18–20; 1 Pet. 3:15).

Third, we should understand that those who do not make every effort to enter God's kingdom through the narrow door will not be able to enter. This means not only nonbelieving Jews and nominal Christians but also Buddhists, Hindus, Muslims, New Agers, New Atheists, and Jehovah's Witnesses. A widespread belief is that everyone will be saved in his or her own way. Some teach that many paths to God exist and we will all eventually reach the same summit. There is a problem with this view. These various paths all lead in widely different ways and have irreconcilable understandings of the nature and character of God, if they even believe in God at all.

A core belief of Buddhism is to escape the continual cycle of suffering in this life by observing the eightfold path that leads to nirvana, which is nothingness. It is described as a candle blown out. Some forms of Buddhism are atheistic, while other adherents of this religion worship a mythical Buddha who has had numerous incarnations.

Hinduism's path is achieving god-consciousness or becoming one with the universe. Escaping the cycle of karma is achieved by various methods, such as embracing a life of asceticism, practicing yoga, repeating one's mantra, or being a devotee of one of the three hundred million Hindu gods. These gods have nothing similar in character to the God of the Bible. Hinduism has a monistic worldview in which there is no distinction between God the creator and His creation. For the Hindus, God is in everything. Since all is one in their monistic worldview, anyone at a high level in the caste system who has practiced one of the methods toward god-consciousness—such as yoga, meditation, or mindfulness—may be or become a god. Thus, Hindus worship their gurus. That is, a Hindu's goal is to attain an altered consciousness through various spiritual practices wherein a person's individual soul (atman) seeks to become one with the larger soul (Brahman) and, since gurus have attained this to a much higher degree than ordinary persons have, they are worshiped as spirit-force deities.

The Muslim straight path is not in pursuit of a union with Allah but submission as a slave to his will as revealed in his sharia law. One's goal is paradise, but it is a goal of uncertainty because one can have no assurance of salvation. Actually, Islam does not have a Savior, but its adherents simply hope their good actions outweigh their bad actions or faults to make them acceptable to Allah, if he wills. Becoming a Muslim is very simple: One must repeat the confession of faith (*shahadah*) and attempt to follow the five pillars of Islamic law. One is to become a slave of Allah, submitting to his will. Muslims have no personal relationship with God as in Christianity. Allah is so transcendent that he cannot be immanent, as Jesus Christ was in His incarnation.

Although the incommunicable attributes of Allah are similar to those of the God of the Bible, he is not the same God. Allah is capricious and does not have the standard of righteousness, truth, faithfulness, justice, and love that is found in the God of the Bible. The Muslim's goal in heaven is not the worship and enjoyment of God's presence but indulgence in paradise in wine and beautiful gardens.

New Agers have a path and worldview quite similar to those of Hinduism. To them all in the world is one. There is no God the creator to whom men are accountable on a day of judgment. There is no evil, nor does one have reason to feel guilt or shame. A New Ager may seek to get beyond himself to the power within him by means of messages revealed through channelers or mediums; a well-disciplined life of meditation; a vegan diet; the practice of yoga; and the power of crystals, amulets, and the stars.

Jehovah's Witnesses trust in their salvation through their work and witness for the kingdom. They have no assurance that they will be among the 144,000 who will be in heaven (see Rev. 14:1–5). Their denial of the triune nature of God, the substitutionary atonement and bodily resurrection of Christ, and the personality and work of the Holy Spirit remove all the essentials of the good news of the Kingdom from their belief. The grace of God is shunned for a theology of works salvation.

None of these religions require one to make every effort to enter through the narrow door to the eternal life of which Jesus spoke. All religions other than Christianity are essentially human-centered and works-oriented. Human pride is not seen in them as something to be destroyed but exalted. The way of the cross and the need for the death of Jesus to save us from our sins is denied. In Paul's letter to the Ephesians, the apostle reminds the believers of the state in which they lived before they became Christians.

> Remember that at one time you Gentiles in the flesh,
> called "the uncircumcision" by what is called the cir-
> cumcision, which is made in the flesh by hands—re-
> member that you were at that time separated from
> Christ, alienated from the commonwealth of Israel
> and strangers to the covenants of promise, having
> no hope and without God in the world. But now
> in Christ Jesus you who once were far off have been
> brought near by the blood of Christ. (Eph. 2:11–13)

Note that Paul says that they had "no hope" and were "with-out God in the world." What was it that made them a part of the new Israel, partakers in the covenant promises? Jesus Christ gave them hope and new life by His sacrificial death on the cross for their sins.

Who Will Be in the Kingdom?

Finally, Jesus made clear to the crowd that questioned Him that day that they would be surprised as to who they would find in the kingdom of God. Many Jews of Jesus' day will not be in heaven, even though Jesus was in their midst. Jesus ate with them and taught in their streets. He opened His message to all of them. They heard the gospel. But they did not receive Jesus' teaching. All they could claim was physical proximity to Him. But a person's salvation does not come from being familiar with Jesus; it comes from having a personal relationship with Him.

The crowds that Jesus spoke to will be surprised since they thought that because they were physical descendants of Abraham, they would be saved. Instead of looking to their contemporaries as their future companions in heaven, they should have looked to the examples of faith found in Abraham, Isaac, Jacob, and all the prophets. The Jewish leaders of Jesus' day were full of corruption, self-righteousness, hypocrisy, and misapplication of the law of God.

These people not admitted into the Kingdom will be anguished over being thrown out and seeing the patriarchs and prophets in the Kingdom. The weeping spoken of in Luke 13:28 denotes an expression of grief; the gnashing of teeth expresses the rage of those who are left out. These people outside the Kingdom are in ultimate frustration and disappointment. Note that the text says that they are "thrust out," apparently with force. Leon Morris comments, "The end result of their attitude is to bring upon them the active opposition of God."[17] Remember, Jesus said, "Whoever is not with me is against me" (Matt. 12:30). Are you making your life count now for Jesus? Will you also be shocked on the day of judgment when "God judges the secrets of men by Christ Jesus" (Rom. 2:16)? Everything we do with our life counts. This includes judgment for not doing what we ought to have done (see Luke 19:20–27). As theologian J.I. Packer warns, "One day, when God brings everything to judgment, we will all discover that what we chose to be and do in this world has determined our destiny for us."[18] Our lives must be ones of service and love for the Lord. That means we must live holy lives because, as Hebrews tells us, "Without holiness no one will see the Lord" (12:14, NIV).

Another surprise would be that people from all nations, races, languages, and cultures will be found in the kingdom of God. To hear of all these Gentiles taking part in the messianic banquet must have astounded the Jews. This feast in the kingdom of God was a symbol of the joy of the end time, an event that the Jews looked forward to. Jesus' teaching was a shock to the Jews of His day because they thought of themselves as the only elect people. Even though the Old Testament is full of passages describing the Gentiles coming to faith and being included in the community of God's people, the Jews did not see it. In fact, in Acts 10 we see that it took a special vision of a sheet let down from heaven for Peter to get the message that the gospel was for the Gentiles too.

In Luke 13, Jesus' words about the Gentiles being at the kingdom banquet were meant to excite the Jews to faith with a holy jealousy. The apostle Paul wrote to the Romans, "Inasmuch as I am the apostle to the Gentiles, I take pride in my ministry in the hope that I may somehow arouse my own people to envy and save some of them" (11:13–14, NIV). Jesus' mention of the nations in the kingdom of God must have stung the Jews because of their extreme pride in themselves (see Matt. 8:10–12). But the true "sons of the kingdom" are not those who are physically descended from Abraham but those who respond to Jesus in faith and receive His word.

The final surprise in what Jesus told the Jews is that "there are those who are last who will be first, and first who will be last" (Luke 13:30, NIV). To whom did the gospel first come? Among whom did Jesus minister? The Jews. Were they not the elect people of God? John Calvin explains Jesus' intention.

> . . . to throw down the vain confidence of the Jews, who, having been chosen by God in preference to all the rest of the world, trusted to this distinction, and imagined that God was in a manner bound to them. For this reason, Christ threatens that their condition

will soon be changed; that the Gentiles, who were at that time cast off, would obtain the first rank.[19]

In large part, the Jews rejected Jesus as the Messiah. Even though they had the Old Testament that pointed to Jesus, they did not come in faith to make Jesus their Lord. Millions of Gentiles, however, will come before them into God's kingdom because they put their faith in Jesus. Even people of great faith today, about two thousand years after Jesus' earthly life was over, will receive greater reward than those who saw Jesus doing miracles and heard Him teaching. So the first shall be last and the last first.

Also consider as a warning from the Lord what Paul wrote in Romans 11. He describes how the branches of the olive tree, which represent the Jews, were cut off so that wild olive branches, which represent the Gentiles, might be grafted in. Then he says in verses 20–21, "Do not become proud, but fear. For if God did not spare the natural branches, neither will he spare you." The same causes that made the Jews become last have had the same effect on Christians. Note what happened across North Africa and Turkey—at one time, these areas were the strongholds of Christianity and today they have a tiny minority of Christians. The same can happen in North America, as has largely happened in Europe. If we trust in our outward connection with Christ and continue in sin, we will be among those "last" who are so far behind that they are shut out completely.

Will you be surprised at the people you see in God's kingdom? Will you be there? Have you thought that attending church, giving your tithe, serving in a ministry, and being with Christians is sufficient to get you into the Lord's presence on the last day?

Have you come to Jesus yourself? Do you have a vital relationship with Him in which you speak to Him daily? All of these should not be surprises for those of us who have a personal relationship with Jesus Christ, built on the forgiveness of our sins through Him. We remember that God's ways are not our ways.

Are you following the crowd or are you making every effort to enter through the narrow door? Are you wholeheartedly devoted to loving and obeying Jesus as your Lord? If not, today is the day to begin doing that.

Discussion Questions

1. What is the narrow door that we must go through to enter into eternal life?

2. Why is the door to eternal life narrow? What are the implications of this for us?

3. How should we strive to enter the narrow door? Why must we strive?

4. What should we understand about the character of the "workers of evil" who are sent away?

5. What surprises should we expect upon entering heaven?

6. What warning should we take from the final surprise?

7

Can a Loving God Send Good People to Suffer in Eternal Hell?

Luke 16:19–31

The poor man died and was carried by the angels to Abraham's side.
The rich man also died and was buried, and in Hades, being in torment,
he lifted up his eyes and saw Abraham far off and Lazarus at his side.
And he called out, "Father Abraham, have mercy on me, and send
Lazarus to dip the end of his finger in water and cool my tongue, for I
am in anguish in this flame."

Luke 16:22–24

"Hell" is often heard in common discourse, usually as an expression giving emphasis to one's point. Seventy-one percent of North Americans still believe there is a hell, but they can't imagine that they will be one of the people going there. A national survey of Americans shows that one in four persons has no idea where they will go after death, while only one-half of one percent believe they are going to hell.[1]

Before we examine Jesus' teaching on hell in the story of the rich man and Lazarus in Luke 16, let us take some time to examine people's objections to the idea of hell and what God has to say about its existence.

A Skeptic's Question

Oftentimes, one hears objections to the Christian faith by those who have no fear of God. One of those common objections is some form of this question: How can a loving God send good people to suffer in eternal hell?

First of all, the way the question is formed means that the questioner comes with a Judeo-Christian worldview. The idea of a loving God does not come from observation of history, non-Christian religious texts, or nature. It comes from the Bible. Anyone from a Muslim, Hindu, Buddhist, or animistic background would not even think of God as loving. A loving God is a personal God with whom we can have a relationship through communication. Such a God is not found in other religions.[2]

But upon reading the Bible, one actually finds that the God of love is also a God of judgment who will ultimately put all things right in the world. So to believe that God is purely love but does not judge anyone, rather only accepts everyone, is an act of faith with no supporting evidence from any source. For God to bring justice is evidence of His love. It would not be loving for the unjust and wicked to not be held accountable for their rebellion against God's authority. By analogy, a loving father is not one who would never discipline his child; similarly, a just governor who establishes peace is not one who would fail to bring down justice on a murderer.

Second, the question implies that most people are good and don't deserve hell. Certainly the person posing the question thinks of himself as a good person. What is a good person? Almost everyone will say that he or she is a good person. Even most people in prison will say that they are innocent. A recent newspaper article tells of a nineteen-year-old young man who shot and killed a fourteen-year-old kid on his bike because the younger teen wouldn't move out of the way in the street quickly enough. The judge said of the older teen, "This was basically a good kid, and in the blink of an eye he became a murderer." Yet all sin proceeds from the heart (see Mark 7:20–23).

"A good person" is really a very relative term. In reality, every person is a sinner before God, who alone is holy. Oh, we all acknowledge that we make a mistake once in a while. None of us is perfect. But to say that we are sinners, wicked, rebellious against God seems a bit extreme. Actually, we all sin against God daily in thought, word, and deed. We don't love God with all our heart, soul, mind, and strength, nor do we love our neighbor as ourselves. Rather we are focused on pride, covetousness, sensuality, self-absorption, self-pity, and blame shifting for everything that is wrong.

Our questioner may go on to say, "I don't have anything against God. I just don't see him or her as relevant to my life." If this is true, how can you see Him to be good? This is evidence of people's total lack of acknowledgement that God shows Himself all around us, as we noted in chapter 1: "For his invisible attributes, namely, his eternal power and divine nature, have been clearly perceived, ever since the creation of the world, in the things that have been made. So [we] are without excuse" (Rom. 1:20). The unbeliever, however, suppresses this natural revelation and denies its truthfulness. As Carl Henry said, "Nobody is without some objective knowledge conveyed by general revelation, a knowledge that renders every person guilty for revolt against light, in view of humankind's attempted suffocation of that revelatory content."[3]

What does this lack of recognizing God's relevance lead to? Paul explains, "Although they knew God, they did not honor him as God or give thanks to him, but they became futile in their thinking, and their foolish hearts were darkened" (Rom. 1:21). Having darkened hearts, those who fail to acknowledge God cannot see His light shining through all that He has made and the signs pointing to His greatness and glory. Consequently they are thankless and do not honor God for giving them life itself. So what do such people do? "Claiming to be wise, they became fools, and exchanged the glory of the immortal God for images resembling mortal man and birds and animals and creeping things" (1:22–23). By rejecting knowledge of God, people become idol worshipers, putting their trust in the creation rather than in the Creator of all. The ultimate end of that is seeing themselves as God, so they must look within themselves for insight and wisdom about the meaning of life.

The sad end of this is the depraved life built on this manner of thinking. Paul continues, "Therefore God gave them up in the lusts of their hearts to impurity, to the dishonoring of their bodies among themselves, because they exchanged the truth about God for a lie and worshiped and served the creature rather than the Creator, who is blessed forever!" (1:24–25).

Paul further explains how God gives up sinners who do not acknowledge Him to dishonorable passions of immorality: "Since they did not see fit to acknowledge God, God gave them up to a debased mind to do what ought not to be done" (Rom. 1:28). What kinds of things? Just to name a few, covetousness, malice, envy, murder, strife, deceit, maliciousness, gossip, slander, hating God, insolence, haughtiness, boasting, inventing evil, disobedience to parents, foolishness, faithlessness, heartlessness, and ruthlessness (see 1:29–31). He concludes, "Though they know God's righteous decree that those who practice such things deserve to die, they not only do them but give approval to those who practice them" (1:32). Wow! After reading that, no one will be able to find themselves innocent.

But God's kindness and forbearance and patience are meant to lead us to repentance (see 2:4). This is where the love of God comes in. He has provided a way of escape from His wrath and judgment. It is through Jesus Christ, who stood in our place of punishment on the cross. He suffered and died for you and me that we may be saved if we put our full trust and faith in Him alone for our salvation.

God's Choice

By God's electing grace and sovereign will, He chooses some to be saved from condemnation and to become His adopted sons and heirs (see John 6:37, 44; Eph.1:4–5; 1 Pet. 1:1–2). If people maintain hard and impenitent hearts, however, not knowing God or His gospel, they store up wrath for themselves on the day of vengeance when God's righteous judgment will be revealed at the end of the age (see 2 Thess. 1:7–9). Nowhere does God promise in the Scriptures to save all people, although He freely offers the gospel to all and desires everyone to be saved (see Ezek. 18:23, 32; 1 Tim. 2:4). The few passages that speak of Jesus loving and dying for "all" or the "world" (John 3:16; 4:42; 1 Tim. 4:10; 1 John 2:2; 4:14) must be understood in the context of the passage and the rest of Scripture. "All" and "world" refer to not just the author's readers but to every type of person—male and female, slave and free, Chinese, Persian, Arab, Indian, and Mexican—rather than only to the Jews. For some it seems unjust of God that He would choose to save only some. Carl Henry remarks, "All love is preferential or it would not be love. The non-elect are condemned not because they are non-elect but because they spurn God's universal revelation in nature and history and in the human conscience and mind."[4]

As to justice, God Himself is the norm for what justice is. Our measure of justice is warped by our fallen human natures. Thus some naturalists see justice as simply a reflection of cultural pressures regarding the current prevalent standard of social obligation with no fixed transcendent basis. But God Himself is that fixed basis for what is just, because justice is part of His very character. It is the foundation of His throne (see Ps. 9:7; 89:14). "The LORD . . . is righteous; / he does no injustice; / every morning he shows forth his justice" (Zeph. 3:5). God is judge of all the earth, and His judgment is infallible. Moses sang of the Lord, "The Rock, his work is perfect, / for all his ways are justice. / A God of faithfulness and without iniquity, / just and upright is he" (Deut. 32:4). So to accuse God of misconduct in His elective grace is to forget that He sets the standard of what is truth and love and justice.

God shows His fairness by condemning sinners not for what they don't know but for rebelling against the light of truth they already have. He demonstrates His mercy by extending redemption to us as fallen humans, a redemption that is not extended to fallen angels. Fallen angels have no opportunity to repent. God's call to turn to Him in faith and repentance goes out to all the world, but many refuse Christ's nail-pierced hands as being unloving and unjust, and they prefer to die in their sins. Everyone will be judged by the light they already have, not by what they don't have. No one is without God's light to one degree or another (see Ps. 9:16; Rom. 1:19–20).

Good Works?

"What about all the good things I have done in my life?" some will say. "Don't they count for something toward my salvation?" Well, it all depends on whether their good works were done in faith and for the glory of God or not. Everybody does some good things in his life, even if it is just helping his mother clean the dishes or giving his children good gifts. This is due to God's common grace that blesses everyone. No one's good works, however, are meritorious toward acquiring his or her salvation. "All our righteous deeds are like a polluted garment" in the sight of God (Isa. 64:6).

"When the goodness and loving kindness of God our Savior appeared, he saved us, not because of works done by us in righteousness, but according to his own mercy, by the washing of regeneration and renewal of the Holy Spirit, whom he poured out on us richly through Jesus Christ our Savior" (Titus 3:4–6). Our good works are the evidence of true faith in Christ Jesus, and they were prepared beforehand by God that we should walk in them (see Eph. 2:10). So what is the outcome of our good works?

[God] will render to each one according to his works:
to those who by patience in well-doing seek for glory
and honor and immortality, he will give eternal life;
but for those who are self-seeking and do not obey
the truth, but obey unrighteousness, there will be
wrath and fury. There will be tribulation and distress
for every human being who does evil . . . but glory
and honor and peace for everyone who does good.
(Rom. 2:6–10)

Jesus gave us a parable of the end of the age, when He will
be seated on His throne as king in heavenly glory to judge all
the nations. He will separate the peoples into two groups—the
sheep on His right and the goats on His left. After commending
those on His right for their good works toward the least of these
brothers, He will turn to those on His left.

"Depart from me, you cursed, into the eternal fire
prepared for the devil and his angels. For I was hungry and you gave me no food, I was thirsty and you
gave me no drink, I was a stranger and you did not
welcome me, naked and you did not clothe me, sick
and in prison and you did not visit me." Then they
also will answer, saying, "Lord, when did we see you
hungry or thirsty or a stranger or naked or sick or in
prison, and did not minister to you?" Then he will
answer them, saying, "Truly, I say to you, as you did
not do it to one of the least of these, you did not do
it to me." And these will go away into eternal punishment, but the righteous into eternal life. (Matt.
25:41–46)

So living a righteous life through the righteousness we have obtained through Christ determines our eternal destiny. Our salvation does not depend on our good works, but rather on the gift of faith (see Eph. 2:8–9) we have received through the Holy Spirit. It produces good works through our life for which we will receive an eternal reward.

Even in the life of the Gentile Cornelius, the good works, alms, and prayers he offered were due to the faith he already had (see Acts 10:2) in the same God as that of the Jews (see 10:22). Cornelius is not an example of one who was outside the knowledge of God's Word, but rather one who had the same believing status as an Old Testament believer.[5]

He was not a prime example of what inclusivists such as Pinnock claim to be a "pagan saint,"[6] a person who can be a saved believer through his good works and belief in a supreme being even though he is not a Christian.[7] Inclusivists base their belief upon Peter's statement, "God shows no partiality, but in every nation anyone who fears him and does what is right is acceptable to him" (10:34–35). Peter was used by God to introduce the new-covenant gospel of Jesus' death and resurrection and the sending of the Holy Spirit to the Gentiles and to show that these were not only for the Jews. So this was the new understanding Peter had concerning God having "no partiality."

Both Jew and Gentile were to be saved through the same message. For this reason both Peter and Paul urgently pleaded for their audience of both Jews and Gentiles to repent and believe in the crucified and risen Christ for forgiveness of their sins and as the one who will judge the living and the dead (see 10:39–43; 13:29–41; 17:30–31).

The Nature of Hell

Jesus taught more about the reality of hell than anyone else in the Bible. This is overlooked by those who simply think of Jesus as always going about doing good and talking about love. But His primary message called us to repent because the kingdom of God was at hand (see Mark 1:15).

The reality of hell is made vivid in Jesus' parable of the rich man and Lazarus. Jesus does not make the point that it is a sin to be rich or that all the poor are saved. Some in liberation theology tend to think this way, giving a Marxist twist to the interpretation of Scripture. What Jesus does teach is the great peril those are in who do not live out the principles of the kingdom of God—especially putting into practice love for one's neighbor. There is great spiritual danger in the selfish use of wealth, so much so that it leads one to eternal punishment in anguish and pain (see Ezek. 16:49 concerning Sodom). By not caring for the needs of others, one is living selfishly, disregarding the image of God in each person who should be loved and cared for. Such a person thinks that he is self-sufficient and that he acquired his wealth and status without the help of God.

The rich man has no personal name, hinting that his identity was found only in his wealth, which he lost once in hell (see Ps. 9:5). Lazarus, on the other hand, has a name that likely reflects his character as one who trusted in the help of God. He is the only person named in any of Jesus' parables. This is important, as it emphasizes the continuing worth of the individual. "According to Buddhist belief, man is worthless, having only temporary existence. In Christianity man is of infinite worth, made in the image of God, and will exist eternally. Man's body is a hindrance to the Buddhist while to the Christian it is an instrument to glorify God."[8]

As Sri Lankan pastor and theologian Tissa Weerasingha explains, "Individual identity is of a permanent nature and man is not a mere 'process' in a flux of continuity, although there is impermanence in man in the sense that mind/body complex in its present state will not last forever. A person in this life is identifiable as the same in the life hereafter."[9] Jesus makes this clear in this parable of the rich man and Lazarus: humanity is made up of spiritual beings that have distinct identities that last eternally. It is in this point of failure to understand the true nature of humanity that Buddhism falls short.

We see a great contrast between the rich man and Lazarus, both in their earthly lives and in their lives to come. The rich man arrived through the gate of his estate in his gold-trimmed chariot with his driver steering beautiful white horses. He looked with disgust upon the beggar Lazarus lying there next to his gate in rags with a cupped, uplifted hand. Lazarus, sick with sores, had no one to care for him but the unclean dogs, while the rich man was comfortable and at ease in his mansion, where he dressed in expensive imported purple outerwear and a fine linen inner garment. He feasted sumptuously on delicacies like lobster, filet mignon, mahi mahi, truffles, and rich dark chocolate sprinkled with gold flakes. Afterward, he took baths in his hot mineral springs and got a massage from his masseuse after a hard day of planning as to how he could expand his landholdings.

Is there anything wrong with this picture? Nothing specific about the lifestyle of the rich man was sinful; rather, the problem was his neglect of the poor, his self-satisfaction, and his pride. As the Lord said through Micah, "What does the LORD require of you / but to do justice, and to love kindness, / and to walk humbly with your God?" (Micah 6:8). The rich man was likely proud of what he had accomplished in his life by pushing all his competition out of the way, and he looked down on the beggar as a worthless person who used up good resources and offended his eyes. But the Lord says, "Whoever mocks the poor insults his Maker" (Prov. 17:5). The rich man's sin was that. While he lived in luxury, he did nothing to relieve the suffering of poor Lazarus at his own gate.

After both men died, the rich man called to Abraham, the father of our faith and all Israel, asking for help: "Father Abraham, have mercy on me, and send Lazarus to dip the end of his finger in water and cool my tongue, for I am in anguish in this flame" (Luke 16:24). Note the rich man's attitude toward Lazarus, still expecting him to be his servant and water boy. "But Abraham said, 'Child, remember that you in your lifetime received your good things, and Lazarus in like manner bad things; but now he is comforted here, and you are in anguish'" (16:25). This reflects the truth of the proverb, "Whoever closes his ear to the cry of the poor / will himself call out and not be answered" (Prov. 21:13). Unless we repent of our sins, we also will not be heard in our time of need. Jesus' parable shows us that hell is a place of continual separation from the comfort and joy of the presence of God and of continual anguish. It is pictured as a hot place where one's thirst is never assuaged.

Abraham continues to illuminate the rich man's dilemma: "Besides all this, between us and you a great chasm has been fixed, in order that those who would pass from here to you may not be able, and none may cross from there to us" (Luke 16:26). There is no second chance, no opportunity to change one's mind.

Once we have reached our eternal destiny, it will never change. That is a sobering thought. There exists no place of temporary suffering, no purgatory. This invented doctrine has no scriptural foundation.

We also learn from this passage that hades, the place of the dead, is not a place of annihilation, of simply returning to dust and nonexistence. Hell, like heaven, is a place where people's souls continue in eternal existence. The question we all face is, where will we be upon our death? There are only two places for continued eternal existence: eternal death in hell or eternal life in the new heavens and new earth.

Elisabeth Elliot described hell like this: "Hell is the place where those whose motto is 'My will be done' will finally and forever get what they want. Hell is agony and blankness and torture and the absence of all that humanity was originally destined to be. The glory has terminally departed. It is the heat of flames (not of passion—that will have long since burned out) and the appalling lifelessness of solid ice, an everlasting burning and an irreversible freezing."[10]

Tim Keller, pastor of Redeemer Presbyterian Church in Manhattan, writes, "Hell . . . is the trajectory of a soul, living a self-absorbed, self-centered life, going on and on forever. . . . Hell is simply one's freely chosen identity apart from God on a trajectory into infinity."[11] It is seen in a process of disintegration through addictions that leads to isolation through blaming others and circumstances. When we build our lives on something other than God, that thing becomes the focus of our happiness. This leads to a loss of all humility and being out of touch with reality, in which one is certain that he or she is right and considers everyone else an idiot. This disintegration continues on forever. It leads to no one asking to leave hell because heaven is believed to be ridiculous. People going to hell would rather have their "freedom" than salvation, Keller continues.

> Their delusion is that, if they glorified God, they would somehow lose power and freedom, but in a supreme and tragic irony, their choice has ruined their own potential for greatness. Hell is, as [C.S.] Lewis says, "the greatest monument to human freedom." As Romans 1:24 says, God "gave them up to . . . their desires." All God does in the end with people is give them what they most want, including freedom from himself. What could be more fair than that?[12]

C.S. Lewis put it this way: "All that are in Hell choose it. Without that self-choice it wouldn't be Hell. No soul that seriously and constantly desires joy will ever miss it."[13] The greater grief of those who are damned will be remembering not only that their downfall was their own doing but that they attained it at such cost and pain. They affected their ruin by resisting the Holy Spirit; by overcoming the power of God's mercy, love, and provision; and by refusing to listen to the Word of God, the power of reason, and the urging of their own consciences. They continued to walk in danger of the wrath of God, resisting His revealed will. Their lives would have been much easier lived in sobriety and peace than in suffering from drunkenness, poverty, shame, and sickness. Instead of contentment, they preferred covetousness and ambition, though it cost them anxiety and fear, late nights, and distracted minds. Although their uncontrolled anger resulted in self-torment; though revenge and envy consumed their spirits; though immorality destroyed their health, their good names, and their assets, "yet [would] they do and suffer all this, rather than suffer their souls to be saved. With what rage will they lament their folly, and say, 'Was damnation worth all my cost and pains? Might I not have been damned on free cost, but I must purchase it so dearly!'"[14] How justly will those who are damned suffer in hell for what they worked so hard to earn. "For the wages of sin is death, but the free gift of God is eternal life in Christ Jesus our Lord" (Rom. 6:23).

God's Justice

Although God is a God of love, He is also a God of justice. Both attributes of God are equally emphasized in the Scriptures. If we have one without the other, we have a distorted image of who God really is. Look at how Psalm 145 describes God, for instance.

> The LORD is gracious and merciful,
>   slow to anger and abounding in steadfast love.
>
> The LORD is good to all,
>   and his mercy is over all that he has made. . . .
> The LORD is righteous in all his ways
>   and kind in all his works. . . .
> The LORD preserves all who love him,
>   but all the wicked he will destroy.
>
> (145:8–9, 17, 20)

The wicked who refuse to submit to God's lordship in their life will suffer their just reward. The author of hell's torments is God Himself. Since it was God sinners offended (see Isa. 59:1–15), so it is God who will punish them for their grievous offenses. The torments of hell are for God's enemies. If we are not for Christ, we are against Him, and we are His enemy (see Matt. 12:30; Luke 11:23). We are warned, "It is a fearful thing to fall into the hands of the living God" (Heb. 10:31).

God's place of torment for the ungodly is purposely ordained to glorify the justice of God, Paul explains.

> Has the potter no right over the clay, to make out of the same lump one vessel for honorable use and another for dishonorable use? What if God, desiring to show his wrath and to make known his power, has endured with much patience vessels of wrath prepared for destruction, in order to make known the riches of his glory for vessels of mercy, which he has prepared beforehand for glory—even us whom he has called? (Rom. 9:21–24)

God's Judgment

The effects of God's torment of the damned are extreme because His divine vengeance is implacable. Neglect and abuse of the mercy, goodness, and grace of Christ will be avenged for eternity. Isaiah illustrates God's wrath on the wickedness of Babylon as an image of what all will suffer who have not followed God's ways and been blessed with receiving His mercy.

> Behold, the day of the LORD comes,
>   cruel, with wrath and fierce anger,

to make the land a desolation
>> and to destroy its sinners from it. . . .
I will punish the world for its evil,
>> and the wicked for their iniquity;
I will put an end to the pomp of the arrogant,
>> and lay low the pompous pride of the ruthless.
>>>>>>>>>> (Isa. 13:9–11)

At the end of this age, our Lord Jesus will be seated on a great white throne and before Him will appear all the dead, both great and small. The books of our lives will be opened and we will answer for everything recorded there, including every secret word. The apostle John saw it in his vision.

> The dead were judged by what was written in the books, according to what they had done. And the sea gave up the dead who were in it, Death and Hades gave up the dead who were in them, and they were judged, each one of them, according to what they had done. Then Death and Hades were thrown into the lake of fire. This is the second death, the lake of fire. And if anyone's name was not found written in the book of life, he was thrown into the lake of fire. (Rev. 20:12–15)

"The lake of fire" is another description for hell, a place of all-consuming judgment. We are told in Scripture that the devil will be thrown into the lake of burning sulfur, where he "will be tormented day and night forever and ever" (20:10). Blackest darkness has been reserved forever for the godless (see Jude 13).

Isaiah wrote, "'There is no peace,' says my God, 'for the wicked'" (Isa. 57:21).

The greatest aggravation of the torments of hell is its eternity. Paul wrote of the vengeance that Jesus will inflict on those who do not know God and do not obey the gospel of our Lord Jesus, saying, "They will suffer the punishment of eternal destruction, away from the presence of the Lord and from the glory of his might" (2 Thess. 1:9). Isaiah wrote the word of God, speaking of "the dead bodies of the men who have rebelled against [God]. For their worm shall not die, their fire shall not be quenched, and they shall be an abhorrence to all flesh" (Isa. 66:24). The English Puritan Richard Baxter wrote the following:

> When a thousand million of ages are past, they are as fresh to begin as the first day. If there were any hope of an end, it would ease the damned to foresee it; but For ever is an intolerable thought! They were never weary in sinning, nor will God be weary of punishing. They never heartily repented of sin, nor will God repent of their suffering. They broke the laws of the eternal God, and therefore shall suffer eternal punishment.[15]

Opportunity to Repent

Do we have an opportunity to repent? We do while we are alive. Some, however, propose what is called divine perseverance or postmortem evangelization, like theology professor Gabriel Fackre, who says that God gives the unevangelized an opportunity for salvation after death because God will not condemn anyone until He has seen what their response is to Christ.[16] But the author of Hebrews warns us, "It is appointed for man to die once, and after that comes judgment" (Heb. 9:27); and King David sang concerning the Lord, "In death there is no remembrance of you; / in Sheol who will give you praise?" (Ps. 6:5). If postmortem evangelization were possible, what would be our motivation for evangelization while people are still living? Wouldn't it be better to leave those who have never heard of Christ in ignorance and darkness, knowing that they will have a chance to repent after death than to take all the sacrifices and risks, as did the apostles and as have missionaries throughout church history, to bring the good news to all peoples of the world? The apostles would not have sensed the urgency to proclaim the gospel to both Jew and Gentile if there were another opportunity for repentance and faith after death. We will have no second chances or reincarnations.

Those holding to postmortem evangelization take First Peter 3:18–20 and 4:6 as their primary texts of support: Christ "went and proclaimed [or preached] to the spirits in prison, because they formerly did not obey, when God's patience waited in the days of Noah" (3:19–20). But what we see in this passage is the Spirit of the preincarnate Christ preaching through Noah, "a preacher of righteousness" (2 Pet. 2:5, NIV), for 120 years when God patiently waited for that generation to repent before the flood. The "Spirit of Christ" in Noah "prophesied about the grace that was to be [theirs]" and "predicted the sufferings of Christ and the subsequent glories" (1 Pet. 1:10–11).

Christ's preaching through Noah of His coming death and resurrection was illustrated in type through the deliverance of Noah and his family through water, an antitype of baptism.

He preached a message of repentance and faith to those people whose souls were now separated from their bodies (see Heb. 12:23), called "spirits in prison" (1 Pet. 3:19) or souls in hell (see Rev. 20:13). Peter again confirmed that as a past event, "the gospel was preached even to those who are dead" (1 Pet. 4:6) but who were alive at the time of Noah. His contemporaries had no excuse for not repenting; but they believed Noah's message to be preposterous, and they hardened their hearts to Christ.

With this understanding of the text, we see that no reference is made to a second chance being given those who have died. Rather, we are to make a defense for the "reason for the hope that is in [us]" and "suffer for doing good, if that should be God's will" (3:15, 17). As "Christ suffered in the flesh," so we are to "arm [ourselves] with the same way of thinking" and "live . . . for the will of God" (4:1–2). If there is another opportunity for salvation after death, what is the point in witnessing and suffering for the sake of Christ?

Returning again to Jesus' parable of the rich man and Lazarus, we read the rich man's final plea to Abraham.

> "I beg you, father, to send him to my father's house—for I have five brothers—so that he may warn them, lest they also come into this place of torment." But Abraham said, "They have Moses and the Prophets; let them hear them." And he said, "No, father Abraham, but if someone goes to them from the dead, they will repent." He said to him, "If they do not hear Moses and the Prophets, neither will they be convinced if someone should rise from the dead." (Luke 16:27–31)

The rich man implies in these comments that he and his family were never given enough information about the afterlife. He denies responsibility, shifts the blame, and remains spiritually blind, not even asking to be taken out of hell. Wow! What a solemn warning to us.

We have so much opportunity to hear the clear revelation of God's Word to us and advance notice of the wrath to come unless we repent. It is easily available to us, and good lessons on it can be heard in many churches throughout the country. Yet most people think the teaching of the Word is either ridiculous or only helpful for those who are weak.

So too did the religious leaders in Jesus' day. They ignored or obfuscated God's clear teaching and thought that they were saved because of their outward conformity to the law of God, although their hearts were far from Him. They asked Jesus for some miraculous sign that they might recognize His divine mission. Yet even when he complied with their request—especially by rising from the dead—they still refused to believe in Him. Their hearts were hardened, leading to their self-condemnation. This is the same circumstance for the majority of people who take the wide path to hell.

In the second psalm, we read a prophecy of Jesus Christ's reign over the nations. The rulers of the world plot against Him, but "he who sits in the heavens laughs; / the Lord holds them in derision. / Then he will speak to them in his wrath, / and terrify them in his fury, saying, / 'As for me, I have set my King / on Zion, my holy hill'" (2:4–6). The Lord is speaking of establishing Christ's rule in Zion, the symbol of the dwelling place of God in heaven.

Now therefore, O kings, be wise;
  be warned, O rulers of the earth.
Serve the LORD with fear,
  and rejoice with trembling.
Kiss the Son,
  lest he be angry, and you perish in the way,
  for his wrath is quickly kindled.
Blessed are all who take refuge in him.

          (Ps. 2:10–12)

May each of us be wise, take our refuge in Christ, and find our hope in Him alone. Let us show our allegiance and trust in Him by kissing the Son and calling on Him for mercy while we are alive.

Discussion Questions

1. How is the love of God demonstrated to us?

2. What relationship do our good works have to our salvation?

3. Why is God's attribute of justice important? How does God demonstrate His justice?

4. Is hell a real place? What do we know about what it is like?

5. Can someone who has gone to hell ever get out of it?

6. Is there any opportunity for someone to repent and receive salvation after death?

7. In light of the parable of the rich man and Lazarus, what are we called by God to do?

8

Paul's Approach to World Religions

Acts 17:16–34

*Paul, standing in the midst of the Areopagus, said: "Men of Athens,
I perceive that in every way you are very religious. For as I passed along
and observed the objects of your worship, I found also an altar with
this inscription, 'To the unknown god.' What therefore you worship as
unknown, this I proclaim to you."*

Acts 17:22–23

In today's urban and transitory world, we continually meet
people from a variety of faiths and philosophical systems.
On one corner may be a mosque and across the street an
evangelical church with a Gnostic philosophy center, Hindu
yoga studio, Masonic lodge, Mormon temple, and Jehovah's
Witnesses Kingdom Hall just a few blocks away. The different
worldviews represented by each of these buildings affects how
their adherents live—from their eating, manner of dress, and relationships to their burial, education, and worship. But do these

people really know God? Does God make a difference in their lives? And if they claim to believe in and pray to God, which god is it? These questions are important because their answers determine not only the course of our present life, but also our eternal destiny.

We find in Acts 17 that Silas and Timothy had been preaching the Word of God with Paul in Berea, a city in the region of Macedonia. But Paul was forced to escape due to persecution from the Jews and he fled south to Athens, where he awaited the arrival of Silas and Timothy. His evangelistic team had temporarily been broken up.

Athens, the leading city of Greece, had reached its zenith of cultural prominence in architecture, poetry, and philosophy in the early fifth century BC. Although it had been conquered by the Romans in 146 BC, it was still one of the great intellectual and cultural centers of the ancient world. By Paul's day, it had been superseded by Corinth politically as the capital of the province of Achaia. It was a free city with a population possibly of only ten thousand.

It is significant to note in Paul's going to Athens that his missionary strategy was to reach major urban centers, particularly provincial capitals, as a means to reaching the whole region with the gospel. It remains unclear if going to Athens was part of his original intention or simply the result of the persecution that forced him in that direction.

Provoked to Preach

Very prominent in the city was the Acropolis Hill with the beautiful Parthenon, built six centuries before Paul arrived there. Also in the numerous temples and in the agora (the marketplace), Paul saw many sculptured idols. Statues of the god Hermes were particularly prominent. How did Paul respond to all he saw? "While Paul was waiting for them at Athens, his spirit was provoked within him as he saw that the city was full of idols" (Acts 17:16).

The provoking of Paul's spirit was the work of the Holy Spirit, who causes the believer to be moved with anger at blasphemy toward God's holiness by unbelievers in their lawless deeds, as was Lot in Sodom (see 2 Pet. 2:8). Jesus was moved to such anger when the Temple was made a "den of thieves," and he drove out the money changers (see Matt. 21:12–13; John 2:14–17). Thus Jesus fulfilled the prophecy of David in the Psalms, "Zeal for your house has consumed me" (Ps. 69:9).

Mixed with our anger over God's pure worship corrupted, we are also moved with compassion for the lost, with sadness for their ignorance and love for those whom Christ is calling to Himself. Such provocation motivated Paul to speak and act on what he observed. Those professed believers who are not moved by, but pass over as nothing, the blasphemy of God and who fail to honor God at least as much as they do their earthly fathers are not worthy to be called God's children. Paul was pricked not to simply rest and wait for his companions but to speak out the truth in the face of the falsehood all around him.

Evan Hopkins wrote concerning how those who go out with the gospel as foreign missionaries need to be prepared for such occasions.

> One of the first things he will be told on reaching a foreign shore is that there are many roads to

one town, and it matters little which is taken. The mind of many a young missionary has been baffled to answer this plea, and largely because of insufficient mental preparation beforehand. Armed with a thorough knowledge of the Word of God and a sympathetic understanding of the ancient beliefs of the people to whom he is being sent, he will find himself in a position at the same time to hold fast the faith and hold forth the Word of Life against all opposition.[1]

Paul was thoroughly prepared mentally, educationally, and spiritually for the challenge, "so he reasoned in the synagogue with the Jews and the devout persons, and in the marketplace every day with those who happened to be there" (Acts 17:17). We see in this verse that Paul took a two-pronged approach to his ministry in Athens. On the Sabbaths, he spoke about Jesus as the risen Christ in the local synagogue to Jews and Greek proselytes devoted to the worship of God, while the rest of the week he reached out with his message in the local marketplace to whoever would listen.

Pagan Philosophies

Since Athens was a university city, "some of the Epicurean and Stoic philosophers also conversed with him. And some said, 'What does this babbler wish to say?'" (17:18). Athens had been a center of philosophy for centuries and two major schools of thought dominated. The tenets of these philosophies continue to mold the beliefs of many modern religions and cults.

Epicureanism was based on the teaching of its founder, Epicurus (342–270 BC), who taught that the chief end of humanity is pleasure and freedom from pain, passions, superstitious fears, and anxiety about death. For Epicureans, pleasure was the only good and pain the only evil. Consequently, virtue was to be sought only because it brought the most enjoyment. Their view of pleasure was lofty and they had a scorn for sensualism.

Because they denied a future life and a coming judgment, they lived according to the philosophy, "Let us eat and drink, for tomorrow we die" (1 Cor. 15:32). Many people live like this on our university campuses today. Epicurus believed that gods did not exist or, if they did, denied that they were interested in the lives of people or that they had influence in the world's affairs, like deism. They had an elementary atomic theory and belief that the universe was not created, but was the result of a chance "concourse of atoms," much like the philosophy of evolution. Epicureanism was practically materialistic and atheistic, denying the immortality of the soul as do secular humanism and communism today. It seems to resemble Buddhism as they sought to avoid all desires and denied the existence of God and the soul.

Zeno (340–265 BC), a Cypriot, founded Stoicism, so named for Zeno's teaching from a raised part of the portico, or stoa, of the agora. His philosophy stressed living in harmony with nature, an idea we see in Eastern philosophy. Ethically, Zeno taught dependence on reasoning, exercise of individual self-sufficient powers, and obedience to the dictates of duty. He viewed God pantheistically as the "world-soul" in which everything was God and God was everything. There was no distinction between the Creator and His creation, as we see also in Mormonism and Eastern philosophy. One can see how this philosophy is similar to Hinduism of today, which also has a pantheistic worldview and states that our goal is to eventually become part of the Brahman godhead through the elimination of bad karma.

For Stoics, a distinction between virtue and sin did not exist because they saw no difference between our holy God and people's accountability to Him for their thoughts, words, and actions. Since for them God was impersonal and humans were part of God, they had no pangs of conscience over sin. Rather, they believed in resignation to or conquest of circumstances on one's own, "but they were fatalists and considered absolute apathy the highest moral attainment."[2] Such fatalism is prevalent among Muslims, who repeatedly say inshallah, meaning "if God wills," as an excuse for not doing what has been agreed upon or ought to be done. Epicureanism and Stoicism were two alternatives to dealing with life apart from the revelation of God found in Christ in the Gentile world. Both Epicurean and Stoic philosophy sought peace of mind. Such peace, however, is only possible through having a right relationship with our creator God through Jesus Christ, who gives us a peace that passes all understanding.

Without Christ, we are in conflict with ourselves, our neighbor, and the God who made us and calls us to live righteously. The philosophers were skeptical and critical of Paul's teaching, lacking a clear understanding of what he was saying. To them, the most basic Christian truths were absurd. They called him a "babbler," a word that alluded to a bird that picked at scraps in the gutter. Hence the word referred to a worthless loafer who acquired mere scraps of learning and peddled assorted ideas. "Others said, 'He seems to be a preacher of foreign divinities'—because he was preaching Jesus and the resurrection" (Acts 17:18).

It appears that they mistakenly thought Paul was preaching about two divinities, likely mistaking resurrection (*anastasis*) as a goddess consort to the God named Jesus. This reminds us how people from other worldviews will always interpret what we say through their own lenses of understanding. So Muslims, when we talk about the one triune God, understand us to be saying that we worship three gods—God, Jesus, and Mary. They deny that God could have a son and they understand the Holy Spirit to be the angel Gabriel. Therefore, they often accuse Christians of *shirk*, the unpardonable sin of associating partners with Allah. The non-Christian's understanding of God is veiled by personal perspective (see 2 Cor. 4:3–4). Paul explains, "The natural person does not accept the things of the Spirit of God, for they are folly to him, and he is not able to understand them because they are spiritually discerned" (1 Cor. 2:14).

Proclamation Before the Areopagus

God opens doors for our proclamation of the good news found in Christ so that His chosen ones can hear and respond in faith.

> They took [Paul] and brought him to the Areopagus, saying, "May we know what this new teaching is that you are presenting? For you bring some strange things to our ears. We wish to know therefore what these things mean." Now all the Athenians and the foreigners who lived there would spend their time in nothing except telling or hearing something new. (Acts 17:19–21)

At one time, the Areopagus was a court or council of Ares, the Greek god of thunder and war, which met on the Hill of Ares (or Mars Hill) to preside over murder trials. In Roman times, the Areopagus was the chief judicial council of the city that exercised jurisdiction on matters such as education and religion. It met in the northwest corner of the agora in the royal portico. It was here that the Epicureans and Stoics brought Paul, perhaps partly in jest and partly in derision at his teaching, but not likely in a serious attempt to seek the truth. But the fathers of Athens did take seriously their task to uphold the reputation of the city for its intellectual vigor and interplay of competing philosophies. Their questioning of Paul was likely not a trial but an investigation out of curiosity as to what this new teaching was.

> Paul, standing in the midst of the Areopagus, said: "Men of Athens, I perceive that in every way you are very religious. For as I passed along and observed the objects of your worship, I found also an altar with this inscription, 'To the unknown god.' What therefore you worship as unknown, this I proclaim to you." (Acts 17:22–23)

Paul began his address to the council with courtesy by commending them for how "very religious" they were. He sought to win over their hearing, yet he may also have been attempting to help them see the irony in the fact that, for all their religiosity, they were completely superstitious and lacked knowledge of the true God.

Paul proceeded to note an inscription he had found on one of the statues to a god: 'To the unknown god.' His hearers would likely have seen this as a positive thing while, for Paul as a Jew, it was completely abhorrent. Picking up on this as a point of contact, he introduced the God who had made Himself known and called men to account through repentance. There was no real connection between the one true God and "the unknown god" that the Athenians worshiped as if unconsciously worshiping the true God. True worship of God is not possible apart from the Lord first revealing Himself to us through His special revelation found in the Bible. He must be known to be worshiped. This is the problem with those who claim that Muslims worship the same God as Christians. Allah remains unknown and unknowable, while the one triune God has revealed and brought us into an intimate relationship with Himself.

It should be noted that Paul took a very different approach in his message here than he had in the Jewish synagogue of Pisidian Antioch (see Acts 13:16–41), where he referred to Jewish history and quoted from the Scriptures, which had been fulfilled in Jesus Christ. Nor did Paul repeat the approach he had taken in Lystra, when the pagan people started to sacrifice to him and Barnabas as gods. There he spoke of the living God who had made heaven and earth and gave us rain and fruitful seasons to satisfy our hearts as a witness to His glorious majesty (see 14:13–18). Instead, Paul adapted his message again to his audience, taking them from what they knew to what God had revealed. He put into practice what he had explained to the Corinthians about his approach to ministry: "I have become all things to all people, that by all means I might save some" (1 Cor. 9:22). By beginning with common ground, Paul was able to lead some to understand "the work and person of Jesus as the apex of God's redemptive work for humanity."[3]

British missions statesman Evan Hopkins, of a previous generation, wrote this analysis:

> The chief purpose of the outgoing missionary is not to challenge a comparison between his faith and that which will oppose him; it is rather to declare the good news of Christ's gospel, leaving the hearer to decide for himself the supremacy of that of which he is told. But at the same time it is a task which demands an intelligent grasp of the modes and manner of thinking of the non-Christian, and every would-be missionary should begin here and now to equip himself with a rational understanding of just where the Message he brings meets the unsatisfied needs of the heathen heart, and how and why the indigenous faith is inadequate.[4]

This is exactly what Paul was doing. Obviously, Luke summarized the message of Paul in his account here in Acts to bring out the main points Paul was making. Luke was skillful in highlighting the suitability of Paul's messages to each audience.

Paul continued, "The God who made the world and everything in it, being Lord of heaven and earth, does not live in temples made by man, nor is he served by human hands, as though he needed anything, since he himself gives to all mankind life and breath and everything" (Acts 17:24–25). In proclaiming the God who made the universe and all that it contains "Lord of heaven and earth", Paul was using a concept found in the Hebrew Scriptures as well as one that would have been acceptable to the Greek philosopher Plato. He also used language familiar to Greeks, saying "world" rather than using the Hebrew terminology of "the heaven and the earth." In a similar fashion, it is helpful for us to use terminology with which our audiences can identify. For example, in speaking to a Muslim, we might refer to God as Allah, Jesus as *Isa*, and the Bible as *Kitab*.

In referring to the biblical conception of God, Paul corrected the Athenians' false view of God and the fallacies of their system of belief. Doing this is so important because false views of God are the most basic error of all world religions and cults. A right view of God is absolutely essential to the Christian faith and proper worship of Him. The gospel cannot be reconciled with pantheism, polytheism, or naturalism.

When Paul said God "does not live in temples made by man," he was repeating a concept already found in higher forms of paganism. In the fifth century BC, Euripides asked, "What house built by craftsmen could enclose the form divine within enfolding walls?" But Paul's argument was profoundly biblical. King Solomon prayed at the dedication of the Temple, "Will God indeed dwell on the earth? Behold, heaven and the highest heaven cannot contain you; how much less this house that I have built!" (1 Kings 8:27). Isaiah proclaimed, "Thus says the LORD: / 'Heaven is my throne, / and the earth is my footstool; / what is the house that you would build for me, / and what is the place of my rest? / All these things my hand has made, / and so all these things came to be, / declares the LORD'" (Isa. 66:1–2). An earthly temple cannot contain God because He is spirit and He is omnipresent. Next, Paul addressed God's relationship to humanity: "He made from one man every nation of mankind to live on all the face of the earth, having determined allotted periods and the boundaries of their dwelling place" (Acts 17:26). This teaching struck at the heart of Athenian pride and their belief in Greek racial superiority. This kind of pride is common with many ethnic groups around the world. The Athenians boasted that they had originated from the soil of their Attic homeland and were not like other people. Paul, however, affirmed the oneness of humanity from a common ancestor without naming Adam. He also undercut the deistic view of the Epicureans in saying that God had determined specific times for the events in our lives and the places where each of us would live. God certainly exercises His sovereignty by being involved in the affairs of this world. As the psalmist says, "Whatever the LORD pleases, he does, / in heaven and on earth" (Ps. 135:6).

God's involvement with humankind is so "that they should seek God, and perhaps feel their way toward him and find him" (Acts 17:27). God has called each of us to seek Him. The prophet Isaiah proclaimed, "Seek the LORD while he may be found; / call upon him while he is near; / let the wicked forsake his way, / and the unrighteous man his thoughts; / let him return to the LORD, that he may have compassion on him, / and to our God, for he will abundantly pardon" (Isa. 55:6–7). Our seeking of God should be accompanied by the hope that as we feel our way toward Him, we might find Him. Paul's phrasing about what seekers might do to find God is unusual. He could have been referring to the Hellenistic manner of philosophical searching for truth and the divine without any real hope of success. But the scriptural sense is that of the thankful and longing heart reverently seeking the God whose goodness and blessing it has experienced (see Jer. 29:13).[5]

Paul proceeded to support his points by quoting from Greek poets who were viewed by his audience as recognized authorities.

In Acts 17:27–28 he said, "He is actually not far from each one of us, for 'In him we live and move and have our being.'" Paul here quoted Epimenides of Crete (ca. 600 BC) from his poem "Cretica" in which Minos, Zeus' son, honors his father.[6] Paul continued, "As even some of your own poets have said, 'For we are indeed his offspring.'" This quote is from the Cilician poet Aratus' (ca. 315–240 BC) poem "Phaenomena."

Then Paul admonished, "Being then God's offspring, we ought not to think that the divine being is like gold or silver or stone, an image formed by the art and imagination of man" (Acts 17:29). Paul rejected Greek polytheism and Stoic pantheism. Likewise we too must reject images created from human imagination because they limit God, who is distinct from His creation. He is much more than all we can think or imagine. The fullness of His majestic splendor and glory cannot be contained by our puny minds. God is Spirit, He is everywhere, and He is in sovereign control of the universe. "Who has measured the Spirit of the LORD? . . . Behold, the nations are like a drop from a bucket, / and are accounted as the dust on the scales. . . . To whom then will you compare me, / that I should be like him? says the Holy One" (Isa. 40:13, 15, 25).

By quoting the Greek poets, Paul was finding common ground with his audience, using authorities who in some respect supported his message. However, he sanitized and baptized the poets' words for his own purposes of sharpening his message to touch the Athenians' hearts. Similarly, we can contextualize our gospel presentation to our audience using passages from their own texts that support our premise. Those bringing the gospel to Muslims will frequently quote from the Qur'an when it is supportive of a Christian doctrine. However, we must be careful not to quote passages that have a completely different meaning to the Muslim than the Christian because of the Muslim's particular definition of identical terms. We also need to be careful not to cause our audience confusion about our source of authority. Quoting their sources should be merely to provide a point of contact and establish common ground.

Although Paul used pagan poet quotations, his message was thoroughly consistent with the teaching in his epistles. In editing Paul's message for his orderly account in Acts, Luke highlighted the significant points that particularly addressed the worldview of the Greek philosophers in Athens. This does not mean that Paul necessarily left out saying anything about the cross of Christ and His grace. To explain Christ's resurrection, he would had to have referred to Christ's crucifixion.

Paul's message was also consistent with the preaching of Jesus. "Jesus came into Galilee, proclaiming the gospel of God, and saying, 'The time is fulfilled, and the kingdom of God is at hand; repent and believe in the gospel'" (Mark 1:14–15). To repent is to turn one's life in another direction. It is to forsake a life of sin and follow Christ wholeheartedly. It is a call to be held accountable for one's life. Thus Paul continued, "The times of ignorance God overlooked, but now he commands all people everywhere to repent, because he has fixed a day on which he will judge the world in righteousness by a man whom he has appointed; and of this he has given assurance to all by raising him from the dead" (Acts 17:30–31). Paul assured his listeners that they were all accountable to the God who had created them and given them life. Also, history does not just go on interminably, as is believed in pantheism and naturalism. Rather, a day of judgment is coming. As the author of Hebrews states, "Just as it is appointed for man to die once, and after that comes judgment, so Christ, having been offered once to bear the sins of many, will appear a second time, not to deal with sin but to save those who are eagerly waiting for him" (9:27–28). This is the blessed hope of the Christian.

John DeVries, president of Mission India, told how a literacy primer he wrote for teaching people to read tells the story of the Bible in a summary way. It began with the creation of the world and humankind and ended with Christ's second coming and the end of the age. This was seen as amazingly good news to the thousands of Indians from a Hindu background who read this. It meant that for poor outcasts, there was a future and a hope rather than the endless cycle of reincarnation without any real expectation to eventually reach nirvana.

Why would God send a judge? Judgment comes because of humanity's sin. For those of us who believe and have had our sins washed away, the day of God's judgment will be a time of rejoicing to be with our Lord. But for those who refuse the free offer of God, it will be a time of great fear and gnashing of teeth. The man appointed to be our judge is no ordinary person but rather one who has risen from the dead. He is now Lord of heaven and earth and has authority over all things. Paul was a witness to the risen Christ whom he dramatically encountered on the road to Damascus. God then called Paul to be His witness to the Gentiles to attest to this amazing fact of history.

Response

How did this sophisticated assembly respond to the message? "When they heard of the resurrection of the dead, some mocked. But others said, 'We will hear you again about this'" (Acts 17:32).

Perhaps those who said they wanted to hear Paul again were politely dismissing him but more likely, they secretly hoped that what he said was true.

The majority of Greeks, however, sought wisdom and thus considered the message of Christ's crucifixion a folly (see 1 Cor. 1:22–23). They also objected to the concept of resurrection. Had Paul spoken of the immortality of the soul, most of his audience, except for the Epicureans, would have assented to what he said. But to most of the Athenians, the idea of a bodily resurrection from the dead was simply impossible. They regarded the body as earthly and evil, while the soul was the seat of the divine in a person. Five hundred years earlier, the poet Aeschylus (525–456 BC) wrote of the god Apollo saying upon the inauguration of the court of the Areopagus, "When the dust has soaked up a man's blood, once he is dead, there is no resurrection" (Eumenides 647–48).[7] So it is for most people today as well.

For the Christian, however, the body is good as created by God and will be re-created upon our resurrection. Of course, that is only possible by the direct intervention of God into the affairs of humanity by a miracle. Yet this is exactly what God did in order to conquer sin, death, and Satan and gain the ultimate victory for His eternal kingdom. The resurrection was the ultimate proof for the Christian community that God was reconciling Himself with the world through Christ (see 2 Cor. 5:15, 19). God acted in a unique way through Jesus that was never to be repeated again and was the decisive act in history. It is only through the resurrection that the believer in Christ has any hope at all of a blessed eternal future. This is the good news that Christ brought. Paul's message was not well received overall. The city fathers' decision as to whether to grant Paul permission to continue teaching seems to have been postponed until another meeting. Yet, a few did respond to the message with gladness and followed Paul. One of these was Dionysius, a member of the council of Ares. Later tradition names this man as the first bishop of Athens. Another was a prominent woman named Damaris. However, we do not hear of a church being formed in Athens during the apostolic age.

In writing to the church in Corinth, Paul spoke of the household of Stephanas, the members of which he had baptized as the first converts in Achaia (see 1 Cor. 1:16; 16:15), the region that included both Athens and Corinth. Could these believers have come to Corinth with Paul from Athens? It often appears that in regions where a long-established system of belief is entrenched, Satan keeps hold of the people with more tenacity. That is often seen today in areas of the world where some of the major world religions dominate. Yet God still calls us to reach all people with the gospel, as he used Paul to do as well.

We must remember that Paul's going to Athens may not have been a part of his original outreach strategy, but rather the result of flight from persecution and a place to wait for his companions. He actually had not intended to do serious ministry there until Silas and Timothy arrived. But moved by the Spirit through being provoked by the idolatry of the city, he began to preach. Paul did what he later instructed Timothy to do: "Preach the word; be ready in season and out of season" (2 Tim. 4:2). God used Paul to bring His chosen ones to Himself there, although we are not told what subsequently happened to these individuals. The gospel was not being firmly established there because of the hardness of heart and intellectual pride of the people who were steeped in their pagan philosophy and idolatry.

It was their attitude toward the Word of God more than a lack of effectiveness in Paul's preaching that caused them to reject the gospel. Luke would not have given us the extensive detail of Paul's ministry in Athens and the highlights of Paul's message if they were not intended to be instruction for us to learn from and imitate. Remember, few are chosen who go through the narrow gate to life, and broad is the road to destruction.

What is your response to the call of God as seen in Paul's preaching to the Athenians? You may find all around you people enmeshed in a quagmire of relativism, naturalism, and pantheism, with no true hope of a future. Are you ready to respond to the challenge of Jesus to call them to repentance and faith in what He has done for them, that they may be forgiven and made new creations in Christ? If you are a believer and now sense that God is calling you to proclaim the gospel to those holding to worldly belief systems, pursue the challenge by preparing yourself intellectually, culturally, and spiritually. Then go to these people under the power of the Holy Spirit through prayer.

Discussion Questions

1. Have you ever felt provoked by something ungodly? What did you do about it? What is a proper Christian response?

2. What approach did Paul take with his audience? What can we learn from this for our own witness to others?

3. How should we prepare ourselves for witness to those from other religions?

4. What new things could we learn about God and His relationship with us from Acts 17:16–34?

5. Was Paul's ministry in Athens a failure? Why or why not?

9

Christian Tolerance
1 Peter 3:8–18

All of you, have unity of mind, sympathy, brotherly love, a tender heart, and a humble mind. Do not repay evil for evil or reviling for reviling, but on the contrary, bless, for to this you were called, that you may obtain a blessing.

1 Peter 3:8–9

In recent years, terrible atrocities have been committed in various parts of the world because of a lack of tolerance for those with whom the perpetrators differ. We think of massacres in Nigeria, Indonesia, Pakistan, Sri Lanka, India, Iraq, and Syria; bombings in London, Madrid, Brussels, and Istanbul; mass shootings in Tunisia, Kenya, Paris, Dhaka, and San Bernardino; and beheadings in Libya, Saudi Arabia, Iraq, and Syria. As I write this, the worst shooting massacre in American history just occurred when an American-born Muslim killed forty-nine people at a gay nightclub in Orlando, Florida. Many of our leaders interpret numerous terrorist acts, especially in our country, as actions done out of hate. Yet usually these acts are inspired by an ideology and a political motivation. R.R. Reno, editor of *First Things*, explains.

> Our leaders cannot imagine a rational anti-Americanism. This is due in part to the narrowing effect of multiculturalism. Paradoxically, instead of broadening our capacity to entertain ways of thinking not our own, multiculturalism has made us parochial. We compliment ourselves endlessly for our tolerance, inclusiveness, and diversity. Since we are so tolerant of others, we assume, there is no reason others shouldn't tolerate us. Since we are never offended, we must be inoffensive. When Barack Obama and Hillary Clinton say that history is on our side, this is what they mean: There is no valid argument against our ascendancy or our way of thinking. Our multicultural leaders are incapable of seeing the world through the eyes of a conservative Muslim, or of any religiously conservative person.[1]

Today we are living in a world that has a greater mixture of religions, races, ethnicities, and ideologies than perhaps at any other time in history. Now practically everyone meets others from backgrounds different from their own. This raises many questions about how we can live in a community with others peacefully and respect their views when they are so contrary to our own. It takes the virtue of tolerance. What is an intolerant person? Donald McGavran has defined them thus: "Intolerant persons are those who not only believe they are absolutely right, but forbid others to hold beliefs which differ from theirs. Intolerant people force others to believe as they do."[2] This is the very nature of dictatorships, such as we see in Kim Jong Un's North Korea and in Iran and Saudi Arabia today. It is often seen in cults, as well. At times, we also see it manifested by those who represent the world's major religions. Unfortunately, it has also been found at various times historically among Christians who have a twisted understanding of the Bible's teachings or lack of understanding of what it says. The Christian, however, is to be tolerant of others and must also respond to other's intolerance with grace, as we will examine later in First Peter 3.

In addressing the topic of tolerance, we must distinguish between various types: legal, social, and intellectual.

Legal Tolerance

Legal tolerance is when everyone's religious rights, including those of minorities, are protected by law. It should be the goal of Christians today, whether they are in the majority or a minority. It is only just. Tolerance needs to include the right to change one's religion. This and other aspects of tolerance should be demanded to be in every country's constitution and enforced by the authorities. Tolerance is found in the Universal Declaration of Human Rights, which has been adopted by most countries in the world, yet it is often not enforced by them. All the Muslim majority countries stretching from Morocco to Afghanistan state that they have freedom of religion in their constitution; yet they actually don't, as they enforce imprisonment or death for a Muslim converting to another religion and restrict the activities of those from other faiths. Similarly, conversion from Hinduism to another religion is against the law in numerous Indian states, where reconversion has been forced on some who left their original Hindu faith for Christianity. It has even resulted in martyrdom.

Christians should be allowed to build and repair churches and establish schools and seminaries in Islamic countries, just as Muslims should be allowed to do in countries where they are a minority. Although each religious group should have equal rights, this does not mean that Christians should not seek to have an influence on society and raise the moral standards by enacting laws that encourage and support marriage between a man and a woman; sexual purity; life for the unborn; care for the elderly, sick, and handicapped; and the just rights of minorities. The purpose of government is to protect the weak from the strong, uphold everyone's just rights, and maintain peace for the common good. This is only truly possible when there is freedom as opposed to a majority forcing a minority to submit to an ideology, as is the case with the "protected" *dhimmi* who have second-class status in Muslim societies and are forced to pay an extra poll tax.

While Muslims in the West need to be protected and given freedom to practice their faith, their Islamic sharia law should not supersede the US Constitution and law of the land. The two systems are incompatible. Some concentrated Islamic communities in Western countries are presently applying sharia law in their community, ignoring the laws of their state. This leads to much tension.

Today, legal tolerance for freedom of religion is being challenged, even in the United States, as the present US government administration has changed from promoting freedom of religion to allowing freedom of worship, both in domestic and foreign policy. What this means is that a person is free to exercise his or her religion in a house of worship or at home but not in public. This ideology is practiced by most Communist, Muslim, and other tyrannical governments. But the founders of the American republic specifically sought to avoid this kind of tyranny by declaring that the state could not limit the "free exercise" of one's religion (emphasis added).[3]

The implications of this change in interpretation mean that Christians are forced to act against their conscience in many matters—for example, requiring pharmacists to sell abortifacient drugs; forcing tax payers to absorb the cost of abortions; demanding that teachers or professors teach evolution as fact without allowing them to offer the alternative of intelligent design; mandating clerks to grant marriage certificates to gay and lesbian couples; and requiring business owners to provide services even when they totally disagree with what the buyer is using their service to promote.

Where this conflict of interests is currently becoming most acutely felt is in the realm of Christians practicing and speaking their beliefs publicly and the LGBTQ community declaring our message to be hate speech, inciting violence, and thus demanding our silence. Already some pastors are being threatened and several have been arrested in a few Western countries for speaking in their churches on biblically moral topics that are construed to be hate speech. A statement by Mat Staver, founder and chairman of Liberty Counsel, asserts that a report from the US Commission on Civil Rights attacks religious freedom, suggesting that "the words 'religious freedom' and 'religious liberty' have become merely code words for intolerance, Christian suprema-cy, racism, sexism, homophobia, Islamophobia, and therefore must yield before LGBT anti-discrimination laws." Staver also states that the report calls for laws that "eliminate exemptions or accommodation for religious convictions."[4] As Christians, we are likely to see more and more legal challenges when it comes to living out our moral convictions in the public sphere.

Social Tolerance

Social tolerance means holding respect for all people, no mat-ter what their views, social status, financial standing, national or-igin, race or ethnicity, or sexual orientation. The Christian basis for this is, first, that God "made from one man every nation of mankind to live on all the face of the earth" (Acts 17:26). All of us have a common ancestry and are therefore blood brothers. In addition, we cannot expect Christian views and ways of life from those who are not Christians. So we should show respect and friendliness toward our gay neighbors, racist colleagues, Muslim classmates, or Marxist professors, even though we hold radically different views from them on life. By this means we can be a witness to the light of Christ in us. We need to listen to others. This does not mean that we need to promote their viewpoints to the public as a means of giving them equal time. Rather, within our power we should uphold truth, justice, and love toward all.

Second, we are all made in the image of God (see Gen. 1:26–27), meaning that everyone's life has infinite value because all people are made to have an intimate relationship with their cre-ator. We must therefore respect every person as someone who reflects the image of God and may embody His character as God works in him or her. In fact, the ultimate value of a person is that God sent His unique, one-and-only Son to appear among us as a man and suffer and die for us that we may be redeemed from our sins.

Third, for those who are in Christ Jesus by faith, there is no distinction between Jew and Gentile, slave and free, male and female (see Gal. 3:28) such as the rest of the world makes. We who are Christians are all one in our common faith and we must love all even as we are loved by God. We must show good neighborliness to every believer. We are "to speak evil of no one, to avoid quarreling, to be gentle, and to show perfect courtesy toward all people" (Titus 3:2).

Scriptural injunctions written by Paul to the believers in Rome, where religious persecution was prevalent, enjoined them to live as follows:

> Live in harmony with one another. Do not be haughty, but associate with the lowly. Never be wise in your own sight. Repay no one evil for evil, but give thought to do what is honorable in the sight of all. If possible, so far as it depends on you, live peaceably with all. Beloved, never avenge yourselves, but leave it to the wrath of God, for it is written, "Vengeance is mine, I will repay, says the Lord." To the contrary, "if your enemy is hungry, feed him; if he is thirsty, give him something to drink; for by so doing you will heap burning coals on his head." Do not be overcome by evil, but overcome evil with good. (Rom. 12:16–21)

These radical ideas are difficult to live by, but they are life and community transforming. May God give us the power to execute them. Most of us are familiar with situations in which we see someone who is not part of our group, church, or denomination doing a work in the name of Christ. Should we denounce such people and seek to hinder their work because they are not part of us? Certainly not! Just because they are not part of our group does not mean they are not doing a God-glorifying work. Consider how Jesus responded to this kind of situation with His disciples.

> John said to him, "Teacher, we saw someone casting out demons in your name, and we tried to stop him, because he was not following us." But Jesus said, "Do not stop him, for no one who does a mighty work in my name will be able soon afterward to speak evil of me. For the one who is not against us is for us. For truly, I say to you, whoever gives you a cup of water to drink because you belong to Christ will by no means lose his reward. (Mark 9:38–41)

It was not that this man John was speaking of was not a follower of Christ, but that he was not one of the twelve apostles who had received Christ's official commission. Jesus noticed pride in John's question and declined to denounce this man doing works of the kingdom of God. Rather, all such persons who are supportive of the cause of Christ should be acknowledged. Indeed, even those who do small acts of mercy in the name of Jesus will be rewarded. Jesus told His disciples on several occasions that He would suffer many things and be rejected by the

Jewish religious leaders, that He would be killed, and that on the third day He would be raised (see, for example, Luke 9:22, 44). So Jesus began to make His way purposefully from Galilee in the north going southward toward Jerusalem. To get there, He had to pass through Samaria. Now, the Samaritans and Jews deeply hated each other, so the Jews traveling to festivals in Jerusalem were often not welcomed in Samaritan villages on the way. For that reason, most pilgrims to the Temple traveled the longer route alongside the Jordan River. Luke tells us what happened as Jesus and His disciples made their way through Samaria.

> When the days drew near for him to be taken up, he set his face to go to Jerusalem. And he sent messengers ahead of him, who went and entered a village of the Samaritans, to make preparations for him. But the people did not receive him, because his face was set toward Jerusalem. And when his disciples James and John saw it, they said, "Lord, do you want us to tell fire to come down from heaven and consume them?" But he turned and rebuked them. And they went on to another village. (9:51–56)

Notice the extreme anger of James and John at this village that had refused hospitality to them. They wanted to call upon God to bring down fire to destroy them as the prophet Elijah had done to those who sought to kill him hundreds of years before (see 2 Kings 1:10–12). This was a normal Jewish response toward the Samaritans. But Jesus did not allow retaliation and judgment. He had come not to destroy people's lives but to save them. So instead, Jesus moved on to another village that would be hospitable. This should be our response. We ought not to take judgment of others into our own hands but leave that up to God in His timing. On another occasion while passing through Samaria, Jesus sat by a well at noontime while His disciples went into a town to buy lunch. A Samaritan woman with a bad reputation came to draw water from the well and Jesus asked her for a drink. She was surprised that a Jewish rabbi had spoken to her, not only because she was a woman but also because she was a Samaritan. Moreover, He had asked her for a drink. After Jesus offered the woman living water welling up to eternal life, He asked her to call her husband. When she responded that she didn't have one, Jesus said to her, "'You are right in saying, "I have no husband"; for you have had five husbands, and the one you now have is not your husband. What you have said is true.' The woman said to him, 'Sir, I perceive that you are a prophet'" (John 4:16–19).

Then she proceeded to bring up the religious subject that separated Jews from Samaritans: whether the proper place of worship was on Mount Gerizim or in Jerusalem. Jesus responded to her.

> "You worship what you do not know; we worship what we know, for salvation is from the Jews. But the hour is coming, and is now here, when the true worshipers will worship the Father in spirit and truth, for the Father is seeking such people to worship him. God is spirit, and those who worship him must worship in spirit and truth." The woman said to him, "I know that Messiah is coming (he who is called Christ).

When he comes, he will tell us all things." Jesus said
to her, "I who speak to you am he." (John 4:22–26)

Notice how Jesus overcame the intolerance that was prevalent between Jews and Samaritans in His day. He spoke openly,
asking for a drink. Common courtesy in that hot weather would
mean meeting such a human need, yet Jesus used it as an opportunity to overcome prejudices and address the mistaken ideas
that the Samaritan woman had.

He engaged her in dialogue in order to convince her of the
truth. He boldly stated what true worship was and where the
revelation that brings salvation comes from. He revealed His
identity as the promised Messiah who had come to bring eternal
life. As a result, the life of this woman and the lives of everyone
in her town were turned around.

Many Samaritans from that town believed in him because of the woman's testimony, "He told me all that
I ever did." So when the Samaritans came to him,
they asked him to stay with them, and he stayed
there two days. And many more believed because of
his word. They said to the woman, "It is no longer
because of what you said that we believe, for we have
heard for ourselves, and we know that this is indeed
the Savior of the world." (4:39–42)

Developing social tolerance is often closely connected with
intellectual tolerance, as is the case in the above example.
Demonstrating such tolerance can have a transformative impact
on society.

Intellectual Tolerance

Third, Christians must tolerate differing intellectual views as something others have a right to believe. We cannot force anyone to agree with our opinions. These are things that people become convinced of through logical and reasonable argument, deduction, and reception of the truth. Being tolerant does not mean that we cannot share our convictions with others or that our faith is merely a private matter; it's simply that we have to share in a respectful manner.

What the various religions of the world need to confront today is the difficulty that accompanies pluralism, as noted by Clark Pinnock.

> What makes pluralism so challenging today is the "relativistic mindset of late modernity," that is, "an ideology of pluralism which celebrates choice in and of itself and claims that choice is good no matter what is chosen." . . . Any diversity of choices is tolerable except one: "the mentality that believes that some choices are right and others wrong, some beliefs true and others false. That cannot be tolerated."[5]

In other words, this position of pluralism is an intolerance that contradicts its premise by defining what is not tolerable and making a value judgment on it.

We cannot accommodate every opinion as being true or valid, however. Obviously some views are false and evil and must be rejected. To accept everybody's opinion as equally valid is not a virtue. To do so is illogical and harmful.

For the Christian, all truth and goodness find their ultimate expression in Jesus Christ, who claimed to be "the truth" (John 14:6). What is contrary to Jesus is by definition the opposite of goodness and truth. This does not mean that everything is either black or white in how one would define it. Most always one will find a mixture of truth, beauty, and goodness intertwined with deceit, ugliness, and evil. But Christianity is based on the premise that all truth is God's truth. We are an intolerant religion when it comes to the matter of truth and error. We are not intolerant of people but of error. Just as a mathematician cannot accept two plus two as equaling five, so Christians insist on holding to the truth over error. That is why Jesus boldly explained the truth to the Samaritan woman at the well.

In our relativistic age, anyone who strongly believes in anything and tries to persuade others is considered intolerant. Christians believe Jesus to be unique, not just another prophet as many before Him; He is the special revelation of God in human form called the incarnation. He is the one that previous prophets predicted would come. Through His death for our sins on the cross and His resurrection on the third day that brought victory over sin, death, and Satan, Jesus has authority as king over all things. Through Jesus we have access to God the Father as He continually intercedes for us. All these facts of the gospel continually challenge those from other faiths and those relativists with no faith. True believers in Christ cannot but share the good news of forgiveness from sins and the gift of eternal life. For those who see tolerance as almost the highest of virtues, the claims of Christ to being the only way, the absolute truth, and the source of life (see 14:6) are intolerable. So for us to proclaim the faith in public is seen to them as anathema.

For example, in an open forum such as an American public school today, one can teach about any religion as it pertains to history, culture, and literature; but when it comes to mentioning Christianity, it is feared to be violating the law of separation of church and state. But this view is totally contrary to the intention of the founding fathers of America, who simply did not want to establish one denomination as the state church. God was acknowledged by our founders as sovereign ruler in everything that was done in government, even by those who were non-Christian deists. On the other hand, our society considers teaching a worldview in which God does not exist or have anything to do with us is not teaching religion. But life is religion, and certainly such instruction is teaching a religion of secular humanism and relativism that says there is no God who intervenes in the affairs of humanity. Secularism has a philosophical basis that permeates all areas of life. If our society does not teach about God and what He requires of us, we will have no basis for ethics, morality, and a proper understanding of reality.

Although many see tolerance as the new virtue of our age, tolerance often carries with it a double standard that prevails. Christian protests and displays against abortion or LGBTQ rights are usually denounced, maligned, or torn down and their representatives restricted or punished in some way, even with arrest. Protests are acceptable only if they support a liberal cause, even if those liberal causes are obviously racially motivated. For the Christian, however, while tolerance is extremely important, if we tolerate evil, we are culpable for that.[6]

To deny the right of Christians to teach their faith in a Muslim society also denies Muslims the opportunity to know what the Bible truly says, leading to many misunderstandings, just as the reverse does for Christians in regard to Islam. So a restriction on the importing and printing of Bibles and Christian literature in majority Muslim countries is a form of intolerance. It is because of principles from the Bible on ethics, the rule of law, exploration of the universe, rights of women and children, and hope for the future that many countries with large Christian populations have prospered so much. And it has been the application of biblical principles that has led to attention to human rights in the face of genocide, torture, abortion, sexual slavery, and dehumanization of populations.

David Hewetson of Australia wrote, "As I see it tolerance in religion has only one role: it is there to preserve the rights of all men everywhere to believe what they choose to believe." In our day of supposed "tolerance," however, it is used not just to protect human rights but as a criteria as to whether something is true or false. Just because we all rightly should have the freedom to believe whatever we want to believe, this does not mean that all beliefs are equally correct or above criticism. For instance, a person may believe that the world is flat. He should not be persecuted for that. We ought to do all we can to protect the rights of such a person to hold to that belief. Freedom to believe such error, however, does not make this person's ideas something that should be accepted as scientific fact. To disagree is not intolerance but simply common sense. Hewetson continued, "So tolerance cannot decide what is right or wrong, true or false, and we should not ask it to. It already has a most valuable, indeed essential, role. It preserves our right to an opinion, no matter how mistaken others may think us. And it allows us to be tolerant of other people's beliefs without necessarily agreeing with them."[7] Tolerance is meant to preserve everyone's freedom to believe as they wish without necessarily agreeing that their opinions are true.

The Bible teaches that God has given all people general revelation in what He has made. That makes it possible for everyone to know that there is a God who created the world by His design, power, and intelligence. God's attributes of eternal power and divine nature are "clearly perceived . . . in the things that have been made" (Rom. 1:20). Additionally, the law of God is written on the hearts of all, which is borne witness to by each person's conscience (see 2:15). Consequently, those from all the religions of the world have some things in common with those in other religions, particularly in the area of ethics. The truths that people find in general revelation about the nature of God and the nature of reality should be seen as preparation for their reception of God's special revelation, seen in the Judeo-Christian Scriptures known as the Holy Bible, which reveal Jesus Christ as the revelation of God to us. General revelation leaves the world in anticipatory hunger waiting for God's special revelation of Christ in Scripture. Michael Cassidy from South Africa has well-articulated our position.

> So everything that is true in other religions is a preparation for the Gospel. So although we are open to people of other faiths and tolerant of their different beliefs, we nevertheless avoid the openness of indifference to truth—truth being coherence with the facts as they are—but embrace the openness that invites everyone into the quest for knowledge and certitude in Christ.[8]

Since Jesus Christ claimed that He Himself was the truth, anything that contradicts what He has revealed is untrue and so must be seen as such. This is the difficult but necessary intolerance of truth. Sri Lankan Christian leader Ajith Fernando said the following:

> If a person builds his life on an untruth, we have the responsibility to direct him to the truth. And that means bringing him to the point of discarding the untruth in order to accept the truth. If we see a person trying to drink a dangerous cyanide compound, believing it to be harmless, we cannot ignore the situation by stating that this is his personal opinion which he is entitled to hold and with which we must not interfere. We would do everything in our power to persuade him against drinking the substance. John Stott asks, "How can Christians be intellectually tolerant of opinions we know to be false or actions we know to be evil?" He calls this "unprincipled indulgence."[9]

We have to get involved. We must try to persuade people to see that only through Christ is there hope of eternal life and deliverance from the condemnation we deserve for our sins. However, such persuasion must not turn to coercion, imposition, deception, or manipulation. It is only the Spirit of God that can transform hearts and bring people to a conviction of the truth of the gospel. We are simply to be ambassadors of the message of reconciliation that God has given us to proclaim (see 2 Cor. 5:19–20).

Christian Response to Intolerance

Lord Alton, a United Kingdom member of parliament, reported, "A Pew Research Centre study found that religious repression was recorded in 151 of 185 countries studied in the last 10 years."[10] A recent survey has indicated that a majority of Americans, especially among evangelical Protestants, agree with the statements "Christians increasingly are confronted by intolerance in America today" and "Religious liberty is on the decline in America."[11]

But as our culture has rapidly become more secular and anti-Christian and embraced an increasing mixture of various religions, Christians need not become fearful or panic. The church has always been in a culture hostile to biblical faith. It began in an oppressive society ruled by the Roman Empire. Then the church had no social, political, or economic clout. The early church was planted and grew in a society that was filled with idol worship, temple prostitutes of both sexes, child sacrifices, and mystery cults.

The government required enforced worship of the Roman emperor. Believers in Christ struggled, suffered, and were martyred in such a society. All this occurs today. But this is as Paul told us: "Indeed, all who desire to live a godly life in Christ Jesus will be persecuted" (2 Tim. 3:12).

Peter gives us clear instruction about how we ought to respond in the face of oppression and intolerance as believers in Christ.

> Have unity of mind, sympathy, brotherly love, a tender heart, and a humble mind. Do not repay evil for

evil or reviling for reviling, but on the contrary, bless, for to this you were called, that you may obtain a blessing. For "Whoever desires to love life / and see good days, / let him keep his tongue from evil / and his lips from speaking deceit; / let him turn away from evil and do good; / let him seek peace and pursue it. / For the eyes of the Lord are on the righteous, / and his ears are open to their prayer. / But the face of the Lord is against those who do evil." Now who is there to harm you if you are zealous for what is good? But even if you should suffer for righteousness' sake, you will be blessed. Have no fear of them, nor be troubled, but in your hearts honor Christ the Lord as holy, always being prepared to make a defense to anyone who asks you for a reason for the hope that is in you; yet do it with gentleness and respect, having a good conscience, so that, when you are slandered, those who revile your good behavior in Christ may be put to shame. For it is better to suffer for doing good, if that should be God's will, than for doing evil.

For Christ also suffered once for sins, the righteous for the unrighteous, that he might bring us to God, being put to death in the flesh but made alive in the spirit. (1 Pet. 3:8–18)

We see here that Christ is an example for us of unjust suffering for righteousness' sake. This means that we must be humble in our approach toward others, without an arrogant attitude that suggests that we are superior in any way. Rather, we must acknowledge that all we have and are comes from God. Salvation is a free gift that we cannot claim any part in obtaining. Our response to those who question our faith or slander us must be "with gentleness and respect."

We must also be able to answer people "having a good conscience" in that we are honest about our beliefs and where we stand. We are not to operate in underhanded, deceptive ways. Some Christians, attempting to contextualize their faith to the culture of Islam in an Islamic society, have called themselves Muslims because they submit themselves to God ("Muslim" means "one who submits to God"), but these individuals come across as deceptive in that they do not hold to the Muslim faith but instead are followers of *Isa* (Jesus). I would question whether this approach functions with a "good conscience." We are to be "as shrewd as snakes and as innocent as doves" (Matt. 10:16, NIV).

One way we can be honest in our interactions with those of other faiths is to dialogue with them. Christians share many common concerns with people from other religions, but we all tend to box people into stereotypes of what we think they are like. We usually don't really know what people are thinking until we meet with them. Therefore, organizing what I like to call "Meetings for Better Understanding" (MBUs) is a useful strategy for interreligious dialogue without argument or debate.[12] MBUs are not an attempt to compromise on one's commitments but an effort toward true understanding of where people from other faiths stand on a variety of issues. For example, a Muslim and Christian leader may each speak from their own perspective on a particular topic with the meeting moderated by someone explaining the process and fielding concluding questions from the audience. Venues can be alternated between a mosque and a church with refreshments served afterward for friendly interaction between both communities. Usually people from other religions will not have heard what Christians really believe but will know only what is taught within their religion about Christians, which is often a distortion of the truth. So MBUs build bridges rather than walls.

Although many Christians suffer unjustly, we must remember that we cannot retaliate for wrongs against us. Jesus taught us, "You have heard that it was said, 'Eye for eye, and tooth for tooth.' But I tell you, do not resist an evil person. If anyone slaps you on the right cheek, turn to them the other cheek also" (Matt. 5:38–39, NIV). Establishing justice to correct wrongs in society is the role of the government instituted by God (see Rom. 13:1–4), but vengeance is the Lord's, both in this earthly life and in the hereafter (see Nah. 1:2; Rom. 12:19; Heb. 10:30).

As Christians, we are called to live as strangers, sojourners, and exiles in this world (see Lev. 25:23; 1 Pet. 2:11) because we are on a pilgrimage to our heavenly home (see Gen. 47:9; Heb. 11:8–10). We live in two kingdoms—the kingdom of this world with political leadership and the kingdom of God that indwells the hearts of believers. Although our faith should influence everything in society to the glory of God and we must recognize that God is sovereign over all things, we are not to establish a Christian political state that imposes the Christian faith on anyone. This was the mistake of the Roman Catholic Inquisition and it sometimes occurred in colonialism as well, especially in Latin America, with miserable results. Rather, we are to exemplify the life of Christ in our personal lives and as a Christian community that wins people willingly and with reason, without deception or economic incentive. (Actually, it would be impossible for someone to become a true Christian through economic incentive, since being born again is a work of the Spirit through the proclamation of God's Word.)

A Christian must show respect and love toward all people, even those with whom he differs strongly. This means that we must live by the Golden Rule that Jesus taught us: "Whatever you wish that others would do to you, do also to them, for this is the Law and the Prophets" (Matt. 7:12).

If we apply this to freedom of conscience, we must stand up not only for our rights as Christians in a secular society but also for the rights of the Muslim, Buddhist, Hindu, Sikh, Jew, animist, and atheist. Freedom of conscience for everyone is a Christian principle worth dying for. Christian statesmen should firmly defend the non-Christian's right to believe as he or she does. If we selfishly demand our own rights and forget to defend religious freedom generally for all, in the end we will lose our own freedom.

Legal coercion does not bring about the kingdom of God. We cannot expect to bring in Christian values to society by establishing a Christian state. A pluralistic democratic order has been found to be the best option we have in this fallen world for living together in relative peace. To attempt to legally coerce people to enter the kingdom of God will lead to utter failure because the nature of God's kingdom is spiritual. We enter it through faith and receive it as a gift from God. Citizenship in God's kingdom is voluntary, never coercive. Jesus responded to Pilate at His trial, "My kingdom is not of this world. If my kingdom were of this world, my servants would have been fighting" (John 18:36).

As Christians, we must resist all forms of coercive secularization or ideological pluralism that restricts public expressions of our faith. This is not because we want to establish our faith by law; because of the spiritual nature of our faith, that is impossible. Rather, it is because to repress the free exercise of religion and persuasion is as wrong toward Christians as it is toward secularists and those from other religions. Tolerance is an outworking of the very nature of the gospel. Its pragmatic expression is seen in the development of a democratic and free society. John Piper explains, "For Christians, tolerance is not purely pragmatic. The spiritual, relational nature of God's kingdom is the ground of our endorsement of pluralism—until Christ comes with rights and authority that we do not have."[13]

Prayer is the one response we definitely must resort to when we are the confronted with intolerance. Remember, "the king's heart is a stream of water in the hand of the Lord; / he turns it wherever he will" (Prov. 21:1). Only God can change people's hearts and turn them in a favorable way to work toward common goals, even if they don't agree with our premises. This is how we are instructed in Scripture:

> I urge that supplications, prayers, intercessions, and thanksgivings be made for all people, for kings and all who are in high positions, that we may lead a peaceful and quiet life, godly and dignified in every way. This is good, and it is pleasing in the sight of God our Savior. (1 Tim. 2:1–3)

Rather than having a response of fear to the apparent downward spiral of our society, we ought to grieve before God about the situation and bring it before Him in prayer. Jesus grieved over Jerusalem as He approached the city just before His death, knowing the judgment that was coming on those who lived there (see Luke 13:34–35; 19:41–44). Let us plead before God as Abraham did for the righteous in the city of Sodom. Let us shine forth as light in the midst of darkness and as salt preserving the good from decay.

Remember, we must learn the discipline of radical discipleship that Jesus called us to when He authoritatively spoke, "You have heard that it was said, 'You shall love your neighbor and hate your enemy.' But I say to you, Love your enemies and pray for those who persecute you, so that you may be sons of your Father who is in heaven" (Matt. 5:43–45).

Although we must insist on holding to the truth, making right judgment regarding people based on the fruit that they bear (see 7:15–20), we must remember not to be judgmental toward others when we may be equally guilty,[14] as Jesus taught us.

> Judge not, that you be not judged. For with the judgment you pronounce you will be judged, and with the measure you use it will be measured to you. Why do you see the speck that is in your brother's eye, but do not notice the log that is in your own eye? Or how can you say to your brother, "Let me take the speck out of your eye," when there is the log in your own eye? You hypocrite, first take the log out of your own eye, and then you will see clearly to take the speck out of your brother's eye. (7:1–5)

If we carry a condemning attitude toward others, we fail to demonstrate forgiveness, which is necessary if we expect to be forgiven by God (see Matt. 6:15).

Finally, we can work toward common goals for a better society with many groups with whom we otherwise might have little in common. Thus those from many religions can unite against the secularism that is engulfing our society. Together, we can confront the social ills of gambling, prostitution, slave trafficking, corruption, single parenthood and divorce, abortion, AIDS, the gay and confused sexual-identity agenda, gay marriage, drugs, gangs, graffiti, and pollution. We should work together to address humanitarian concerns and nation building that meet the needs of all in the community. On a global level, countries need to uphold the rule of law and the protection of minorities. This was included in the justice that the Old Testament prophets continually spoke of concerning care for the poor and the sojourner. Lord Alton pleaded the same in his writing.

> Can the great faiths motivate their followers to be peace-makers, peace-builders, protectors of minorities, and practitioners of pluralism, tolerance, mutual respect, and the upholding of the rule of law? Could global society devote comparable energy into countering religious extremism as the energy which has been used to spread religious extremism? Countries have to make the cause of those who suffer for their religion or belief the great cause of our times.[15]

Hopefully we will all learn to listen and appreciate where others are coming from and respectfully allow people to hold to their positions, even if we strongly disagree with them. Tolerance is necessary if we are going to live together in this world in peace.

Discussion Questions

1. How would you distinguish between legal, social, and intellectual tolerance?

2. How did Jesus illustrate tolerance for us?

3. How can a Christian maintain belief in the uniqueness of Christ as the way, the truth, and the life and yet not be intolerant toward others?

4. What should Christians be intolerant about? Why? How should that be expressed?

5. Have you experienced intolerance? What did you do about it?

6. How should a Christian respond to intolerance?

7. What steps can we take to promote understanding and tolerance?

10

Freedom from Sin, Freedom to Do Good

John 8:31–36

*Truly, truly, I say to you, everyone who practices sin is a slave to sin.
The slave does not remain in the house forever; the son remains forever.
So if the Son sets you free, you will be free indeed.*

John 8:34–36

Most people in the world long for freedom, unless they are in a position of wealth, privilege, and power, and the latter are usually the people who have put those longing for freedom in their oppressed state. Principles found in the Christian Bible form the foundation on which our modern conception of freedom is founded.

Historian Philip Jenkins quotes Jürgen Habermas, a venerated leftist philosopher whose proclamation astonished his admirers.

> Christianity, and nothing else, is the ultimate foundation of liberty, conscience, human rights, and democracy, the benchmarks of Western civilization. To this day, we have no other options [to Christianity]. We continue to nourish ourselves from this source. Everything else is postmodern chatter.[1]

Yet, even when we have political, economic, and personal freedom, all of us are still under the oppression of our own enslavement to sin. Even those in positions of privilege and power suffer their own form of enslavement. It is to this that the gospel of Christ brings all of us true freedom.

Freedom

"Freedom" is a word that has a variety of meanings to different people. To many it refers to human rights, such as the four freedoms Franklin Roosevelt spoke of on January 6, 1941.

"Freedom of speech and expression—everywhere in the world . . . freedom of every person to worship God in his own way . . . freedom from want . . . and freedom from fear." For some, to live free is to live under law rather than in a chaotic society run by anarchists. For others—those with a rebellious spirit—to be free is to live without law, a state sought by anarchists in the Exarchia neighborhood of Athens, Greece. A dominant idea in American culture regarding freedom is to be free from unjust oppression. We see this desire engraved on the Statue of Liberty in New York Harbor: "Give me your tired, your poor, your huddled masses yearning to breathe free."[2] But it is important that we distinguish between two types of freedom: freedom from external restraint and freedom from inward bondage. Usually we think of freedom in the first sense. Everyone wants to be master of his fate and the captain of his soul. People get anxious and rebellious when under restraint and want to break the yoke of oppression. They want to rule and not be ruled, to have self-determination. Thus we have the patriotic hymn saying, "My country, 'tis of thee, sweet land of liberty!"

In the New Testament, however, we have no such direct call to political freedom. The believers in Jesus' day were under political domination, even oppression, by the Romans. They could not vote, have freedom of speech, or have trial by jury. About half the population was enslaved. Yet Paul wrote to believing slaves, "Were you a bondservant when called? Do not be concerned about it. (But if you can gain your freedom, avail yourself of the opportunity)" (1 Cor. 7:21). Why was slavery not a major concern for Paul and Jesus? Because by being in Christ, we are the Lord's free men.

"Compare Paul the prisoner with Nero the Emperor. Which of these was the more truly free, the apostle in prison with a soul set free from the bonds of sin, or the emperor on his throne the slave of every evil passion?"[3] Historian and Church of England clergyman Charles Kingsley has said, "There are two freedoms—the false, where a man is free to do what he likes; the true, where a man is free to do what he ought."[4] Clearly this is where most people are confused about the true meaning of freedom. It is why revolutionaries often have misplaced priorities. This does not mean, however, that we should not move to promote political, economic, and personal freedoms, as these too are rooted in biblical truths. It is clear in the New Testament that our greatest and deepest need for deliverance and freedom is from inward bondage. This is what Jesus promised to those who continue in His Word. Only such freedom is real and sufficient for our needs. Everywhere we see people, however, who have this inward bondage but seek release from it in the wrong places. Some seek it through transcendental meditation by which one seeks to eliminate all thoughts other than a one-word mantra such as "om," thus inviting demonic spirits and their lies into one's life. Others seek internal freedom through ecstatic experiences, such as in the Islamic Sufism practice of *dhikr*—repeatedly saying one of the names of Allah while twirling in a dance of increasing tempo to a crescendo of collapse. In much of the world dominated by animism, this freedom requires the appeasing of spirits through gifts given as sacrifices and offerings, sometimes even consisting of human organs. Still others seek internal deliverance from bondage through indulgence in sensual pleasures of unbridled sex, gluttony in comfort foods, thrills of dangerous feats, or the buzz that comes from alcohol or drugs. Such forms of escapism do not lead to the truth of God that brings freedom from controlling bad habits, bad thoughts, war of words, hatred, unforgiveness, jealousy, envy, bitterness, and rebellion.

Jesus spoke pointedly about freedom, which we see in chapter 8 of John. He said, "The truth will set you free" (8:32), and, "If the Son sets you free, you will be free indeed" (8:36). What did he mean by this? First, freedom means being set free from ignorance of spiritual things; and second, it means being set free from sin. The means for obtaining this freedom is found only in Christ. It comes through the truth found in Him and the salvation He freely provided for us through His redemptive crucifixion and resurrection from the dead.

The Truth Will Set You Free

As some of the Jews heard Jesus teaching, they came to believe in Him. For many of them, however, their profession of belief was merely outward. They had an intellectual belief without a heart commitment. Jesus knew their hearts, so He urged them to remain—to continue or abide—in His word. Jesus' "word" means the entirety of His teaching; so when He said that, He meant that they were to believe and obey what He taught them. This is what it means to have real faith. To "abide in" Jesus' word is to put oneself into subjection to Jesus' lordship. To abide in Jesus' word produces a growing discipleship. Following initial belief in Jesus, discipleship is a lifelong process of growing in faith and obedience to the Lord, by which we become liberated from the bondage of sin. Through a process called sanctification, we become more and more holy and conformed to the image of Christ (see Rom. 8:29; 2 Cor. 3:18).

God is the one who initiates our true knowledge of Him—which is His will for us—and He reveals our sinfulness as He delivers us from our darkness and blindness. As King David exclaimed, "In your light do we see light" (Ps. 36:9). In this vein Jesus went on to say, "You will know the truth, and the truth will set you free" (John 8:32). Truth is associated with the very person of Christ. In the prologue to his Gospel, John says, "Grace and truth came through Jesus Christ" (1:17). Jesus made the claim, "I am the way, and the truth, and the life" (14:6). Knowledge of the truth makes one a disciple of Jesus. He was communicating to His disciples that truth was essentially part of Him. The truth spoken of here is not facts that dispel ignorance in science, philosophy, or engineering. Rather, it is the truth bound with the person and work of Christ. It is saving truth. It is the truth that saves us from the depravity of our sin and shame. The only way to know this truth is through believing and obeying Jesus' word.

Jesus saw His ministry as the fulfillment of Isaiah's prophecy, "He has sent me to proclaim liberty to the captives" (Luke 4:18).[5] Most people do not realize that they are in bondage; they think they have some special place or privilege. The Jews thought they were protected from bondage because they were sons of Abraham. These unbelieving Jews gave an incredible response to Jesus, having been offended upon hearing that they needed to be liberated: "We are offspring of Abraham and have never been enslaved to anyone" (John 8:33). They were thinking in a purely external sense of political freedom. Even though they made this claim, however, there was really no basis for it. For much of Israel's history, the descendants of Abraham were enslaved in Egypt; after settling in Canaan they were often dominated by the Philistines, then by the Assyrians, Babylonians, Persians, Greeks, and Syrians, and now, by this time, the Romans. But Jesus had in mind a different kind of liberation—that of the soul set free from sin.

Slaves to Sin

Many people think that freedom is the license to do whatever a person wants, to break all bonds and enjoy life without restraint. Thus free thinkers accept any idea that comes down the pike with no means for evaluating its validity or truthfulness, and free livers reject all authority and the restraints of God's moral code as found in the Ten Commandments. Whatever is true for you is fine, they say, but it may not be the same truth for me. Everything is relative. However, under this way of thinking, there is no true freedom because in it, there can be no absolute truth. It leads only to slavery and death.

This is illustrated in Jesus' parable of the prodigal son, who went away with his father's inheritance and spent it all on wild living, only to end up starving as he ate the food of the pigs he had been hired to care for. Only in knowing the truth can we have true freedom to love God and others as we are called to. Consequently, we are all slaves of sin unless we have experienced the gracious intervention of God into our life.

> True freedom is the ability to do what is right. It takes obedience in order to have true freedom. I can sit at a piano and be at liberty to play any keys that I want, but I don't have freedom, because I can't play anything but noise. I have no freedom to play Bach, or even "Chopsticks." Why? Because it takes years of practice and obedience to lesson plans to be truly free at the piano. Then, and only then, does one have the freedom to play any piece of music.
>
> The same is true of freedom in living. To be truly free, we must have the power and ability to be obedient.[6]

Although many have come to the United States to gain relief from political tyranny, they still remain in bondage to their own passions. For some, this bondage is the idolatry of greed—the need to get the almighty dollar. For others, it is addiction to sexual passions, gambling, or alcohol. For still others, it is the inability to control their temper, filthy language, jealousy, or lust for power. All sin has enslaving power, whether the sins of the flesh that are outwardly seen or the secret sins of the heart.

People frequently seek the vain pursuit of a life without bounds, imagining it will bring freedom. But to go beyond the bounds established by God leads to slavery and death. Just as an animal taken out of its natural habitat will die, so people die when they try to live outside God's established order in relation to Him. To take a fish out of water to enjoy the great freedom of the air is not freedom but sure death. God established its boundaries for life. He has also established physical and moral boundaries within which we are to live and find true freedom.

Jesus answered the Jews, "Everyone who practices sin is a slave to sin" (John 8:34). The apostle Paul develops this idea further in Romans 6:12–23, where in part he asks, "Do you not know that if you present yourselves to anyone as obedient slaves, you are slaves of the one whom you obey, either of sin, which leads to death, or of obedience, which leads to righteousness?" (6:16).

How many of us have experienced this slavery to sin ourselves, knowing what is right and trying to change but continually making excuses for ourselves and rationalizing why we don't need to change? Many religions claim to bring release or freedom from this bondage but ultimately have no real solution. They demand fasting, pilgrimages, demanding tasks, inflicted pain, or deprivation. They always depend on human efforts, which are futile. They demand that people keep the law in order to be good but do not offer the inner change or the power necessary to make it possible. Peter warns us that false prophets and false teachers "promise . . . freedom, but they themselves are slaves of corruption. For whatever overcomes a person, to that he is enslaved" (2 Pet. 2:19).

In Buddhism, there is no recognition of human sin in the sense of moral evil because there is no sin against a supreme being. Consequently, "there is no ultimate difference between good and evil; nor is there any emphasis upon human sinfulness. There is bad karma, which produces misery, but that is really part of an impersonal cosmic order from which one should seek to become disengaged."[7] Jerry Yamamoto explains the consequence of this.

> If karma is an impersonal force, however, then people themselves find it quite easy to become impersonal concerning their own actions. And so, they say: "It was my karma which made me do it." Or, "I am who I am because of my karma." Karma focuses on the responsibility of individuals for their own actions but, because it is an impersonal force, it allows people to disregard both the responsibility and the consequence of their own actions.[8]

Thus, "Buddhist karma tends to engender fatalism, hopelessness, self-excusing, and pessimism in the majority of the population."[9] So when a Christian speaks of sin to a Buddhist, they usually think we are talking about crime, having broken the law, rather than our moral offense to God's holiness and rebellion against His authority over us. Satan seeks to keep us in this slavery to sin and incite us to sin that leads to death. We must make a choice. As Bob Dylan sang, "You're gonna have to serve somebody. . . . It may be the devil or it may be the Lord, but you're gonna have to serve somebody."[10] When we are in bondage, we are not free to will and to work good as we know we ought to.

Humankind lost its free will when Adam fell from a right relationship with God by deciding he wanted to be like God Himself. Ever since then, every member of humanity has been born with a depraved heart that is enslaved in sin (see Job 14:4; 15:14; Ps. 51:5; Rom. 5:12, 19; Eph. 2:3). "None is righteous, no, not one" (Rom. 3:10). This does not mean that there is no good in us, for we are made in the image of God (although deeply affected through the Fall) and by God's common grace we contribute much good to society, but our minds and hearts are perverted and "debased" (1:28) such that we cannot please God. "No one does good" that merits anything or justifies anyone before God (3:12). "No one understands; / no one seeks for God" by his own will (3:11).

People's understanding is clouded by a fog so that "the natural person does not accept the things of the Spirit of God, for they are folly to him, and he is not able to understand them because they are spiritually discerned" (1 Cor. 2:14). Our wills are enslaved by sin. Paul explains this, saying, "I know that nothing good dwells in me, that is, in my flesh. For I have the desire to do what is right, but not the ability to carry it out. For I do not do the good I want, but the evil I do not want is what I keep on doing" (Rom. 7:18–19).

Jesus answered the Jews who held to their own self-righteousness, "Truly, truly, I say to you, everyone who practices sin is a slave to sin. The slave does not remain in the house forever; the son remains forever" (John 8:34–35). Jesus was making a very important point, and we recognize this because He called our attention to it by introducing it with the words "truly, truly." Since everyone is a sinner, we are all slaves to sin. Jesus was talking about sin's power to control us. Although we may try, we cannot live without sinning in thought, word, and deed. The Jews thought that because they were descendants of Abraham, they were safely within the family of God. They were not, however, because they had not believed in God's Son. Soon even Jerusalem and the Temple would be destroyed and the Jews scattered. Only those who abide in Jesus' word are true sons. A son will not be sold and moved to another place as a slave may be. A son is the inheritor of his father's property and his rights cannot be taken away, while a slave has no security and can lose his privileges at any time. But we may become a son of God with assured rights as His child for eternity: "In Christ Jesus you are all sons of God, through faith" (Gal. 3:26). As God's children we are free, with all the rights and privileges of being joint heirs with Jesus Christ.

Free Indeed

Despite this promise of freedom in Christ, we are helpless to save ourselves. Our only hope is the intervention of God. Paul went on to exclaim, "Wretched man that I am! Who will deliver me from this body of death? Thanks be to God through Jesus Christ our Lord!" (Rom. 7:24–25). "There is therefore now no condemnation for those who are in Christ Jesus. For the law of the Spirit of life has set you free in Christ Jesus from the law of sin and death" (8:1–2). This freedom is provided for us by God the Father sending Jesus Christ to come in the flesh and live like us, yet without sin. He took upon Himself our sin at the cross and suffered the punishment we deserved (see 2 Cor. 5:21; Gal. 3:13). Jesus conquered Satan and his demonic powers through His triumph over sin and death at the cross and resurrection (see Col. 2:15). Through His death, He destroyed the power of the devil so that He could "deliver all those who through fear of death were subject to lifelong slavery" (Heb. 2:14–15). Now that we are set free from sin, the devil no longer has a means of accusing us before God: "Who shall bring any charge against God's elect? It is God who justifies. Who is to condemn? Christ Jesus is the one who died—more than that, who was raised—who is at the right hand of God, who indeed is interceding for us" (Rom. 8:33–34). Through His death and resurrection, we are set free from our bondage to sin when we look by faith to Jesus as our Redeemer. We are set free from the fear of death. This is the freedom we are promised by Jesus in the light of His truth if we continue in His word. He said, "If the Son sets you free, you will be free indeed" (John 8:36).

This freedom from sin and its consequences of eternal condemnation comes to us totally freely—by the grace of God alone. It is not based on human effort, good works, keeping the law, sacraments, or ascetic practices but through faith in Christ alone. Paul strongly condemns the idea that human effort can be added to God's grace for salvation (see Gal. 1:6–9; 5:12). Our obedience to God's moral law is the fruit of faith given to us by the Holy Spirit. The Spirit works in us through our hearing of God's Word to produce faith in us (see Rom. 10:17; 1 Cor. 1:21; 1 Thess. 1:5; 1 Pet. 1:23).

Without faith, it is impossible to please God (see Heb. 11:6). We are accountable before God, and He calls us to repentance from sin and the obedience of faith (see Luke 5:32; Acts 20:21; Rom. 1:5).

Call on Him! We can claim God's promises, by faith, to be free from whatever besetting sin still controls our lives. When we do so through obeying and trusting God's promises by His enabling power, we become free to obey His commandments and receive eternal life. God's grace raises us from spiritual death so that we can be born again through the living and abiding word. Then, by our obedience to the truth revealed in the Word of God, our souls are purified (see 1 Pet. 1:22–23) and we are conformed to the image of Christ to be like Him in full humanity and holiness.

John opens the book of Revelation with a doxology of praise to Jesus: "To him who loves us and has freed us from our sins by his blood . . . , to him be glory and dominion forever and ever" (1:5–6). This is a major theme throughout the Scriptures. God applies the work of Christ to us through His Spirit: "The Lord is the Spirit, and where the Spirit of the Lord is, there is freedom" (2 Cor. 3:17). The Spirit gives us freedom from guilt, shame, condemnation, sin, death, and blindness to God's truth as revealed in the gospel and empowers us to live a life of love based on the holy character of God. The Spirit also gives us access to God's loving presence.

The Spirit also gives us freedom to discern how to live by faith for God's glory. Thus we are no longer guided by ascetic regulations as seen in all religions other than Christianity. Paul asked the Colossian believers who were confused:

> If with Christ you died to the elemental [controlling] spirits of the world, why, as if you were still alive in the world, do you submit to regulations—"Do not handle, Do not taste, Do not touch" (referring to things that all perish as they are used)—according to human precepts and teachings? These have indeed

> an appearance of wisdom in promoting self-made re-
> ligion and asceticism and severity to the body, but
> they are of no value in stopping the indulgence of the
> flesh. (Col. 2:20–23)

These rules have no value in changing our inner self, the heart, and our relationship with God and others. In fact, they can be an impediment to our relationship with God; since the practitioner may be deceived into thinking that they are leading him into gnostic secret knowledge revealed from angels or into a higher level of oneness with the godhead, while in reality they are leading him into doctrines of demons.

On the other hand, not practicing ascetic regulations does not mean being free to do whatever we may have an inclination to do. As Paul instructed the Corinthian church regarding eating meat offered to idols, he wrote, "'All things are lawful,' but not all things are helpful. 'All things are lawful,' but not all things build up. Let no one seek his own good, but the good of his neighbor" (1 Cor. 10:23–24). We should not offend our brother's weak conscience, which may be offended by what we might feel free to do. Paul goes on to conclude how we should be guided by our freedom.

"So, whether you eat or drink, or whatever you do, do all to the glory of God. Give no offense to Jews or to Greeks or to the church of God, just as I try to please everyone in everything I do, not seeking my own advantage, but that of many, that they may be saved" (10:31–33).

It is tragic to think that many misinterpret the Christian faith to be a stricter law, a curbing of human liberty, an imposition of restrictions. (For some Christians, this kind of thinking can be due to the mistaken legalistic approach they take to the Christian life.) But in actual fact, Christianity breaks bonds and offers deliverance and redemption, as prophesied by Isaiah, whom Jesus quoted to imply that He Himself was the fulfillment of the prophecy.

> The Spirit of the Lord is upon me,
>   because he has anointed me
>   to proclaim good news to the poor.
> He has sent me to proclaim liberty to the captives
>   and recovering of sight to the blind,
>   to set at liberty those who are oppressed,
> to proclaim the year of the Lord's favor.
>
> (Luke 4:18–19)

The fulfillment of this liberation is the testimony of millions of people who have experienced it in their own lives. Many have been delivered from addictions, bad habits, bitterness, anger, and depraved thoughts that they had no control over. Now they can claim the promise of God: "No temptation has overtaken you that is not common to man. God is faithful, and he will not let you be tempted beyond your ability, but with the temptation he will also provide the way of escape, that you may be able to endure it" (1 Cor. 10:13). Innumerable people have found a peace that passes all understanding in the midst of suffering, trouble, and loss. They have given up bitterness and anger and become free to love, even their enemies. Broken relationships have been restored. Justice has been established. Sexual addictions and a false sense of one's sexual identity have been discarded. True disciples of Jesus have been set free from ignorance of God's spiritual truth and from the power of sin, themselves, and

Satan. Rather than being conformed to this world, they have been transformed by the renewal of their minds (see Rom. 12:2), thinking God's thoughts after him as informed by His Word.

Once we have been set free from sin by Christ, we are no longer to live under its bondage. Paul wrote to the Romans, "We know that our old self was crucified with him in order that the body of sin might be brought to nothing, so that we would no longer be enslaved to sin" (6:6). He further explains to the Galatians, "For freedom Christ has set us free; stand firm therefore, and do not submit again to a yoke of slavery" (Gal. 5:1). "For you were called to freedom, brothers. Only do not use your freedom as an opportunity for the flesh [fallen sinful desires], but through love serve one another" (5:13). Peter taught the same idea: "Live as people who are free, not using your freedom as a cover-up for evil, but living as servants of God" (1 Pet. 2:16).

Now that we have been set free, we are free to obey God and live for Him. We can forsake the deeds of our sinful nature and produce the fruit of the Spirit: "love, joy, peace, patience, kindness, goodness, faithfulness, gentleness, self-control." That is because we have "crucified [died to] the flesh with its passions and desires" (Gal. 5:22–24). "The fruit of the Spirit is not a checklist to work through but the unified blossoming of a heart liberated by the gospel of grace."[11] Now we are actually free to love our neighbor as ourselves in obedience to our Lord as we walk by His Spirit. This brings glory to God and fulfills our purpose for being alive.

Discussion Questions

1. From what do you long to be freed? Fear, want, oppression, bitterness, unforgiveness, or sin?

2. What does freedom mean to you? How should it be lived out?

3. How do some people abuse or misuse freedom to indulge the flesh? How does this actually enslave them?

4. How has Christ freed us from the power of Satan? What result has that produced for us who believe?

5. How do knowing and living the truth relate to having true freedom?

6. What is the freedom a believer in Christ enjoys?

11

Waging Peace in a Religiously Violent Age

Matthew 5:9–12

Blessed are the peacemakers, for they shall be called sons of God.
Blessed are those who are persecuted for righteousness' sake, for theirs is
the kingdom of heaven.

Matthew 5:9–10

In Sri Lanka, dozens of churches have been burned in recent years by Buddhist monks concerned that Buddhists are converting to Christianity. Hundreds of churches in Indonesia have been burned since 2000, and Muslim extremists beheaded three Christian girls who were on their way to school. An eighty-four-year-old French priest had his throat slit by a Muslim terrorist. "All told, 810 attacks on French Christian places of worship and Christian cemeteries took place in 2015."[1] Hindu radicals in India have burned churches, killed evangelists, burned alive an Australian missionary and his son, and passed anticonversion laws in five of India's states. Each of these religions claims to be a religion of peace, yet when their followers are confronted with the gospel, they fly into a rage. Jesus taught us to be peacemakers in the midst of a troubled world. In following His command, however, we will face great revilement and persecution.

Being a Peacemaker

Jesus taught in the Beatitudes, "Blessed are the peacemakers, for they shall be called sons of God" (Matt. 5:9). Peace is not merely the absence of trouble, but the presence of all things good. But maintaining peace does not mean being inactive when a dangerous or threatening situation develops. To not do anything is to cause greater trouble to develop. Peace may demand taking action to face issues, dealing with them, and conquering them. Thus, the making of peace may actually occur through struggle.

When Jesus called those who make peace "sons of God," He was using a typical Hebrew expression, since the language is not rich in adjectives. For example, it adds "son of" to an abstract noun, as when Barnabas is called "son of encouragement" instead of "an encouraging man." So when Jesus says "Blessed are the peacemakers, for they shall be called sons of God," He means that peacemakers are doing a godlike work. A person who makes peace is doing the very work that the "God of peace" is doing (see Rom. 15:33; 2 Cor. 13:11; 1 Thess. 5:23; Heb. 13:20). Jesus was given the title "Prince of Peace;" it was said of His rule that "of the increase of his government and of peace there will be no end" (Isa. 9:6–7); and the angels announcing His birth proclaimed, "On earth peace among those with whom he is pleased!" (Luke 2:14). Thus Jesus is our model as a peacemaker.

He was intent on one thing: the salvation of the world, bringing peace to men and women's hearts through peace with God.

This involves a change of heart. In order to become peace-makers, it is evident that we must first have peace ourselves. Jesus did not come proclaiming the kingdom of God so that we would become more comfortable in our sins, but so that we would repent and live a life in the Spirit in a new community characterized by peace. Since we are alienated from God, others, and ourselves by our sin, we must first be reconciled with God before we can become peacemakers. God the Father sent His unique Son to be the means of our reconciliation with Him, because He bore the judgment for sin that we deserve. Having been reconciled with God through Christ's atonement for our sin and the forgiveness offered us through faith in Jesus Christ, we can make peace with others and with ourselves because we are able to forgive, even as we were first forgiven by God.

As peacemakers, we become agents of the kingdom of heaven. Our assignment from God is to make "the kingdom of the world . . . become the kingdom of our Lord and of his Christ" (Rev. 11:15) as He works through us. We are all supposed to become peacemakers on a continual basis. One who divides people does the work of the devil, whereas one who brings reconciliation and peace does the work of God. Conflicts arise in all human relationships—between husband and wife, father and son, brother and sister, members of the same church, neighbors, colleagues at work, and nations. Our old human nature calls out to be first rather than last, to be served rather than to serve, to demand rights rather than lose them for the sake of the honor of Christ, to satisfy its lusts and appetites rather than live a life of sacrifice and self-denial. But we are to constantly work as God's peacemakers in our homes, communities, schools, and workplaces, as well as between religious and ethnic groups and internationally. We must look to Jesus as our model and our help in times of tension.

Does this mean that we become doormats and let others continually take advantage of us? Not at all. Such a response does not produce peace for anyone. Just as the apostle Paul appealed to his rights as a Roman citizen, when defending himself before those who sought to have him imprisoned and put to death, we too should claim our legal rights. Moreover, we should take a stand for what is just and right in the eyes of God. We should also make appeals on behalf of our brothers and sisters who are being persecuted for their faith. Many believers have been saved from suffering and death due to the appeal of Christians through the international community and our government. A Moroccan believer who had been arrested for his Christian activity, for instance, was standing before the judge when the judge received a phone call from Rabat, the capital city, telling him to release the believer because of pressure from the US government on his behalf.

Persecuted for Righteousness' Sake

Religious violence is nothing new, but it certainly is alive and active. In the days of the Roman Empire, Christians were burned at the stake and forced to fight lions in the arena. Emperor Nero ordered Christians to be wrapped in pitch and set on fire as burning torches to light his gardens. He had some sewed into animal skins and then set his hunting dogs on them to tear them to pieces. He tortured them on the rack, poured molten lead on them, and cut off body parts. The torture and death of Christians continues today. Although it is hard to know precisely, it is estimated that ten thousand martyrs die for the sake of Christ each year. In war zones, that number is much higher.[2] Recently, a Turkmen pastor in Iran, who was a convert from Islam, was kidnapped by the secret police. His body was dumped in front of his home a few hours later. Jesus taught us that this would come, saying, "They will lay their hands on you and persecute you . . . and some of you they will put to death. You will be hated by all for my name's sake" (Luke 21:12–17).

Jesus went on in the Beatitudes, "Blessed are those who are persecuted for righteousness' sake, for theirs is the kingdom of heaven" (Matt. 5:10). This is not a call for us to go out and get ourselves persecuted. It is not a request for us to have a martyr complex based on self-pity. Nor does this verse teach that we are to do foolish, insulting, or unnecessarily offensive things to convey the gospel, as this is not for righteousness' sake. We must not do things like loudly broadcasting sermons to the neighborhood as a means of witnessing to them and thereby disturbing the peace. When we get shut down by the police for such behavior, we should not think that we are being persecuted. Nor is it persecution for righteousness' sake if we act fanatically, such as by bombing an abortion clinic or shooting an abortionist. We ought not to claim persecution for wrongdoing. Peter warned, "Let none of you suffer as a murderer or a thief or an evildoer or as a meddler" (1 Pet. 4:15). Even suffering for endorsing a cause, be it Christianity or another, is not the same as suffering for the sake of righteousness, which is living like Christ. That means that when we stand firm on the truth, speak the truth in love, stand up for justice, treat all people equally with love and respect, and proclaim the gospel, we can expect to suffer the consequences from the world.

We should also expect strong opposition to the Christian faith if we take the words of Christ seriously. Jesus said to His disciples, "Remember the word that I said to you: 'A servant is not greater than his master.' If they persecuted me, they will also persecute you. If they kept my word, they will also keep yours. But all these things they will do to you on account of my name, because they do not know him who sent me" (John 15:20–21). Paul also warned Timothy of persecution: "Indeed, all who desire to live a godly life in Christ Jesus will be persecuted" (2 Tim. 3:12). He told the Philippians, "It has been granted to you that for the sake of Christ you should not only believe in him but also suffer for his sake" (Phil. 1:29).

Such suffering is an honor because it is by participating in the sufferings of Christ that we are drawn into deeper union with Him. Then the power of His resurrection is manifested in us throughout our Christian life (see 3:10). Paul sent Timothy to the Macedonian church to exhort and strengthen the believers' faith as they suffered persecution, saying, "[Let] no one be moved by these afflictions. For you yourselves know that we are destined for this. For when we were with you, we kept telling you beforehand that we were to suffer affliction, just as it has come to pass, and just as you know" (1 Thess. 3:3–4). To follow Christ is not easy; it involves suffering for the sake of His righteousness.

In contrast to those who know the Lord and seek to be peacemakers are the wicked who do not know the Lord. They continually cause trouble for the believers: "'Peace, peace, to the far and to the near,' says the Lord, / 'and I will heal him. / But the wicked are like the tossing sea; / for it cannot be quiet, / and its waters toss up mire and dirt'" (Isa. 57:19–20).

Why are nonbelievers in Christ so disturbed by Christians who stand by their convictions? Let's take Muslims for example. Islam is a religion that is deeply political in outlook. In fact, some consider Islam to be more of an ideology than a religion. Muslims view the world as consisting of the House of Peace or Islam, in which everyone lives in submission to Allah, and the House of War, whose members Muslims are obligated to bring into submission to Allah—thus their use of both preaching (*da'wah*) and the sword (jihad) to spread Islam. Wherever their faith spreads, they always seek to gain political control of their community and, in so doing, to Islamize the community, defend the rights of Muslims, and *dhimmify* (or put under "protection") the non-Muslim community. *Dhimmis* have restrictions on rights to property, education, jobs, marriage, worship, building and repair of churches, sharing and teaching their faith, the role of women, and testimony in a court of law. Furthermore, they traditionally pay a poll tax not imposed upon Muslims in order to receive "protection" for not serving in the Islamic army that fights for the cause of Islam. Non-Muslim men are not allowed to marry Muslim women, but Muslim men may marry up to four non-Muslim women. By marrying non-Muslim women and raising their children as Muslim, they seek to grow the Islamic faith.

It is common for Christian minorities in Islamic countries to suffer from false accusations as an excuse for Muslims to harass, imprison, and sometimes even kill them. Muslim extremists may use the Qur'anic verse that says, "Whoever kills a human being, except as punishment for murder or other villainy in the land, shall be regarded as having killed all mankind" (Qur'an 5:32). Muslim author Irshad Manji writes, "The spirit of that verse forbids aggressive warfare, but the clause beginning with except is readily deployed by militant Muslims as a loophole."[3] Any foreign representative from "Christian" lands occupying an Islamic country is seen as fair game in light of that loophole, particularly in countries such as Iraq or Afghanistan. Actually, any Christian, Jew, or idol worshiper is not considered innocent to Muslims. To a Muslim, only Muslims are innocent. As stated by Imam Abdul Makin, leader of an East London mosque, "Non-Muslims are never innocent, they are guilty of denying Allah and his prophet." This is confirmed by numerous verses from the Qur'an and the hadith.[4]

Several years ago, a bomb was thrown into a worship service in Pakistan at a Christian school for children of foreigners. Several were killed and injured. Another Pakistani church, with no foreigners in the congregation, was sprayed with machine-gun fire. On Easter Sunday 2016 in Lahore, Pakistan, a suicide bomber killed 74 and injured over 340, targeting Christian families with small children as they picnicked in the Gulshan-e-Iqbal Park. Such is the hostility of the world toward believers.

The cross of Christ continually remains a symbol of derision and hostility (see 1 Cor. 1:23). Muslims deny that Jesus actually died on the cross. "How could God allow his prophet to suffer and to die at the hands of the Jews?" they might ask. They even believe that when Jesus comes back again, he will break all the crosses. The cross is repulsive to those who do not understand that Jesus took our shame and guilt and crucified it with His death. The cross exposes our sin and evil nature, but the world hates the light that shines on the cesspool of our inner hearts.

Jesus had victory over all our shame and guilt by His resurrection from the dead. Those who deny the crucifixion of Christ, or are repulsed by what it stands for, also reject the victory over sin, guilt, shame, death, and Satan that is found in Christ's resurrection from the dead. It is through this event of the cross and resurrection that we obtain the righteousness of Christ by faith and are justified before God (see Rom. 3:21–26; 5:9, 18). Such faith is repulsive to the world.

When Christians take a firm stand for what is right, true, good, and just, they will be the object of derision and persecution for righteousness' sake. As Jesus taught His disciples about what it would be like in the end times, He gave them a message.

> Nation will rise against nation, and kingdom against kingdom. There will be great earthquakes, and in various places famines and pestilences. And there will be terrors and great signs from heaven. But before all this they will lay their hands on you and persecute you, delivering you up to the synagogues and prisons, and you will be brought before kings and governors for my name's sake. This will be your opportunity to bear witness. Settle it therefore in your minds not to meditate beforehand how to answer, for I will give you a mouth and wisdom, which none of your adversaries will be able to withstand or contradict. You will be delivered up even by parents and brothers and relatives and friends, and some of you they will put to death. You will be hated by all for my name's sake. But not a hair of your head will perish. (Luke 21:10–18)

Note here that God sovereignly works out His purposes for each person through persecution. For some it will mean death, for others not a hair of their head will be destroyed. But through it all, persecution becomes an opportunity for us to bear witness to the God of love and peace who sent His Son to die for us.

Jesus extended the principle of being peacemakers further on in His Sermon on the Mount: "I say to you, Love your enemies and pray for those who persecute you" (Matt. 5:44). Paul taught the same principle: "Bless those who persecute you; bless and do not curse them. . . . Repay no one evil for evil" (Rom. 12:14–17). This means that we are to do the right thing, even when we may not feel like it. Those who torment us at the office or, if we are persecuted by the law, at the police station must be responded to in love. We are to lend a helping hand when someone needs it. We must give relief to the victims of the tsunami in Indonesia and Sri Lanka and to those suffering from the earthquake in Pakistan, even if we view them as our religious enemies. The way we can develop the feeling of love for our enemies is to pray for them. This will produce a remarkable change in our attitude. Through our response of love, our witness will lead some to find the true path to life in Christ.

Rejoicing in Persecution

Jesus went on to tell us, "Blessed are you when others revile you and persecute you and utter all kinds of evil against you falsely on my account. Rejoice and be glad, for your reward is great in heaven" (Matt. 5:11–12). How can the Christian rejoice in his persecution? Only by having a right knowledge from God's Word. We cannot find the answer in reason or feeling or even our conscience, which can be warped to allow us to do whatever we want—even committing immorality. We must cling to the Scriptures that reveal the will of God. It is there that we learn to rejoice in persecution and to know that God has His purposes for it and is in control of our suffering.

First of all, we can rejoice in our persecution because it is evidence that we are united to Jesus Christ, who said to His disciples, "If you were of the world, the world would love you as its own; but because you are not of the world, but I chose you out of the world, therefore the world hates you" (John 15:19). When we are hated by the world that is under the control of Satan, we know that we are united with Christ, who has called us to be one with Him. This gives us assurance that we have a place with the Lord forever.

Second, we can rejoice in our persecution for righteousness' sake because we know that the Holy Spirit is at work in our lives to conform us to the sinless image of Jesus Christ. As we turn from a life of sin to a holy life, our transformation will be noticed by the world—and strongly rejected by some. When we don't give in to the pressure to slack off at the factory or construction site, to gossip in the office, to steal a colleague's research at the laboratory, or to participate in wild drinking parties and extramarital affairs, we can rejoice in God's gracious and supernatural work of transforming us through His power.

Third, related to the previous point, we can rejoice in our persecution in that it is a means by which God purifies us. We are to endure hardship as discipline. The Lord rebukes and disciplines us out of love, that we may share in His holiness (see Heb. 12:4–11). Peter wrote to the believers suffering in Asia that the trial of their faith was a means for God to purify their lives—just as gold was refined in the fire (see 1 Pet. 1:6–7). He went on to say at the end of his letter, "After you have suffered a little while, the God of all grace, who has called you to his eternal glory in Christ, will himself restore, confirm, strengthen, and establish you" (1 Pet. 5:10). The psalmist also claimed that affliction led him in the right way: "Before I was afflicted I went astray, / but now I keep your word" (Ps. 119:67). Having gone through the furnace of persecution, we can rejoice in knowing that we will come through it more like Jesus.

Fourth, we can rejoice in persecution because it produces in us a supernatural Christian radiance. It gives us a contagious joy of living for God that is noticed by the world. If we rejoiced while everything always went well for us, how would we be any different from any other person in the world? But when we are able to rejoice during unfavorable circumstances, we see the supernatural power of God in our lives. When Paul and Silas were in prison in Philippi, for example, they prayed and sang hymns of praise to God (see Acts 16:25).

Fifth, we can rejoice in our persecution because we know that we have the promise of reward. Jesus said, "Rejoice and be glad, for your reward is great in heaven" (Matt. 5:12). This is a promise of spiritual reward, of being in close fellowship with Jesus forever. Looking toward a reward is not wrong but of great encouragement to us. By faith, Abraham looked "forward to the city with foundations, whose architect and builder is God" (Heb. 11:10, NIV). "By faith Moses . . . [chose] rather to be mistreated with the people of God than to enjoy the fleeting pleasures of sin. He considered the reproach of Christ greater wealth than the treasures of Egypt, for he was looking to the reward" (11:24–26). Jesus too looked forward to the glory that awaited Him after His suffering. The author of Hebrews says that we should be "looking to Jesus, the founder and perfecter of our faith, who for the joy that was set before him endured the cross, despising the shame, and is seated at the right hand of the throne of God" (Heb. 12:2).

Sixth and finally, we can rejoice in our persecution knowing that God will always be with us. His Holy Spirit indwells us and empowers us for bold witness. Jesus promised that the Spirit would be with us forever. When Shadrach, Meshach, and Abednego were cast bound into the fiery furnace, the king looked and saw four people in there, unbound and unhurt, with the appearance of one like "a son of the gods" (Dan. 3:25). Similarly, the Spirit of Jesus will be with us in our most severe trials to strengthen and help us.

Having the knowledge from God's Word of each of these points helps us to triumph through whatever trials and persecutions we may face. For most of us, dramatic persecution and even martyrdom will not happen, as most of us live in environments that have been blessed by the suffering of generations of Christians before us—who won the privileges we now enjoy. But these privileges are continually challenged by nonbelievers who seek to bring us into darkness and submission to tyranny. We are called to stand firm under the attacks of the Evil One. Many of us may even be persecuted by our friends, who challenge our faith and urge us to doubt God's goodness when we face great loss, such as the death of a loved one, loss of work, or chronic illness. Job was persecuted by his three friends, who accused him of great sin which they asserted must be the reason for his tragic losses. Yet God sees our sufferings for His sake. He remembers us and will greatly reward us for our endurance to the end.

Let us rejoice in our persecution for Christ's sake. If you have not known persecution, even in small ways, perhaps you need to examine your life to see if it is conformed to that of Christ. Let us seek the righteousness of Christ in our lives that will either repel those going down the wide road to destruction or attract those who are seeking the truth.

Discussion Questions

1. What does it mean to be a peacemaker?

2. How are we to be peacemakers in our circles of influence?

3. For what can the Christian rejoice as he goes through persecution?

4. Have you had any experience with persecution? What did you learn through it?

5. If you have not suffered for your faith in any way, can you find ways in which your life and values are different from that of the world?

12

Unity in a Divided World

John 17:20–23

I do not ask for these only, but also for those who will believe in me through their word, that they may all be one, just as you, Father, are in me, and I in you, that they also may be in us, so that the world may believe that you have sent me.

John 17:20–21

Unity is something that many people of the world long for. They see our world divided into so many factions and camps over politics, economics, religion, race, and ethnicity—each of them with a continual desire for more power. When the illusion that the world was progressing and getting better and better was shattered by World War I, the League of Nations was created. Before long the world was again divided in a horrible conflict in World War II. The beleaguered League of Nations became the United Nations. Yet this global body has not been able to broker peace and unity in the world.

Regional and ethnic/religious political alliances exist as well, such as the Organization of African Unity, the Organization of American States, and the Arab League. Yet they too have deep divisions and remain largely ineffective.

Other organizations have sought to bring the world together through sports, such as the Olympics and FIFA (International Federation of Association Football). While there are many admirable aspects to the Olympics, every four years politics again raises its ugly head to cause division, boycotts, tragedies, and accusations between peoples over human rights.

Early in human history, people spoke a common language and worked together to build a tower to the heavens to worship a false god that could descend on the stairway of the ziggurat,[1] and they used the stars in the zodiac to determine their future rather than trust in God. They sought to be self-sufficient and independent from God through their social unity and technology.[2] But, in judgment, God confused their language and caused them to be scattered over the world in order to fill it. As the people of Babel called to one another, "Come, let us make bricks . . . , let us build . . . , let us make a name for ourselves" (Gen. 11:3–4), they were calling for unity for a common purpose, yet apart from God. Humanity is always in search of community and unity. The building of the city of Babylon and its tower was an attempt at that.

Nations today organize as the United Nations or NATO or OPEC in an attempt to achieve common goals. About fifty years ago, a song rang out about the dawning of the Age of Aquarius in which all humankind would live together in peace. But have that "harmony and understanding, sympathy and trust abounding" come? Actually, things seem worse than ever. The international community often speaks out about one particular issue or another, but there is always a dissenting group; then, whenever some "ism" threatens universal harmony, there is an attack on whatever steps out of conformity to the family, tribe, nationality, or religion. This division between peoples is evident not only in our variant languages but also in our deep-seated commitments to our own tribes, people groups, or economic statuses. These divisions have been allowed by God, as He separated the nations in judgment. God established family, government, and the church, so, by definition, some are included in each of these and others excluded. The brotherhood of humanity, apart from relationship with God, is only a myth. "If history proves anything, it proves that the tower will never be completed. The ultimate community builder is God, not man."[3]

Where can we find unity in this world? Is it in the church? Unity is one of the marks of the church for which Jesus prayed in His high priestly prayer in John 17. We see the Christian church, however, divided into many branches: Roman Catholics, Orthodox, Coptic Christians, Assyrians, Anglicans, Liberal Protestants, Evangelical Protestants, Reformed Christians, Lutherans, Baptists, Anabaptists, Pentecostals, charismatics, and so forth. We can find many reasons for these various groupings, such as theology, history, ethnicity, leadership, organizational structure, language, and culture. Yet this variety of churches reflects only their outward structure, which does not reflect the true nature of the spiritual unity that exists between true believers in Christ. That is evident through its relationships, buildings, organizations, and institutions, yet the visible church is not the same as the invisible church—the true people of God. The visible church is marked by both the wheat and the weeds coexisting in the same field. Jesus taught us that not until the end of the age will the weeds—the unbelievers who are part of the visible church—be gathered up by the angels and burned (see Matt. 13:39–42).

But even as true believers, we are divided by misunderstandings, gossip, various interpretations of Scripture, traditions, musical styles, and cultural ethnocentricity. For that reason, Jesus prayed for us. But the unity Jesus prayed for among His people was not organizational unity. Outward unity does not produce the results Christ prayed for. The Roman Catholic and Orthodox answer to the question of unity is that everyone should come together under the leadership of the institutional church led by the pope or patriarch. Yet during the Middle Ages, when there was largely one united church organizationally, the church was ineffective, tyrannous, superstitious, and ignorant while seeking to establish a political empire as the kingdom of God on earth. Although we have been called and born into the family of God, we continue to struggle with indwelling sin and the effects of the Fall. We become divided over our pride, jealousy, envy, wanting to be served rather than to serve, and following men rather than the Lord. Not until the consummation of all things upon Jesus' return will we be transformed into the perfect image of Christ and lose the continuing effects of sin and imperfect knowledge that keep us divided. Then our love for one another will be completely perfected.

In the meantime, we are called to strive toward the same unity seen between the three persons of the Godhead: Father, Son, and Holy Spirit. That is possible only through the power of the Spirit at work in our midst. The Spirit works in our lives through our knowledge of the gospel. Having unity in our understanding of the gospel—that salvation is only by the grace of God, not by our works, and only by the justification that we receive through faith in Christ as revealed in Scripture—is the only basis upon which we can have real unity in the truth.

Although our unity as Christians is based upon the truth we know in Christ—that we have been forgiven of our sins and called to His service—we must also strive for outward unity that is visible to the world. It must be a unity through which people may say, "We know they are Christians by their love for one another" (see John 13:35). In Jesus' prayer for His disciples shortly before He faced His death, He prayed, "Holy Father, keep them in your name, which you have given me, that they may be one, even as we are one" (17:11). The unity of the Persons of the Trinity is a pattern for our own unity as believers through Christ. Jesus prayed also for those of us living today.

> I do not ask for these only [that is, His disciples], but also for those who will believe in me through their word, that they may all be one, just as you, Father, are in me, and I in you, that they also may be in us, so that the world may believe that you have sent me. The glory that you have given me I have given to them, that they may be one even as we are one, I in them and you in me, that they may become perfectly one, so that the world may know that you sent me and loved them even as you loved me. (17:20–23)

Our unity as Christians is a vital part of our witness to the world, because such unity is not seen in the world. Jesus continues today to intercede before the Father on our behalf so we may be one as He is one with the Father. Three images of unity are frequently used in Scripture to help us understand what we are called to as God's people. They are one body, one family, and one fellowship.

One Body

The first image we often find in Scripture to describe unity is that of a body. Looking at three texts, we see the body presented first, as one unit with many parts made for service together; second, as the one loaf of bread that we partake of in the Lord's Supper; and third, as one growing body built up through a common faith. The image of Christians being one body is a vivid one, as the church can be seen in light of how our own bodies function. There are many parts, but each is basically indispensable, and losing one would make us handicapped.

Paul wrote to the church in Corinth about how each believer has spiritual gifts for the edification of the body and service: "Just as the body is one and has many members, and all the members of the body, though many, are one body, so it is with Christ. For in one Spirit we were all baptized into one body—Jews or Greeks, slaves or free—and all were made to drink of one Spirit" (1 Cor. 12:12–13).

Paul went on to explain that because we are one body, each part is indispensable. The foot cannot say that it is not part of the body because it is not a hand nor can an ear say that because it is not an eye, it is not part of the body or has no need of it. "But God has so composed the body, giving greater honor to the part that lacked it, that there may be no division in the body, but that the members may have the same care for one another. If one member suffers, all suffer together; if one member is honored, all rejoice together. Now you are the body of Christ and individually members of it" (1 Cor. 12:24–27). What is unique about the body is that it is built to work. But its parts cannot work separately—only together as a unit. All that God has gifted each member of the body to do for service must be done together in love.

When Paul instructed the early church concerning the Lord's Supper, he reminded them of our unity as believers through our common faith in Christ: "The cup of blessing that we bless, is it not a participation in the blood of Christ? The bread that we break, is it not a participation in the body of Christ?

Because there is one bread, we who are many are one body, for we all partake of the one bread" (10:16–17). As Christians, we illustrate to the world our unity as one body when we break bread from the one loaf representing the body of Christ, who is the head.

Paul wrote the Ephesian church to strive toward unity in the body through sound teaching based on their common faith. Some people are of the opinion that doctrine divides. All we need is to have a common experience of fellowship together, they say, and we can be united. Actually, the opposite is true. Through first having a unity in the faith, we can then have unity for fellowship and service. Paul wrote accordingly to the Ephesians.

> I therefore, a prisoner for the Lord, urge you to walk
> in a manner worthy of the calling to which you have
> been called, with all humility and gentleness, with
> patience, bearing with one another in love, eager to

maintain the unity of the Spirit in the bond of peace. There is one body and one Spirit—just as you were called to the one hope that belongs to your call—one Lord, one faith, one baptism, one God and Father of all, who is over all and through all and in all. . . . And he gave the apostles, the prophets, the evangelists, the shepherds and teachers, to equip the saints for the work of ministry, for building up the body of Christ, until we all attain to the unity of the faith and of the knowledge of the Son of God, to mature manhood, to the measure of the stature of the fullness of Christ, so that we may no longer be children, tossed to and fro by the waves and carried about by every wind of doctrine, by human cunning, by craftiness in deceitful schemes. Rather, speaking the truth in love, we are to grow up in every way into him who is the head, into Christ, from whom the whole body, joined and held together by every joint with which it is equipped, when each part is working properly, makes the body grow so that it builds itself up in love. (Eph. 4:1–16)

This unity will be gloriously manifested when Christ returns but should be forming us now into one body, with Christ as the head. As part of that body, we cannot be separated from each other or we die. We must function together through our unity in the faith.

One Family

As Christians, we are brothers and sisters in the family of God. We have been adopted as orphan children by our loving heavenly Father; we are now children of the King and have been given all the rights that this position entitles us to. But every believer in Christ shares in those privileges, and we have all been called to love one another as true members of the same family.

The basis for this love and commitment to one another is what God has done for us. It is not a matter of our determining and willingly committing ourselves to love our brothers and sisters from our own strength and will. This we could never do in our own power. Rather, as John wrote in the prologue to his Gospel, "To all who did receive him [Christ], who believed in his name, he gave the right to become children of God, who were born, not of blood nor of the will of the flesh nor of the will of man, but of God" (1:12–13). By God's power, we become one family.

One common idea is that all humanity is one brotherhood. At a human level that is true—we all share a common ancestor and we are all equally made in the image of God. Yet at a spiritual level, only those who are born of God by His Spirit are God's children and thus share in the brotherhood of the family of God. Just as we are born into an earthly family without having chosen its members, so we are born into God's family. Having been born into His family, our brothers and sisters are not in relationship with us by choice but by birth. The relationship simply exists, so we must love our family members. We grow together and so learn to love together. In one of his psalms, David expressed our calling in the world, saying, "Behold, how good and pleasant it is when brothers dwell in unity!" (Ps. 133:1). Our unity as a Christian family needs to be expressed and experienced in tangible ways. As the early church began in Jerusalem, a close unity existed among the believers as one family. They shared all they had so that each person's needs would be met: "The full number of those who believed were of one heart and soul, and no one said that any of the things that belonged to him was his own, but they had everything in common" (Acts 4:32). Being in the same family, we have a special responsibility to one another to care for each other. As Paul expressed it, "As we have opportunity, let us do good to everyone, and especially to those who are of the household of faith" (Gal. 6:10). When disaster strikes, such as a flood, hurricane, earthquake, fire, war, or famine, we must be there to help each other in that time of need to rebuild people's houses and feed the hungry.

One Fellowship

The third image for Christian unity is that of fellowship. The word refers to sharing something or having something in common. For the Christian, it refers to a common experience of the gospel. The New Testament speaks of our fellowship with the Father (see 1 John 1:3), the Son (see 1 Cor. 1:9; 10:16), and the Holy Spirit (see 2 Cor. 13:14), so our fellowship with one another is dependent on our experience of an intimate relationship with God.

Deep divisions exist between churches within many denominations. Usually it is between liberals, who reject the supernatural work of God in our lives and the authority of the Bible, and conservatives, who believe in both. Actually, this is a matter of two completely different religions, even though outwardly these groups have the same name and organizational structure. Those who hold to liberalism reject key doctrines of the faith and, consequently, also reject the moral imperatives that go along with it. For them, everything is relative.

True Christian unity can only be based on a common faith in both doctrine and godliness, not in tolerant relativism. Paul encouraged the Philippian believers to stand "firm in one spirit, with one mind striving side by side for the faith of the gospel, and not frightened in anything by [their] opponents" (Phil. 1:27–28). He went on to encourage them to complete His joy by "being of the same mind, having the same love, being in full accord and of one mind" (2:2). Further, Paul pled with the Corinthian believers, who were divided in their loyalties toward Christian leaders, for unity: "I appeal to you, brothers, by the name of our Lord Jesus Christ, that all of you agree, and that there be no divisions among you, but that you be united in the same mind and the same judgment" (1 Cor. 1:10). All these appeals for unity illustrate that a common understanding of our faith among members of the body is foundational to its success.

Unity was modeled by the first Christians in Jerusalem, who "devoted themselves to the apostles' teaching and the fellowship, to the breaking of bread and the prayers" (Acts 2:42). Note their dedication to fundamentals of unity: following the teaching that the apostles had received from our Lord Jesus, fellowship in order to encourage one another in the faith and in their walk with God, the regular administration of the sacraments, and prayer that continually thanked God and brought their concerns and even differences before His throne in glory. As Christians have different understandings on various issues of our faith, this adage is useful to remember: in essentials, unity; in nonessentials, liberty; in all things, charity.

True believers in Christ who have been born from above, but who also happen to be from very different Christian traditions and denominations, can have close fellowship in Christ because they know the same Lord. They can easily work and pray together for a common cause, such as evangelism and works of compassion and mercy. They can encourage one another in love and good works. And they can build one another up in the faith until they express a unity that reflects the oneness they have in Christ. These elements of fellowship are what we as Christians share together. It includes sharing our thoughts and lives together for the glory of God. This can be done practically through church suppers, Bible study and prayer groups, missional teams serving the poor, and ministries targeting special segments of society such as artists, medical students, Chinese restaurant workers, or an indigenous tribe.

Our fellowship with one another flows out of the model of oneness between the three Persons of the one God. Jesus' prayer in John 17 illustrates how His relationship with His Father is uniquely intimate. The amazing thing is that God has also called us to join in that intimate relationship through His Son. By having Jesus in us, we have God in us and can fellowship with Him on a continual basis as we seek Him. Jesus' presence in us is mediated by the Holy Spirit, whom He sent to abide with us forever as a guarantee of our inheritance.

Since each believer is indwelt by the Holy Spirit, we also have sweet fellowship with one another through our common bond in the Spirit. Yet despite this reality, sin still raises its ugly head and believers become divided. A pastor and his elders become torn apart. A church splits, or one group of churches separates itself from another group that it had previously been in fellowship with. We experience misunderstandings, pride, jealousy, a vying for power, and regional and cultural differences.

Paul exhorted the sisters in the Lord at Philippi, Euodia and Syntyche, who had labored side by side with him in the gospel together, "to agree in the Lord" (Phil. 4:2).

We learn from this situation that rather than acting selfishly, we are to rejoice in the Lord always, replacing anxiety with expectant, grateful prayers and contentment in the Lord based on trust in His sovereignty working things out for good through difficult times. Acting reasonably, we should have an attitude of seeking what is best for all and not just ourselves. When we bring everything to God in prayer with thanksgiving for what He has already done, we will enjoy the peace of God.

Paul wrote about similar issues of conflict to the church in Corinth. He appealed to the brothers there to agree by the name of the Lord Jesus Christ and have no divisions among them. He had heard that some said they followed Paul, while others followed Apollos and others Cephas or even Christ (see 1 Cor. 1:10–12). The goal for all of us should be to follow Christ and His example. We should follow Paul's instruction: "Do nothing from selfish ambition or conceit, but in humility count others more significant than yourselves." Each of us must look not only to our "own interests, but also to the interests of others" (Phil. 2:3–4). Paul outlined additional instruction.

> Have this mind among yourselves, which is yours in Christ Jesus, who, though he was in the form of God, did not count equality with God a thing to be

grasped, but emptied himself, by taking the form of
a servant, being born in the likeness of men. And
being found in human form, he humbled himself by
becoming obedient to the point of death, even death
on a cross. (Phil. 2:5–8)

Taking this approach with others—especially those who
are hard to love—is difficult. But we can do all things through
Christ who strengthens us (see 4:13). Notice in the context of
Paul's admonition in First Corinthians 1 that the believers were
divided over the issue of baptism. Yet Paul wrote, "Christ did
not send me to baptize but to preach the gospel, and not with
words of eloquent wisdom, lest the cross of Christ be emptied
of its power. . . . We preach Christ crucified" (1:17–23). This
should be our focus as together we bring the message of reconciliation with God to the world.

One Great Multitude

The deep divisions we see in the world today are being reversed through the grace of God applied by His Spirit in the lives
of believers who proclaim and live the gospel. At Babel, the Lord
scattered the people over all the earth, thus emphasizing that
His will and justice would be accomplished. Our world is still
confused, with one group continually in a struggle with another.
These divisions can even frustrate the attempts of people within
the *same* group to unite in a fight against God. For example, more
Muslims are killed by other Muslims than by people of any other
religion or ideology. God did, however, give His people hope of
a future unity in serving Him. After announcing judgment upon

Jerusalem and the nations, the Lord said through the prophet Zephaniah, "At that time I will change the speech of the peoples / to a pure speech, / that all of them may call upon the name of the LORD / and serve him with one accord" (Zeph. 3:9). One day the Lord will give people clean lips, or unpolluted speech, through the atonement of Christ (see Isa. 6:5–7) and turn them from worshiping pagan gods. Humankind will be cleansed to worship God together as one people and serve Him. This work of service will be universal, done by "all" and unanimous "with one accord."

In contrast to God's judgment in scattering the peoples and causing them to be confused by various languages at Babel, He reversed the events at the beginning of the establishment of the New Testament church. On the day of Pentecost, thousands of Jews and proselytes gathered for the festival from many nations around the Mediterranean and Middle East to worship at the Temple. Jesus' 120 disciples came together in Jerusalem. When the Holy Spirit descended on them, they spoke in various tongues so that the people visiting Jerusalem heard the gospel message in their native language. This miracle from God was a sign of the reversal of God's judgment.

God had scattered the people of Babel through a miraculous change in their language because they had sought in pride to make a name for themselves. On the day of Pentecost, all the people understood God's message, which came to them through people who had never learned their tongue. Rather than scattering people and bringing judgment against them, God visited people to save them and bless them through giving them His triune name. He fulfills His eternal covenant promise to Abraham to bless the nations through his seed, who is Christ (see Gen. 12:2–3; 13:15; 17:4–6; 22:17–18; Ps. 47:9; Gal. 3:16). He sent the Spirit to bring blessing and unity in Christ. The message was now to go to all nations so that each one could hear the gospel in his or her own language.

In a similar way, God will gather around His throne on the last day people "from every nation, tribe, people and language" (Rev. 7:9, NIV)—all those whose sins have been washed away by the blood of the Lamb and have been brought into one body, one family, and one fellowship. This is the true unity that we can expect, and will only be affected by the power of God. John's vision from the Lord of the future redeemed people of God in united worship was of "a great multitude that no one could number, from every nation, from all tribes and peoples and languages, standing before the throne and before the Lamb, clothed in white robes, with palm branches in their hands, and crying out with a loud voice, 'Salvation belongs to our God who sits on the throne, and to the Lamb!'" (7:9–10).

Will you be there in that great crowd? If you are part of His family, let us start now to love one another and work together toward God's will being done on earth as it is in heaven. When we do this, we will become perfectly one so that the world may know that the Father sent Jesus and loves us even as He loves His only Son. It will become the basis for God to bless us with great revival and a turning to Him. We must pray toward this end.

Following are some practical points of application that will lead toward unity.

1. Pray together on a regular basis. When we pray *for* one another and *with* one another, it will be hard for us to work against a fellow believer, hold a grudge, or develop an

unloving attitude. God works through prayer. Without it, He will not bless or grow our churches or the planting of new ones.

2. Repent of any sin and offense we may have brought against another without being quick to defend ourselves. This includes corporate and institutional sin, both of which can be difficult to see when we are enmeshed in them.[4] We are to forgive those who have offended us so that we may be forgiven by our heavenly Father (see Matt. 6:14–15). We must acknowledge our weaknesses and show grace toward others as Christ has shown His grace toward us.

3. Respect one another. In doing so, we will not look down on others as being less worthy than us. We are all sinners saved by grace and in the process of being conformed to the image of Christ. To respect one another, we will have to listen to one another rather than simply dismiss another person's ideas as foolish. If the person is foolish, then he should be corrected with gentleness and respect. And we should be open to being corrected ourselves. So we must be humble toward one another and know that God lifts up the humble but brings the proud down low. As Peter reminds us, "Have unity of mind, sympathy, brotherly love, a tender heart, and a humble mind" (1 Pet. 3:8).

4. Fellowship with one another. Hebrews admonishes us, "Let us consider how to stir up one another to love and good works, not neglecting to meet together, as is the habit of some, but encouraging one another, and all the more as you

see the Day drawing near" (Heb. 10:24–25). Often pastors and other Christian leaders work in isolation and without accountability toward others. This is not biblical or healthy. Through mutual fellowship, we will be motivated to achieve higher goals, resist temptation, and do greater works to glorify the Lord.

5. Seek ways in which we can work together as partners in the common purpose of proclaiming the kingdom of God. We can do this in areas such as theological training, church planting, mercy ministry, publications, conferences, missions, and witness in the marketplace. God does not call everyone to the same work, however; we each have our own gifts and placement for ministry. Working toward a common purpose is based on our common faith and, in doing so, we may often find ways in which we can support one another, even if it is just to share someone's burdens and pray with him or her.

Discussion Questions

1. Is the disunity in the world, whether between Christians or among the peoples of the world, a judgment from God (see Gen. 11)?

2. What are three images for unity given to us in the Scriptures? How can we live out these images within our own circles of influence?

3. What is the basis for Christian unity?

4. What sign did God provide in the early church for creating unity among a diverse people?

5. Looking at the list of steps toward unity, which do you particularly need to work on? What can you begin to do this coming week?

13

Christ's Church Triumphant
Matthew 16:13–18

On this rock I will build my church, and the gates of hell shall not prevail against it.

Matthew 16:18

We live in a world of fierce opposition to Christ and His people. There are weekly incidents of violations against Christians around the world, when our values, morals, places of worship, institutions, and our brothers and sisters around the world are under regular attack for bearing the name of Christ. These attacks are evidence that God is at work, that people from other faiths are coming to Christ, and that satanic forces are being provoked. We rarely see this in the secular media since religious motivations are not reported and real statistics are often underreported. Most attacks are not the type that are newsworthy, although they are expressed as verbal denouncements, discrimination, threats, and loss of freedom to practice our faith and witness.[1] King David expressed dismay at how the wicked shoot their arrows in the dark at the upright in heart. He rejected His enemies' advice to "flee like a bird to [his] mountain" (Ps. 11:1). But would he stand firm under attack? He asked what many in our day are asking: "If the foundations are destroyed, what can the righteous do?" (11:3). The foundations of our Western culture with a Twoist worldview of the creator God and His creation have practically been destroyed. Now even major segments of the church are bowing to the god of this world.

In response to such a loss of a sure footing, David said, "In the LORD I take refuge. . . . The LORD is in his holy temple; / the LORD's throne is in heaven; / his eyes see, his eyelids test the children of man. . . . The upright shall behold his face" (11:1–7). In the Lord we have a sure hope. He is the unshakeable foundation who shall never be destroyed by the lies of Satan. In the gospel, we find that Jesus is the fulfillment of the promise of that solid-rock foundation.

How should the church respond to the devolution of our culture in light of who we are in Christ and what He has already done for us? Certainly it must begin with the foundation of our identity, which is Christ.

Christ the Rock

Jesus traveled with His disciples to Caesarea Philippi, north of the Sea of Galilee, near the slopes of Mount Hermon. This was a particularly pagan region, the ancient site of the shrine of the Greek god Pan. Jesus took this occasion to ask His disciples who people thought He was, as it was crucial to His purpose for coming to earth as the divine incarnate man. They responded, "Some say John the Baptist, others say Elijah, and others Jeremiah or one of the prophets" (Matt. 16:14). Each of these answers reflected various ideas circulating at the time, including a prediction of the return of Elijah (whom Jesus asserted to be John the Baptist—see Mal. 3:1; Matt. 11:7–10, 13–14) and the coming of a prophet like Moses (identified as Jesus the Christ—see Deut. 18:15, 18; John 1:45; 6:14; 7:40; Acts 3:22–23; 7:37).

Jesus continued by asking His disciples who *they* thought He was. Simon Peter replied, "You are the Christ, the Son of the living God" (Matt. 16:16). This was a remarkable statement of spiritual insight. It was an indication that Peter had grasped Jesus' true identity. Jesus answered him, "Blessed are you, Simon Bar-Jonah! For flesh and blood has not revealed this to you, but my Father who is in heaven" (16:17). In that statement, Jesus was essentially saying that Peter's understanding of His identity had not been gained by some normal human observation but by divine revelation. This reflects the consistent teaching throughout Scripture that the spiritual understanding that leads to salvation comes only by God's Spirit (see 1 Cor. 2:11–14).

What was this understanding given to Peter? It was who Jesus was and what He did, or the person of Christ and the work of Christ. Knowing this is essential to salvation, and it is the foundational rock of the church. It is essential for us to understand that Jesus is the Son of God— "very God of very God," as the Nicene Creed states it—in order to appreciate the value of His dying for us on the cross. It is only because Jesus is God that His death is of infinite value and has power to take away our sins. As the Messiah, Jesus came to be our intercessor and sacrifice for sin, yet rule as King and Lord over all. For those of us who believe that, it was revealed to us by God. Keeping this truth in mind, we proceed to Jesus' famous statement to Peter: "I tell you, you are Peter, and on this rock I will build my church, and the gates of hell shall not prevail against it" (Matt. 16:18). What did Jesus mean? Three main interpretations have been given on the first half of the statement.

The first is that Peter himself is the rock, since Jesus used a play on words—"Peter" being Petros in Greek, and "rock" being petra. This is the interpretation of the Roman Catholic Church as well as some Protestants. Protestants who believe this, however, have a different understanding of it than Catholics, believing that Peter was simply the first to make this confession as the representative spokesperson of the apostles, who are the foundation of the church (see Eph. 2:20; 3:5). And they see no mention of Peter's successors, infallibility, or exclusive authority, as Roman Catholics do, in claiming Peter as the bishop of Rome and the first pope.

The second understanding is that Peter's confession, "You are the Christ, the Son of the living God," is the rock. This is the major view among Protestants and the early church fathers.

The third view is that Christ is the Rock, which is the view of Augustine of Hippo, James Montgomery Boice, and others. Nowhere does Matthew hint that Peter was the rock; while elsewhere in Matthew, Jesus teaches on the wise man who built his house upon *the rock*, referring to Himself and His teachings (see 7:24–25). Later in Matthew He quotes Psalm 118:22 to speak of Himself as "the stone that the builders rejected" that "has become the cornerstone" (21:42). Frequently in the Old Testament God is described as the Rock of Israel (see Deut. 32:4, 31; 1 Sam. 2:2; 2 Sam. 22:2, 32; Ps. 18:2, 31).

Being divine, Jesus is also identified as the Rock upon which the church should be built. Paul identified the rock from which water sprang to give drink to Israel in the wilderness as Christ (see 1 Cor. 10:4). In describing the apostles and prophets as foundational to the church, he called Jesus Christ the chief cornerstone of that foundation (see Eph. 2:20), recalling Isaiah's reference to the Lord laying as a foundation in Zion "a stone, a tested stone, a precious cornerstone, of a sure foundation" (Isa. 28:16). Paul continued in his letter to the Corinthians about the foundation upon which we should build, saying, "No one can lay a foundation other than that which is laid, which is Jesus Christ" (1 Cor. 3:11).

Especially importantly, Peter's first letter identifies Jesus Christ as the "living stone rejected by men" and believers as "living stones . . . being built up as a spiritual house" (2:4–5). Peter insisted that Christ is the Rock upon which the church is built, both in his epistle and in his speech before the Sanhedrin (see Acts 4:11; 1 Pet. 2:6–7), while we are stones only in the sense that we have been built upon Jesus, the actual foundation.[2] When Jesus said, "On this rock I will build my church," He was saying that not only is He the foundation of His church, but He is also its builder as "the founder and perfecter of our faith" (Heb. 12:2). So the "rock" is not Peter or his confession, but Christ. Since Jesus is the solid-rock foundation for the church, we know that we can have confidence and assurance that our faith is unshakeable and our hope is secure.

Nothing can move us as we stand on Him. As we see the church and God's people attacked in various ways—from our belief in the integrity of the Scriptures to our understanding that God is our creator to our stand on biblical sexuality—we know that ultimately nothing can shake those of us who are truly His. When I began to study Islam at Temple University with Muslim graduate students, I was regularly challenged about my faith. Initially, some of what my classmates said sounded reasonable from a human viewpoint, yet I found that their challenges only served to strengthen my faith as I found answers to their questions and propositions and as I was forced to dig deeper into Scripture.

The Gates of Hell

Jesus' statement to Peter contains another phrase difficult to interpret: "the gates of hell shall not prevail against it." "Hell" is the translation given to the more literal word "hades," the place of the dead. Most commonly understood is that "the gates of hades" refers to attacks of Satan and his demonic forces upon the people of Christ. It is thought that this promises that Satan will not succeed. The main problem with this view is that the word "gates" does not evoke the image of an attacking army but rather a defensive figure. Thus, a natural way of understanding this phrase is that hades will not be able to resist the forces of the church that attack it. Although the Bible does speak of spiritual warfare, it does not speak of our evangelism and outreach in these terms. But in saying that "the gates of hell shall not prevail against" the church, we have a pictorial way of expressing the truth that the organized powers of evil shall not prevail or win over the church. Believers who hold on to Christ and His teaching will ultimately win a great victory that no one can take away.

Another view of "the gates of hades" or "the gates of hell" is that the gates refer to death. It was common in Jewish thought to perceive of death as one passing through the gates of hades or hell.[3] They represent dominion and power, as seen in Old Testament times when judgments were made by the rulers of a town at the gates of the city. If Jesus meant this view, He was then saying that physical death, whether from natural causes or through mass persecution, would not be able to destroy the church that He was building.[4] All those whom the Father elected and called will come into Christ's kingdom through the work of His Spirit before physical death eventually overcomes them.

But that is not the end! In Peter's sermon on the day of Pentecost, he explained Jesus' resurrection, saying, "God raised him up, loosing the pangs of death, because it was not possible for him to be held by it" (Acts 2:24). He then quoted David's prophesy concerning the Messiah: "You will not abandon my soul to Hades, / or let your Holy One see corruption" (2:27; see also Ps. 16:10). Because of Jesus' resurrection, we too have victory over death. Our Lord is sovereign over the invisible realm of death, which no living person has seen. He remains our hope forever, so even though we do all eventually die physically, we will be resurrected to reign with Him.

The main idea we come away with from this phrase "the gates of hell" is that despite attacks of all sorts, the church will be invincible.[5] Why? Because it is built on Christ as the Rock. We see an example of this in the life of Peter. Jesus said to Simon Peter as the Lord was about to face crucifixion, "Simon, Simon, behold, Satan demanded to have you, that he might sift you like wheat, but I have prayed for you that your faith may not fail. And when you have turned again, strengthen your brothers" (Luke 22:31–32). Since Peter's faith was founded on Jesus Christ the Rock, he came through the strong temptation and eventually faced persecution and imprisonment for boldly preaching the gospel to thousands who came to believe. As long as the church is built on Christ, the gates of the prison house of hades—or death—will never close on us. It is through Christ alone that we have eternal life. This is the hope that you and I have that keeps us from seeing our struggle with sin and the world as wasted effort.

Disarmed Powers and Authorities

We now see Christ is the Rock and mark His victory by His disarming of spiritual powers and authorities. He declared to Peter that "the gates of hell shall not prevail," meaning the dominion of death dominated by Satan will not overcome His church. We are essentially in a spiritual battle for souls.

Paul wrote the believers in Colossae about the victory that Christ already won for us: "Having disarmed the powers and authorities, he made a public spectacle of them, triumphing over them by the cross" (Col. 2:15, NIV). Christ has triumphed with power over the evil spiritual forces that seek to destroy us. Much of the world is in the grip of the influence of these demons, whom the Colossians believed to control their destinies, as some still do today. The world is filled with dark angels who seek to harm us, destroy our faith, and lead us into sin. These demons sought to lead the Colossians into ascetic practices and false teachings about Christ. We see the same movement in the West today in an effort to obtain a higher consciousness with the godhead of the universe and to view Christ as simply another incarnation of a god, human prophet, or seer among many.

The reality of the spiritual battle we face is described by Paul in Ephesians, where we are told how to prepare for it.

> Put on the full armor of God, so that you can take
> your stand against the devil's schemes. For our strug-
> gle is not against flesh and blood, but against the rul-
> ers, against the authorities, against the powers of this
> dark world and against the spiritual forces of evil in
> the heavenly realms. (Eph. 6:11–12, NIV)

Satan "is filled with fury, because he knows that his time is short" (Rev. 12:12, NIV). He is described as "a roaring lion looking for someone to devour" (1 Pet. 5:8, NIV). But his roar is a bluff, a scare tactic to make us afraid of him, for he is chained. We have the victory over him in the power of the Holy Spirit. We are told to resist the devil, standing firm in the faith, and he will flee from us (see James 4:7; 1 Pet. 5:9). Through His death and resurrection, Christ disarmed the enemy as a conquering army would its vanquished foe. At the crucifixion of Christ, a cosmic struggle ensued by which the prince of this world was "driven out" (John 12:31, NIV), "hurled to the earth" (Rev. 12:9, NIV; see also Luke 10:18), and "bound" (Rev. 20:2; see also Matt. 12:29). He cannot withstand the power of God working through us when we stand firm in our faith and call on the Lord Jesus.

We have two pictures of what God did to these spiritual powers and authorities. First, God made a public spectacle of them (see Col. 2:15). To the readers of the letter in Colossae, this would have given the image of a general returning to Rome in triumph after a victorious campaign, with his humiliated enemies following his chariot. Plutarch describes such a triumphal return of General Aemilius Paullus after his capture of Macedonia. A three-day parade had the whole city of Rome out in festive dress to see the silver and gold, the goods, the booty, the captured king, the king's servants and children, the prisoners, the victorious general, and, finally, his army with wreaths of laurel. God made a public spectacle of His defeated foe, Satan, and his dark angels. As God's victory is proclaimed with the spread of His kingdom, Satan's defeat is visible for all to see, displayed each time a person comes to saving faith in Christ. Though he is still around to attempt to ruin us, he knows his days will end soon when he is thrown into the lake of fire (see Rev. 20:10).

Second, God triumphed over the powers and authorities by the cross of Christ. By dying for us, Jesus bought us or redeemed us, paying the ultimate price so that He might give us life. Satan hoped that crucifixion would be the end of Jesus, but the Son of God triumphed over death in His resurrection. That was Satan's defeat. He is a liar, a murderer, and an accuser of the brothers. He seeks our death. "The thief [Satan] comes only to steal and kill and destroy" (John 10:10). We overcome him "by the blood of the Lamb and by the word of [our] testimony" (Rev. 12:11).

The beginning of this defeat of Satan was seen in the proclamation of the kingdom of God by Jesus' seventy-two disciples, whom He sent out like lambs among wolves. When they returned rejoicing that even the demons had submitted to them in Jesus' name, Jesus replied, "I saw Satan fall like lightning from heaven. I have given you authority to trample on snakes and scorpions and to overcome all the power of the enemy; nothing will harm you" (Luke 10:18–19, NIV). Here we see the defeat of Satan and even the demons, who are represented in the snakes and scorpions, as the gospel of Jesus was proclaimed.

The author of Hebrews explains why Jesus came in the flesh: "Since the children have flesh and blood, he too shared in their humanity so that by his death he might destroy him who holds the power of death—that is, the devil—and free those who all their lives were held in slavery by their fear of death" (Heb. 2:14–15, NIV). Satan's hold on the power of death is seen in his inducing people to sin and come under its penalty, which is death: "The one who sins is the one who will die" (Ezek. 18:4, NIV). Jesus came to give us abundant life (see John 10:10), not to escape a meaningless life of suffering, as Buddhism seeks. So He triumphs over Satan by giving us eternal life that will never be taken away from those He loves. No one can snatch us out of Jesus' hand (see 10:28).

In this life we will continue to struggle in our battle with Satan and his legions of demons because his demise will not be complete until the end of the age, when Jesus returns in triumph and glory. Presently, Satan is blinding the minds of unbelievers from understanding and seeing the light of the gospel (see 2 Cor. 4:4). They are deceived from acknowledging the truth about God, from understanding their sinfulness in light of God's holiness, and into believing the philosophies and gods of this age. He can do this because he "disguises himself as an angel of light" (11:14). The devil is scheming against us in an attempt to derail us from remaining faithful to Christ.

But the "deceiver of the whole world" and "accuser of our brothers," Satan, has been thrown down because "the salvation and the power and the kingdom of our God and the authority of his Christ have come" (Rev. 12:9–10). The believers "have conquered him by the blood of the Lamb and by the word of their testimony, for they loved not their lives even unto death" (12:11). But the "devil has come down to [the earth and sea] in great wrath, because he knows that his time is short!" (12:12).[6]

Therefore we must put up our shield of faith to "extinguish all the flaming darts of the evil one" (Eph. 6:16); take up the sword, the Word of God; and pray in the Spirit on all occasions (see 6:17–18). Since we are no longer under condemnation because our sins have been forgiven and our record of debt has been nailed to the cross (see Col. 2:13–14), the ground for Satan's accusations against us has been taken away. His influence over us has lost its advantage and strength. His power is broken, and as Luther's hymn says, "Lo, his doom is sure."

This same Jesus who triumphed over Satan at the cross indwells us by His Spirit. This means that we have a power greater than all the forces of Satan together because we can claim the Spirit to protect us and deliver those who have been captive to demonic forces. Charles Kraft describes our task in light of this.

> Be assured that on our side is a powerful and empowering Lord who is willing to use anyone. On the other side, then, is a kingdom of dark angels working mostly by deceit, fear, and bluff. Jesus has already won the victory. [God uses us as agents for the] . . . rescuing and freeing of the prisoners of war. . . . Let people know and experience the fact that Jesus is King of Kings and Lord of Lords right now as well as in the future.[7]

King Jehoshaphat prayed to God when a vast army from three nations came against him and his kingdom of Judah.

> O LORD, God of our fathers, are you not God in heaven? You rule over all the kingdoms of the

nations. In your hand are power and might, so that none is able to withstand you. . . . O our God, will you not execute judgment on them? For we are powerless against this great horde that is coming against us. We do not know what to do, but our eyes are on you. (2 Chron. 20:6–12)

As all the assembled people of Judah stood before the Lord, the Spirit came upon Jahaziel.

Thus says the LORD to you, "Do not be afraid and do not be dismayed at this great horde, for the battle is not yours but God's. . . . You will not need to fight in this battle. Stand firm, hold your position, and see the salvation of the LORD on your behalf, O Judah and Jerusalem." Do not be afraid and do not be dismayed. Tomorrow go out against them, and the LORD will be with you. (20:15–17)

So Jehoshaphat and all Judah fell down in worship before the Lord, and the Levites "stood up to praise the LORD, the God of Israel, with a very loud voice" (20:19). Early the next morning Jehoshaphat encouraged the people, "Believe in the LORD your God . . . [and] his prophets, and you will succeed" (20:20). Then "he appointed those who were to sing to the LORD and praise him in holy attire, as they went before the army," saying, "'Give thanks to the LORD, for his steadfast love endures forever.' And when they began to sing and praise, the LORD set an ambush against the men of Ammon, Moab, and Mount Seir, who had come against Judah, so that they were routed" and "they all helped to destroy one another" (2 Chron. 20:21–23). In this historical account, we see the great power of God demonstrated to preserve His Old Testament church through the praise of His people as Satan was defeated. Each time Christ's church meets for worship, remembering His triumph on the cross and through His resurrection, it is putting at bay and defeating the satanic powers arrayed to deceive, accuse, and destroy God's people. Knowing what God has done for us in Christ, we see that we are complete in Him. So we rejoice with Paul: "Thanks be to God, who in Christ always leads us in triumphal procession, and through us spreads the fragrance of the knowledge of him everywhere" (2 Cor. 2:14).

Ultimate Triumph over Evil

Although this important passage in Matthew 16 about Christ's founding of the church and its authority has been given numerous interpretations, its basic thrust is well understood. Peter's confession of faith that Jesus is the Christ, the Son of the living God, is foundational to what the church is built on— Christ Jesus Himself. Believing that, we know that hell shall not keep hold of those it seeks to claim. Instead, those with this faith in Christ shall be raised up from death and given new life. Rather than suffering the eternal punishment of being apart from God, the redeemed will be for eternity joint heirs and corulers with Christ in His kingdom. Satan cannot destroy Christ's new creation. This is only possible because as the Christ, the Son of God, Jesus has all authority. Before He ascended to heaven, He met His disciples and said to them, "All authority in heaven and on earth has been given to me" (Matt. 28:18). We need to reflect on this. He has all authority in heaven and on earth. Nothing is out of His control. He knows not only what *has* happened but what *will* happen. He can intervene in any situation we bring to Him in prayer and change it. For those who love God, He will work all things together for good (see Rom. 8:28). The apostle John saw in the revelation given him from Jesus that, as Lord, Christ had authority to open doors of opportunity for the triumph of the gospel.

> To the angel of the church in Philadelphia write:
> "The words of the holy one, the true one, who has
> the key of David, who opens and no one will shut,
> who shuts and no one opens. 'I know your works.
> Behold, I have set before you an open door, which
> no one is able to shut.'" (Rev. 3:7–8)

This is a promise from God about the triumph of the gospel that will go throughout the world. No one can close this door that God has opened, despite the opposition, the flesh, and the devil. As Paul wrote of his stay in Ephesus, "A wide door for effective work has opened to me, and there are many adversaries" (1 Cor. 16:9). So, along with the opportunity for the gospel, we will find fierce opposition. Paul warns believers of coming persecution: "Indeed, all who desire to live a godly life in Christ Jesus will be persecuted, while evil people and impostors will go on from bad to worse, deceiving and being deceived" (2 Tim. 3:12–13). Paul also wrote of the coming rebellion, led by the man of lawlessness who will claim to be God and will come before the appearing of the Lord Jesus.

The mystery of lawlessness is already at work. Only
he who now restrains it will do so until he is out of
the way. And then the lawless one will be revealed,
whom the Lord Jesus will kill with the breath of his
mouth and bring to nothing by the appearance of
his coming. The coming of the lawless one is by the
activity of Satan with all power and false signs and
wonders, and with all wicked deception for those
who are perishing, because they refused to love the
truth and so be saved. (2 Thess. 2:7–10)

This outbreak of opposition to our Lord and His people is
expected. Consequently, many believers will face martyrdom.
Yet they will remain confident that God is in control and that
His triumph is certain. God is even using the atrocities of ISIS
and other radical Islamists to bring many Muslims to faith in
Christ.[8]

A few years ago in Somalia, a staffer for Food for the Hungry
was captured by radical Islamists as he transported food. Two
years before, this man had become a believer in Christ out of
a Muslim background. The Islamists called the people of a local village together for an alleged feast but instead paraded the
"apostate" before them and beheaded him. Then they broadcast
a video of the event as a warning to others. Such martyrdom does
not mean that God has forgotten His people but may rather be
the means by which God strengthens the faith of some and leads
many others to the faith. The people of this world can't stand the
people of God and what we represent. Yes, God allows some of
His saints to suffer death as martyrs, yet those who suffer in this
way will be rewarded gloriously and Christ's church will expand

through their witness of faith that triumphed through death. In Revelation, we see a great city of false worshipers and its sexually immoral powers depicted as prostitutes, kings, and a beast. "They will make war on the Lamb, and the Lamb will conquer them, for he is Lord of lords and King of kings, and those with him are called and chosen and faithful" (Rev. 17:14). But we have this encouraging promise from Christ: "The one who conquers, I will grant him to sit with me on my throne, as I also conquered and sat down with my Father on his throne" (3:21).

Christ Building His Church

The people of God are often persecuted, afflicted, distressed, and brought low, but Christ is still building His church. Although some visible churches, such as the one in Ephesus, may disappear, the true church never dies. God has always had a faithful people. When Elijah thought that he was the only believer in Israel, God reminded him that He had seven thousand people who had not bowed their knee to Baal (see 1 Kings 19:18). Despite the fact that some leave the faith in apostasy, heresy, and distress, many men and women cannot be bought because they will not buy their way into a relationship with God. They have received salvation as a gift from Him by His grace and therefore will not sell out.

Commenting on God's perseverance through His faithful remnant, P.J. Miller has blogged on the subject.

> There have been times of affluence and prosperity when the Church's message was nearly diluted into oblivion by those who sought to make it socially

attractive, neatly organized and financially profitable. It has been gold plated, draped in purple and encrusted with jewels. It has been misrepresented, ridiculed, blotted and scorned.

These followers of Jesus Christ have been according to the whim of the times elevated as sacred leaders and martyred as heretics. Yet through it all, there marches on that powerful army of the meek, God's chosen people that can't be bought, flattered, murdered or stilled. On through the ages they march.[9]

In his book *Decline and Fall of the Roman Empire*, eighteenth-century historian Edward Gibbon describes how it disintegrated from within.

While that great body was invaded by open violence or undermined by slow decay, a pure and humble religion gently insinuated itself into the minds of men, grew up in silence and obscurity, derived new vigor from opposition, and finally erected the triumphant banner of the cross on the ruins of the Capitol.[10]

Similarly today, Christ is building His church in lands such as China on the ruins of the cultural revolution and Marxist atheistic ideology, there being perhaps 100 to 130 million people who have become believers, mostly in recent years, outpacing membership in the Communist party. A revival was held in Iran in the midst of the austerity of Islamic law and the imprisonment of Christians. In the Hindu nation of Nepal, where in the 1950s only a handful of believers existed, a church of close to three hundred thousand is currently the fastest-growing body in the world despite prohibitions against changing one's religion and threats from Maoist revolutionaries.

Christ is still building His church and it will triumph gloriously, with every foe vanquished. As we are promised, "The God of peace will soon crush Satan under your feet" (Rom. 16:20). Paul also recorded this promise of God's tremendous love for His people despite all opposition:

> What then shall we say to these things? If God is for us, who can be against us? He who did not spare his own Son but gave him up for us all, how will he not also with him graciously give us all things? Who shall bring any charge against God's elect? It is God who justifies. Who is to condemn? Christ Jesus is the one who died—more than that, who was raised—who is at the right hand of God, who indeed is interceding for us. (8:31–34)

Nineteenth-century Scottish pastor Robert Murray M'Cheyne wrote confidently, "If I could hear Christ praying for me in the next room, I would not fear a million enemies. Yet distance makes no difference. He is praying for me."[11]

> Who shall separate us from the love of Christ? Shall tribulation, or distress, or persecution, or famine, or nakedness, or danger, or sword? As it is written, "For your sake we are being killed all the day long; / we are regarded as sheep to be slaughtered." No, in

> all these things we are more than conquerors through
> him who loved us. For I am sure that neither death
> nor life, nor angels nor rulers, nor things present nor
> things to come, nor powers, nor height nor depth,
> nor anything else in all creation, will be able to sepa-
> rate us from the love of God in Christ Jesus our Lord.
> (Rom. 8:35–39)

Nothing will separate those God foreknew, predestined, called, justified, and glorified from His eternal love. As Jesus gave His Olivet discourse to His disciples, concerning events soon to come and others some ways off, He assured them of the following:

> They will deliver you up to tribulation and put you
> to death, and you will be hated by all nations for
> my name's sake. And then many will fall away and
> betray one another and hate one another. And many
> false prophets will arise and lead many astray. And
> because lawlessness will be increased, the love of ma-
> ny will grow cold. But the one who endures to the
> end will be saved. And this gospel of the kingdom
> will be proclaimed throughout the whole world as a
> testimony to all nations, and then the end will come.
> (Matt. 24:9–14)

Notice that in the midst of this suffering and apostasy, the gospel will be proclaimed to all peoples of the world before the end of this age. Some years ago, when I had a case of my book *Muslims and Christians at the Table* delivered to Nigeria for a local pastor to distribute, the secret police, who were Muslim, confiscated the shipment. Some of those men read the book, however, and six of them came to faith in Christ! We can look forward to the triumph of the gospel because the Son of God, who looked as if He had been slain, has gathered a great multitude of worshipers around His throne—people He purchased with His blood from every tribe and language and nation (see Rev. 5:9). Christ purchased every kind of person through the merit and power of His sacrifice to accomplish God's eternal purpose and fulfill God's covenant promise to Abraham to bless all nations.

Discussion Questions

1. What is the rock on which Christ will build His church? What supports your view? What significance does this have for our faith?

2. What is meant by "the gates of hell shall not prevail against it?" Does it mean victory over satanic forces against the church, victory by Christ and those who hold to His teaching over false teaching, victory over the dominion of death, or the truth that Christ's church will be invincible?

3. How did Christ triumph over Satan and his demonic forces? How can we participate in that victory?

4. What confidence can we have and what promises can we claim to help us know that Christ's church will ultimately triumph?

Notes

Preface

1. Pew Research Center findings in Mary Eberstadt, "Regular Christians Are No Longer Welcome in American Culture."
2. Peter Jones, *The Other Worldview*, 99.
3. Timothy Keller, "The Bible and Same Sex Relationships: A Review Article."
4. Stephen V. Monsma and Stanley W. Carlson-Thies, "Keeping the Faith on Campus."
5. Catherine Elvy, "Lack of Recognition."
6. Barna Group, "Most American Christians Do Not Believe that Satan or the Holy Spirit Exist."
7. David Wells, "Conversations with the Contributors," in *The Supremacy of Christ in a Post-modern World*, eds. John Piper and Justin Taylor, 163-64.
8. See Sherif Girgis, "Obergefell and the New Gnosticism."
9. Anthony Giddens, *Sociology*, 452.
10. Lea Carawan, "'First They Came' . . . Will History Repeat Itself?"
11. David French, "The American Church Needs to Get Serious about Religious Liberty, Now."
12. Bonnie Pritchett, "Political Attack on California Christian Colleges Advances."
13. See Peter Conn, "The Great Accreditation Farce." Also, J.C. Derrick, "Ontario Court Deals Blow to Christian Law School."
14. Jones, *The Other Worldview*, 78.
15. Michael Keller, "RUF and the Secular Campus."
16. See, as an example, Samuel G. Freedman, "A Laboratory for Interfaith Studies in Pennsylvania Dutch Country."

17. Alister E. McGrath, "A Particularist View: A Post-Enlightenment Approach," in *Four Views on Salvation in a Pluralistic World*, ed. Stanley N. Gundry, 156.

Chapter 1: Is Seeing God in Nature Sufficient for Salvation?

1. Tony Castle, comp., *The New Book of Christian Quotations*, 208.

2. Don Richardson, *Eternity in Their Hearts*, 38.

3. Antony Flew, in Jones, *The Other Worldview*, 25.

4. Blaise Pascal, "Of the Means of Belief," in *Thoughts*, 288.

5. Jones, *The Other Worldview*, 12.

6. Ibid., 12–13.

7. To read a Christian medical response to transgenderism from the Christian Medical and Dental Associations, see "Finding One's Identity Within God's Design" in *World* magazine.

8. R.C. Sproul, *Knowing God*, 27.

9. Tony Castle, comp., *The New Book of Christian Quotations*, 207.

10. Herman Bavinck, *Reformed Dogmatics*, 314.

11. James Montgomery Boice, *Romans*, 156.

12. Michael P. Green, ed., *Illustrations for Biblical Preaching*, 305.

Chapter 2: The Authority of the Bible Among Multiple Revelations

1. Barna Group, "Americans Draw Theological Beliefs from Diverse Points of View."

2. Wells, "The Supremacy of Christ in a Postmodern World," in Piper and Taylor, *The Supremacy of Christ in a Postmodern World*, 28.

3. Ibid.

4. Barna Group, "Most American Christians Do Not Believe that Satan or the Holy Spirit Exist."

5. McGrath, "A Particularist View," in Gundry, *Four Views on Salvation in a Pluralistic World*, 159-62.

6. "International Student Ministry Resource: Hinduism."

7. "Christian Witness to Buddhists," Lausanne Occasional Paper 15.

8. S.J. Aloysius Pieris, "The Buddha and the Christ: Mediators of Liberation," in *The Myth of Christian Uniqueness*, 164.

9. Voddie Baucham Jr., "Conversations with the Contributors," in Piper and Taylor, *The Supremacy of Christ in a Postmodern World*, 167.

10. Wayne Grudem, ed., ESV Study Bible, 2333, 2342, 2423.

11. John R. W. Stott, *The Authority of the Bible*, 10–15.

12. Ibid., 9–16.

13. Ibid., 24.

14. Ibid., 17–27.

15. John Nijenhuis, "Baha'i: World Faith for Modern Man?" 535.

16. Ibid., 539.

Chapter 3: The Lord—He Is God!

1. Castle, *The New Book of Christian Quotations*, 97.

2. Jones, *The Other Worldview*, 109.

3. Meredith Somers, "Washington National Cathedral Hosts First-ever Muslim Prayer Service."

4. Jones, *The Other Worldview*, 105, 110–112.

5. Ibid., 115.

6. Ibid.

7. Sophia Lee, "The Son of God and the 'Sons of the Land.'"

Chapter 4: The Unique Christ in a Pluralistic Age

1. McGrath, "A Particularist View," in Gundry, *Four Views on Salvation in a Pluralistic World*, 171-72.

2. Stephen C. Neill, in J.N.D. Anderson, *Christianity and Comparative Religion*, 42.

3. J.H. Bavinck, *The Impact of Christianity on the Non-Christian World*, 158–59.

4. Throughout Jesus' teaching in John's Gospel, we see seven claims that He made as the "I AM." These include "I am the bread of life" (John 6:38, 45), "I am the light of the world" (John 8:12), "I am the gate" (John 10:7, 9), "I am the good shepherd" (John 10:11, 14), "I am the resurrection and the life" (John 11:25), "I am the way and the truth and the life" (John 14:6), and "I am the true vine" (John 15:1). Additionally, as Jesus was being arrested in the garden of Gethsemane and the soldiers and officials asked for Jesus of Nazareth, He responded, "I am he." The majesty with which He said this caused those who came to arrest this meek peasant to fall back to the ground (see John 18:2–8).

5. Boice, *The Gospel of John*, 121.

6. McGrath, "A Particularist View," in Gundry, *Four Views on Salvation in a Pluralistic World*, 167.

7. Ravi Zacharias, *The Uniqueness of Christ in World Religions*, DVD.

8. Kenneth L. Barker, ed., NIV Study Bible, 1859.

9. Zacharias, *The Uniqueness of Christ*.

Chapter 5: No Other Name

1. Christine Wicker, "How Spiritual Are We?"

2. Charles R. Erdman, *The Acts*, 43.

3. Philip Graham Ryken, *Is Jesus the Only Way?* 37.

4. Inclusivists believe that God saves people only because of the work of Christ but that people may be saved apart from knowing about Christ through belief in God as revealed in His creation and providence. See John Sanders, ed., *What About Those Who Have Never Heard?* 13.

5. Clark H. Pinnock, "Acts 4:12—No Other Name under Heaven," in *Through No Fault of Their Own?*, eds. William V. Crockett and James G. Sigountos, 111.

6. Ibid., 112–13.

7. Carl F.H. Henry, "Is It Fair?," in Crockett and Sigountos, *Through No Fault of Their Own?*, 254.

8. See a more detailed discussion of this paragraph in William V. Crockett, "Will God Save Everyone in the End?," in Crockett and Sigountos, *Through No Fault of Their Own?*, 159-66.

Chapter 6: Enter Through the Narrow Door

1. Stephen Mitchell, ed., *The Enlightened Mind*, 75–76.

2. Ralph Winter, "The Diminishing Task: The Field and the Force."

3. Leon Morris, *The Gospel According to St. Luke*, 225.

4. Robert Jamieson, A.R. Fausset, and David Brown, *Commentary Critical and Explanatory on the Whole Bible*, 113.

5. Alexander MacLaren, *Expositions of Holy Scripture*, 10.

6. Richard Baxter, *The Saints' Everlasting Rest*, 16.

7. Ibid., 105.

8. MacLaren, *Expositions of Holy Scripture*, 9.

9. George Eldon Ladd, *A Theology of the New Testament*, 74.

10. Alfred Plummer, in Norval Geldenhuys, *Commentary on the Gospel of Luke*, 381.

11. MacLaren, *Expositions of Holy Scripture*, 9.

12. S. Wesley Ariarajah, *The Bible and People of Other Faiths*, 27.

13. Ibid.

14. Gavin D'Costa, "The New Missionary: John Hick and Religious Plurality," 67.

15. Ibid.

16. Ibid., 68.

17. Morris, *The Gospel According to St. Luke*, 226.

18. James Packer, *Your Father Loves You*, July 9.

19. John Calvin, *Matthew, Mark, and Luke*, 361.

Chapter 7: Can a Loving God Send Good People to Suffer in Eternal Hell?

1. Barna Group, "Americans Describe Their Views About Life After Death."

2. In Islam, Allah is described as "loving," meaning he provides for all he has created in the Christian sense of common grace. But Allah is not immanent; he is transcendent and unknowable. He reveals his will, but humanity has no relationship with him. Those who submit to Islam are his slaves.

3. Henry, "Is It Fair?," in Crockett and Sigountos, *Through No Fault of Their Own?*, 251.

4. Ibid., 254.

5. Ronald H. Nash, "Restrictivism," in *What About Those Who Have Never Heard?*, ed. John Sanders, 121.

6. Clark H. Pinnock also sees Melchizedek, like Cornelius, as a "pagan saint" in *Four Views on Salvation*, 189. Melchizedek, however, is a type of Christ who obviously knew and led the worship of the true God ("He was priest of God Most High," Gen. 14:18). Jethro, the priest of Midian, Moses' father-in-law, was also not another example of a "pagan saint," as he "rejoiced for all the good that the LORD had done to Israel," "blessed" the Lord for delivering the Israelites, and said, "Now I know that the LORD is greater than all gods," followed by offering sacrifices to God (see Exod. 18:9–12).

7. Nash, "Restrictivism," in Sanders, *What About Those Who Have Never Heard?*, 122.

8. Josh McDowell and Don Stewart, *Understanding Non-Christian Religions*, 71.

9. Tissa Weerasingha, "Buddhism Through Christian Eyes," in *God in Asian Contexts: Communicating the God of the Bible in Asia*, eds. Bong Rin Ro and Mark C. Albrecht, 158.

10. Elisabeth Elliot, *On Asking God Why*, 108.

11. Timothy Keller, *The Reason for God*, 77–78.

12. Ibid., 79.

13. C.S. Lewis, in Keller, *The Reason for God*, 79.

14. Baxter, *The Saints' Everlasting Rest*, 79.

15. Ibid., 89.

16. Fackre, Gabriel, in Sanders, *What About Those Who Have Never Heard?*, 13.

Chapter 8: Paul's Approach to World Religions

1. H.A. Evan Hopkins, ed., *The Inadequacy of Non-Christian Religion*, 6.

2. Erdman, *The Acts*, 125.

3. Richard N. Longenecker, "The Acts of the Apostles," in *John and Acts*, 476.

4. Hopkins, *The Inadequacy of Non-Christian Religion*, 6.

5. I. Howard Marshall, *Acts*, 288.

6. Longenecker, "The Acts of the Apostles," 476.

7. Ibid., 478, and Marshall, *Acts*, 291.

Chapter 9: Christian Tolerance

1. R.R. Reno, "Terrorism Is Not Hate."

2. Donald A. McGavran, quoted in Ajith Fernando, *The Christian's Attitude Toward World Religions*, 153.

3. Chuck Colson, "Redefining the First Freedom: More Than Worship."

4. Mat Staver, Liberty Counsel newsletter, September 17, 2016.

5. Pinnock, quoted in Veli-Matti Kärkkäinen, *An Introduction to the Theology of Religions*, 269.

6. Eileen Scott, "Cemetery of the Innocents," 18.

7. David Hewetson, quoted in Michael Cassidy, *Getting to the Heart of Things*, 154–55.

8. Ibid., 156.

9. Fernando, *The Christian's Attitude Toward World Religions*, 152.

10. Lord David Alton, Jubilee Campaign newsletter, July 15, 2015.

11. "Views on Religious Liberty."

12. For a description on how to develop the MBU approach, see Bruce A. McDowell and Anees Zaka, *Muslims and Christians at the Table*.

13. John Piper, *A Godward Life*, 63–64.

14. While it's true that we must not be judgmental toward other believers when we may be guilty ourselves, it does not mean that we are not to exercise judgment on those who are apostate within the church (see 1 Cor. 5:9–13; 1 Tim. 1:20).

15. Lord Alton, Jubilee Campaign newsletter.

Chapter 10: Freedom from Sin, Freedom to Do Good

1. Philip Jenkins, "Godless Europe?" 120.
2. Boice, *The Gospel of John*, 643–44.
3. James and Edward Hastings, eds., *The Speaker's Bible*, 191.
4. Castle, *The New Book of Christian Quotations*, 91.
5. Morris, *The Gospel According to John*, 456–57.
6. Green, *Illustrations for Biblical Preaching*, 156.
7. David M. Stowe, *When Faith Meets Faith*, 50–51.
8. J. Isamu Yamamoto, *Beyond Buddhism*, 113–14.
9. "Christian Witness to Buddhists," 7.
10. Bob Dylan, "Gotta Serve Somebody."
11. Bryan Chapell, ed., ESV Gospel Transformation Bible, 1581.

Chapter 11: Waging Peace in a Religiously Violent Age

1. Lela Gilbert, "The Unreported Terrorism Targeting France's Catholic Communities."
2. Ruth Alexander, "Are There Really 100,000 New Christian Martyrs Every Year?"
3. Irshad Manji, "When Denial Can Kill," 78.
4. See Robert Spencer, "UK Imam: 'Non-Muslims Are Never Innocent.'" Also see Qur'anic and hadith quotes from MBP Lee, "Whoever Kills a Person (Unjustly)".

Chapter 12: Unity in a Divided World

1. R.C. Sproul, ed., New Geneva Study Bible, 27.
2. Grudem, ESV Study Bible, 69.
3. Janie B. Cheaney, "Babel's Tower," 33.
4. See Jemar Tisby, "Reflections from a Black Presbyterian on the PCA's Overture on Racial Reconciliation."

Chapter 13: Christ's Church Triumphant

1. See, for example, Jones, "Heil to the Coming Progressive Utopia."
2. Boice, *The Gospel of Matthew*, 306.
3. We find phrases like "gates of death" in Job 17:16 and 38:17, Psalm 9:13 and 107:18, Isaiah 38:10, and in Jewish intertestamental literature.
4. Boice, *The Gospel of Matthew*, 308.
5. Just to make sure that we are clear as to what we mean by "church," Christ is speaking of those who have been born of the Spirit, washed of their sins by faith in Him, and clothed in His righteousness. He does not refer to any particular denomination or to a local building where people worship God. Rather, He refers to the mystical body of Christ, of which He is the head. True believers are united as one by a common faith in Christ.
6. As I wrote this, I received news that four Bible translators in the Middle East had been killed and their work destroyed by ISIS. But their agency has pledged to continue and complete the work God has called them to do. Such martyrs are like those John saw in his vision, who defeat Satan through their testimony of giving their lives for Jesus.
7. Charles H. Kraft, *Defeating Dark Angels*, 242.
8. Harriet Sherwood and Philip Oltermann, "European Churches Say Growing Flock of Muslim Refugees Are Converting;" Nadette de Visser, "Why Are So Many Muslim Refugees in Europe Suddenly Finding Jesus?"
9. P.J. Miller, "The Church Triumphant."
10. Green, *Illustrations for Biblical Preaching*, 56.
11. Andrew Bonar, ed., *Robert Murray M'Cheyne*, 179.

Bibliography

Alexander, Ruth. "Are There Really 100,000 New Christian Martyrs Every Year?" *BBC News*. Accessed July 4, 2016. www.bbc.com/news/magazine-24864587.

Allen, W.C. *St. Matthew*. International Critical Commentary. Edinburgh: T&T Clark, 1965.

Alton, Lord David. Jubilee Campaign newsletter, July 15, 2015.

Anderson, J.N.D. *Christianity and Comparative Religion*. Downers Grove, IL: InterVarsity Press, 1970.

Ariarajah, S. Wesley. *The Bible and People of Other Faiths*. Maryknoll, NY: Orbis, 1989.

Barclay, William. *The Gospel of Matthew*, vol. 2. Daily Study Bible Series. Philadelphia: Westminster Press, 1958.

Barker, Kenneth L., ed. NIV Study Bible. Grand Rapids: Zondervan, 1985.

Barna Group. "Americans Describe Their Views About Life After Death." Barna Group. Accessed September 26, 2016. www.barna.com/research/americans-describe-their-views-about-life-after-death/#.V-l06fkrKM8.

———. "Americans Draw Theological Beliefs from Diverse Points of View." Barna Group. Accessed March 3, 2016. www.barna.org/component/content/article/5-barna-update/45-barna-update-sp-657/82-americans-draw-theological-beliefs-from-diverse-points-of-view#.VterCuYzwg4.

———. "Most American Christians Do Not Believe that Satan or the Holy Spirit Exist." Barna Group. Accessed September 26, 2016. www.barna.com/research/most-american-christians-do-not-believe-that-satan-or-the-holy-spirit-exist/#.V-lRYfkrKM8.

Baucham, Voddie, Jr. "Conversations with the Contributors." In Piper and Taylor, *The Supremacy of Christ in a Postmodern World*.

Bavinck, Herman. *Reformed Dogmatics*. Vol. 1, *Prolegomena*. Grand Rapids: Baker, 2003.

Bavinck, J.H. *The Impact of Christianity on the Non-Christian World*. Grand Rapids: Eerdmans, 1948.

Baxter, Richard. *The Saints' Everlasting Rest*. New York: American Tract Society [1836?].

Boice, James Montgomery. *The Gospel of John*. Vol. 1, *The Coming of the Light, John 1:1–4:54*. Grand Rapids: Zondervan, 1975.

———. *The Gospel of John*. Vol. 2, *Christ and Judaism, John 5–8*. Grand Rapids: Baker, 1999.

———. *The Gospel of Matthew*. Vol. 1, *The King and His Kingdom, Matthew 1–17*. Grand Rapids: Baker, 2001.

———. *Romans*. Vol. 1, *Justification by Faith, Romans 1–4*. Grand Rapids: Baker, 1991.

———. *The Sermon on the Mount: Matthew 5–7*. An Expositional Commentary. Grand Rapids: Zondervan, 1972.

Bonar, Andrew, ed. *Robert Murray M'Cheyne*. Carlisle, PA: Banner of Truth, 1960.

Bruce, F.F. *Hard Sayings of Jesus*. Downers Grove, IL: InterVarsity Press, 1983.

Calvin, John. *Matthew, Mark, and Luke*. Vol. 1, *Commentary on a Harmony of the Evangelists*. Translated by William Pringle. Grand Rapids: Baker, 1979.

Carawan, Lea. "'First They Came' . . . Will History Repeat Itself?" Congressional Prayer Caucus Foundation (July 18, 2016). Accessed September 26, 2016. cpcfoundation.com/first-they-came-will-history-repeat-itself.

Cassidy, Michael. *Getting to the Heart of Things: Reflections on Christian Basics*. Brunswick East, Victoria, Australia: Acorn, 2004.

Castle, Tony, comp. *The New Book of Christian Quotations*. New York: Crossroad, 1982.

Chapell, Bryan, ed. ESV Gospel Transformation Bible. Wheaton: Crossway, 2013.

Cheaney, Janie B. "Babel's Tower." *World*, May 1, 1999.

Christian Medical and Dental Associations. "Finding One's Identity Within God's Design." *World*. Accessed September 26, 2016. world.wng.org/2016/06/finding_one_s_identity_within_god_s_design.

"Christian Witness to Buddhists." Lausanne Occasional Paper 15. Lausanne Committee for World Evangelization, June 1980.

Colson, Chuck. "Redefining the First Freedom: More Than Worship." *Breakpoint.* Accessed August 22, 2016. www.breakpoint.org/bpcommentaries/entry/13/27903.

Conn, Peter. "The Great Accreditation Farce." *Chronicle of Higher Education.* Accessed July 4, 2016. chronicle.com/article/The-Great-Accreditation-Farce/147425.

Crockett, William V. "Will God Save Everyone in the End?" In Crockett and Sigountos, *Through No Fault of Their Own?*

Crockett, William V. and James G. Sigountos, eds. *Through No Fault of Their Own? The Fate of Those Who Have Never Heard.* Grand Rapids: Baker, 1991.

D'Costa, Gavin. "The New Missionary: John Hick and Religious Plurality." *International Bulletin of Missionary Research* 15, no. 2 (April 1991): 66–69.

De Visser, Nadette. "Why Are So Many Muslim Refugees in Europe Suddenly Finding Jesus?" *The Daily Beast.* Accessed July 25, 2016. www.thedailybeast.com/articles/2016/05/25/why-are-so-many-muslim-refugees-in-europe-suddenly-finding-jesus.html.

Derrick, J.C. "Ontario Court Deals Blow to Christian Law School." *World.* Accessed July 4, 2016. world.wng.org/2016/06/ontario_court_deals_blow_to_christian_law_school.

DeVries, Simon J. *1 Kings.* Vol. 12, *Word Biblical Commentary.* Nashville: Thomas Nelson, 2003.

Dylan, Bob. "Gotta Serve Somebody." *Slow Train Coming.* Columbia Records, 1979.

Eberstadt, Mary. "Regular Christians Are No Longer Welcome in American Culture." *Time* (June 29, 2016). Accessed June 30, 2016. time.com/4385755/faith-in-america.

Erdman, Charles R. *The Acts: An Exposition.* Philadelphia: Westminster Press, 1919.

Elliot, Elisabeth. *On Asking God Why: And Other Reflections on Trusting God in a Twisted World.* Old Tappan, NJ: Revell, 1989.

Elvy, Catherine. "Lack of Recognition: Christian Leadership Ministry at Dartmouth Faces Discrimination." *Ivy League Christian Observer* 11, no. 3 (summer 2012): 14–16.

Fackre, Gabriel. In Sanders, *What About Those Who Have Never Heard?* 13.

Fernando, Ajith. *The Christian's Attitude Toward World Religions.* Bombay: Gospel Literature Service, 1988.

Freedman, Samuel G. "A Laboratory for Interfaith Studies in Pennsylvania Dutch Country." *New York Times*. Accessed July 1, 2016. www.nytimes.com/2016/04/30/us/alaboratory-for-interfaith-studies-in-pennsylvania-dutch-country.html.

French, David. "The American Church Needs to Get Serious about Religious Liberty, Now." *National Review*. Accessed September 26, 2016. www.nationalreview.com/article/437354/american-evangelicals-religious-liberty-fight.

Geldenhuys, Norval. *Commentary on the Gospel of Luke*. New International Commentary on the New Testament. Grand Rapids: Eerdmans, 1951.

Giddens, Anthony. *Sociology*. Oxford: Polity, 1989.

Gilbert, Lela. "The Unreported Terrorism Targeting France's Catholic Communities." *Hudson Institute*. Accessed August 13, 2016. www.hudson.org/research/12678-the-unreported-terrorism-targeting-france-s-catholic-communities.

Girgis, Sherif. "Obergefell and the New Gnosticism." *First Things*. Accessed July 1, 2016. www.firstthings.com/web-exclusives/2016/06/obergefell-and-the-new-gnosticism.

Glasser, Arthur F. and Donald A. McGavran. *Contemporary Theologies of Mission*. Grand Rapids: Baker, 1983.

Green, Michael P., ed. *Illustrations for Biblical Preaching*. Grand Rapids: Baker, 1989.

Grudem, Wayne, ed. ESV Study Bible. Wheaton: Crossway, 2008.

Gundry, Stanley N., ed. *Four Views on Salvation in a Pluralistic World*. Grand Rapids: Zondervan, 1996.

Hastings, James and Edward, eds. *The Speaker's Bible*. Vol. 11, *The Gospel According to St. John*. Grand Rapids: Baker, 1971.

Henry, Carl F.H. "Is It Fair?" In Crockett and Sigountos, *Through No Fault of Their Own?*

Hewetson, David. *One Road Only*. Sydney: Anglican Information Office, 1980.

Hopkins, H.A. Evan, ed. *The Inadequacy of Non-Christian Religion: A Symposium*. London: Inter-Varsity Fellowship of Evangelical Unions, 1944.

"International Student Ministry Resource: Hinduism," Nashville: National Student Ministries, n.d.

Jamieson, Robert, A.R. Fausset, and David Brown. *Commentary Critical and Explanatory on the Whole Bible*. Grand Rapids: Eerdmans, 1935.

Jenkins, Philip. "Godless Europe?" *International Bulletin of Missionary Research* 31, no. 3 (July 2007): 115–20.

Jones, Peter. "Heil to the Coming Progressive Utopia." *truthXchange* (July 21, 2016). Accessed March 27, 2017. https://truthxchange.com/2016/07/heil-to-the-coming-progressive-utopia/.

———. *The Other Worldview: Exposing Christianity's Greatest Threat*. Bellingham, WA: Kirkdale, 2015.

Jordan, Clarence. *Sermon on the Mount*. Valley Forge, PA: Judson, 1970.

Kärkkäinen, Veli-Matti. *An Introduction to the Theology of Religions*. Downers Grove, IL: InterVarsity Press, 2003.

Keller, Michael. "RUF and the Secular Campus." *RUF Northeast Report* (September 2015).

Keller, Timothy. *The Reason for God: Belief in an Age of Skepticism*. New York: Dutton, 2008.

———. "The Bible and Same Sex Relationships: A Review Article." *Redeemer Report* (June 2015). Accessed October 15, 2015. www.redeemer.com/redeemer-report/article/the_bible_and_same_sex_relationships_a_review_article.

Kraft, Charles H. *Defeating Dark Angels: Breaking Demonic Oppression in the Believer's Life*. Ann Arbor, MI: Vine, 1992.

La Sor, William Sanford. "1 and 2 Kings." In *The New Bible Commentary: Revised*, edited by D. Guthrie and J.A. Motyer. Grand Rapids: Eerdmans, 1970.

Ladd, George Eldon. *A Theology of the New Testament*. Grand Rapids: Eerdmans, 1974.

Lee, MBP. "Whoever Kills a Person (Unjustly) . . . Quran 5:32." *Investigating Philosophies, Culture, History, Myth*. Accessed June 17, 2016. mbplee.wordpress.com/2012/01/03/%C2%A77-whoever-kills-a-person-unjustly-quran-532.

Lee, Sophia. "The Son of God and the 'Sons of the Land.'" *World* (April 2, 2016). Accessed September 26, 2016. world.wng.org/2016/03/the_son_of_god_and_the_sons_of_the_land.

Longenecker, Richard N. "The Acts of the Apostles." In *John and Acts*. Vol. 9, *The Expositor's Bible Commentary*, edited by Frank E. Gaebelein. Grand Rapids: Zondervan, 1981.

MacLaren, Alexander. *Expositions of Holy Scripture: St. Luke 13–24*. Grand Rapids: Baker, 1974.

Manji, Irshad. "When Denial Can Kill." *Time*, July 25, 2005.

Marshall, I. Howard. *Acts*, Tyndale New Testament Commentaries. Grand Rapids: Eerdmans, 1980.

McDowell, Bruce A. and Anees Zaka. *Muslims and Christians at the Table: Promoting Biblical Understanding Among North American Muslims*. Phillipsburg, NJ: P&R, 1999.

McDowell, Josh and Don Stewart. *Understanding Non-Christian Religions: Handbook of Today's Religions*. San Bernardino, CA: Here's Life, 1982.

McGrath, Alister E. "A Particularist View: A Post-Enlightenment Approach." In Gundry, *Four Views on Salvation in a Pluralistic World*.

Miller, P.J. "The Church Triumphant." *My Journey . . . .* Accessed September 23, 2016. pjmiller.wordpress.com/2007/11/17/the-church-triumphant.

Mitchell, Stephen, ed. *The Enlightened Mind: An Anthology of Sacred Prose*. New York: HarperCollins, 1991.

Monsma, Stephen V. and Stanley W. Carlson-Thies. "Keeping the Faith on Campus." *World*. Accessed July 4, 2016. world.wng.org/2016/04/keeping_the_faith_on_campus.

Morris, Leon. *The Gospel According to John*. New International Commentary on the New Testament. Grand Rapids: Eerdmans, 1971.

———. *The Gospel According to St. Luke: An Introduction and Commentary*. Tyndale N. T. Commentaries. Grand Rapids: Eerdmans, 1974.

Nash, Ronald H. "Restrictivism." In Sanders, *What About Those Who Have Never Heard?*

Nijenhuis, John. "Baha'i: World Faith for Modern Man?" *Journal of Ecumenical Studies* 10, no. 3 (1973): 532–51.

Packer, James. *Your Father Loves You: Daily Insights for Knowing God*. Wheaton: Shaw, 1986.

Pascal, Blaise. "Of the Means of Belief." In *Thoughts*, 288. www.bartleby.com/48/1/4.html.

Pieris, Aloysius S.J. "The Buddha and the Christ." In *The Myth of Christian Uniqueness: Toward a Pluralistic Theology of Religions*, edited by John Hick and Paul F. Knitter. Maryknoll, NY: Orbis, 1987.

Pinnock, Clark H. "Acts 4:12—No Other Name under Heaven." In Crockett and Sigountos, *Through No Fault of Their Own?*

———. "A Particularist View: A Post-Enlightenment Approach." In Gundry, *Four Views on Salvation*.

———. *A Wideness in God's Mercy: The Finality of Jesus Christ in a World of Religions*. Grand Rapids: Zondervan, 1992.

Piper, John. *A Godward Life: Savoring the Supremacy of God in All of Life*. Sisters, OR: Multnomah, 1997.

Piper, John and Justin Taylor, eds. *The Supremacy of Christ in a Postmodern World*. Wheaton: Crossway, 2007.

Pratt, Richard, Jr., ed. *Spirit of the Reformation Study Bible*. Grand Rapids: Zondervan, 2003.

Pritchett, Bonnie. "Political Attack on California Christian Colleges Advances." *World*. Accessed July 3, 2016. world.wng.org/2016/07/political_attack_on_california_christian_colleges_advances.

Provan, Iain W. *1 and 2 Kings*. New International Biblical Commentary. Peabody, MA: Hendrickson, 1995.

Reno, R.R. "Terrorism Is Not Hate." *First Things*. Accessed June 15, 2016. www.firstthings.com/web-exclusives/2016/06/terrorism-is-not-hate.

Richardson, Don. *Eternity in Their Hearts*. Ventura, CA: Regal, 1981.

Ro, Bong Rin and Mark C. Albrecht, eds. *God in Asian Contexts: Communicating the God of the Bible in Asia*. Taichung, Taiwan: Asia Theological Association, 1988.

Ryken, Philip Graham. *Is Jesus the Only Way?* Wheaton: Crossway, 1999.

Ryle, J.C. *Matthew*. The Classic New Testament Commentary. London: Marshall Pickering, 1989.

Sanders, John, ed. *What About Those Who Have Never Heard?: Three Views on the Destiny of the Unevangelized*. Downers Grove, IL: InterVarsity Press, 1995.

Scott, Eileen. "Cemetery of the Innocents: Pro-Life Display Ignites Fury at Dartmouth." *Ivy League Christian Observer* 11, no. 3 (summer 2012): 18.

Sherwood, Harriet and Philip Oltermann. "European Churches Say Growing Flock of Muslim Refugees Are Converting." *The Guardian*. Accessed June 6, 2016. www.theguardian.com/world/2016/jun/05/european-churches-growing-flock-muslim-refugees-converting-christianity.

Somers, Meredith. "Washington National Cathedral Hosts First-ever Muslim Prayer Service." *Washington Times* (November 14, 2014). Accessed April 3, 2017. http://www.washingtontimes.com/news/2014/nov/14/national-cathedral-1st-ever-muslim-prayer-service/.

Spencer, Robert. "UK Imam: 'Non-Muslims Are Never Innocent, They Are Guilty of Denying Allah and His Prophet.'" *Jihad Watch*. Accessed September 26, 2016. www.jihadwatch.org/2008/04/uk-imam-non-muslims-are-never-innocent-they-are-guilty-of-denying-allah-and-his-prophet.

Sproul, R.C. *Knowing God*. Downers Grove, IL: InterVarsity Press, 2009.

———. *Lifeviews: Understanding the Ideas that Shape Society Today*. Old Tappan, NJ: Revell, 1986.

————. ed. New Geneva Study Bible. Nashville: Thomas Nelson, 1995.

Staver, Mat. "U.S. Commission on Civil Rights Chairman Attacks Religious Freedom." Liberty Counsel newsletter (September 15, 2016). Accessed March 7, 2017. http://www.lc.org/newsroom/details/091516-us-commission-on-civil-rights-chairman-attacks-religious-freedom.

Stott, John R.W. The Authority of the Bible. Downers Grove, IL: InterVarsity Press, 1974.

Stowe, David M. When Faith Meets Faith. New York: Friendship, 1967.

Tisby, Jemar. "Reflections from a Black Presbyterian on the PCA's Overture on Racial Reconciliation." Reformed African American Network. Accessed July 4, 2016. www.raanetwork.org/reflections-pcas-overture-racial-reconciliation.

"Views on Religious Liberty." World. Accessed September 27, 2016. https://world.wng.org/2016/04/views_on_religious_liberty.

Weerasingha, Tissa. "Buddhism Through Christian Eyes." In Ro and Albrecht, God in Asian Contexts: Communicating the God of the Bible in Asia.

Wells, David. "Conversations with the Contributors." In Piper and Taylor, The Supremacy of Christ in a Postmodern World.

————. "The Supremacy of Christ in a Postmodern World." In Piper and Taylor, The Supremacy of Christ in a Postmodern World.

Wicker, Christine. "How Spiritual Are We?" Parade. Accessed September 26, 2016. parade.com/48408/christinewicker/04-how-spiritual-are-we.

Winter, Ralph. "The Diminishing Task: The Field and the Force." Mission Frontiers. Accessed September 26, 2016. www.missionfrontiers.org/issue/article/the-diminishing-task.

Yamamoto, J. Isamu. Beyond Buddhism: A Basic Introduction to the Buddhist Tradition. Downers Grove, IL: InterVarsity Press, 1982.

Zacharias, Ravi. The Uniqueness of Christ in World Religions, DVD. Norcross, GA: Ravi Zacharias International Ministries, 2005.

PUBLICATIONS

Fort Washington, PA 19034

This book is published by CLC Publications, an outreach of CLC Ministries International. The purpose of CLC is to make evangelical Christian literature available to all nations so that people may come to faith and maturity in the Lord Jesus Christ. We hope this book has been life changing and has enriched your walk with God through the work of the Holy Spirit. If you would like to know more about CLC, we invite you to visit our website:

www.clcusa.org

To know more about the remarkable story of the founding of CLC International we encourage you to read

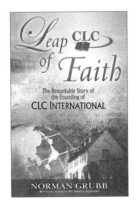

LEAP OF FAITH

Norman Grubb

Paperback

Size 5¹/₄ x 8, Pages 248

ISBN: 978-0-87508-650-7

ISBN (*e-book*): 978-1-61958-055-8

NEIGHBOROLOGY

Dr. David S. Apple

Written as a follow-up to *Not Just a Soup Kitchen*, David Apple's *Neighborology* provides a blueprint for how churches and servant leaders of every ministry can be neighborly helpers. Apple provides insight into developing the heart of a servant by modeling the compassion of Jesus Christ and presenting practical instruction and invaluable resources. This book is a must-read for servants of today and tomorrow.

Paperback
Size 5¹/₄ x 8, Pages 193
ISBN: 978-1-61958-239-2
ISBN (*e-book*): 978-1-61958-240-8